A POETRY OF PRESENCE

**The Wisconsin Project
on American Writers**

A series edited by
Frank Lentricchia

A POETRY OF PRESENCE

THE WRITING OF

WILLIAM CARLOS WILLIAMS

BERNARD DUFFEY

THE UNIVERSITY OF WISCONSIN PRESS

Published 1986

The University of Wisconsin Press
114 North Murray Street
Madison, Wisconsin 53715

The University of Wisconsin Press, Ltd.
1 Gower Street
London WC1E 6HA, England

First printing

Printed in the United States of America

For LC CIP information see the colophon

ISBN 0-299-10470-2

Permission to use quotations from the following works by William Carlos Williams has been granted by New Directions Publishing Corporation: *The Collected Earlier Poems,* copyright 1938 by New Directions Publishing Corporation; *The Collected Later Poems,* copyright 1944, 1948 by William Carlos Williams; *Imaginations,* copyright 1970 by Florence H. Williams; *Paterson,* copyright 1946, 1948, 1949, 1951, 1958 by William Carlos Williams, copyright 1963 by Florence Williams; *Pictures from Brueghel,* copyright 1954, 1955, 1962 by William Carlos Williams. *Many Loves,* copyright 1936, 1942, 1948 by William Carlos Williams, 1961 by Florence Williams; *"Rome"* Journal, copyright 1978 by the Estate of Florence H. Williams. Reprinted by permission of New Directions Publishing Corporation.

The province of the poem is the world. When the sun rises, it rises in the poem and when it sets darkness comes down and the poem is dark.

Paterson 3

We are talking about the spatial and temporal phenomenon of language, not about some non-spatial, non-temporal phantasm.

Wittgenstein, *Philosophical Investigations,* #108

CONTENTS

PREFACE

Rather than a study of William Carlos Williams's "poetry," "prose," "fiction," or "plays," this book is a study of all these considered as an interrelated and interdependent web of "writing." The author's text, in this case, is made up of all that he wrote. He never approached any literary genre without a predisposition to remake it—to wrest it out of existing categories and give it a personal character shaped by the power of "invention" he so greatly valued. The result was a mingling of poetry and prose, of drama with lyric poetry, of critical essay with testament, exclamation, and exhortation. His fiction shows the same fascination with objects as do his poems. The poems themselves were often first written as prose before they were recast, implying that writing was to the author a field of language present for whatever possibility the moment might afford.

The book is organized around a concept of writing as linguistically present action, one derived particularly from Kenneth Burke's *A Grammar of Motives* and developed by attention to the poet as an "agent" working in relation to a "scene" (the geographical and cultural "local" that Williams clung to) that was his subject and his ambiance, an interaction upon which he in turn drew for the "agencies" around which any given case of writing crystallized. His work, finally, was informed by "purpose" generated out of the whole of his dramatic sense of himself as literary actor seeking embodiment of a dynamic and altering whole. After an opening chapter in which Burke's interactive scheme is briefly described, the book proceeds to an examination of Williams's principle writings in the lights that seem most immediate to them: the pervasiveness of scene in *In the American Grain* and the fiction; of agent or poetic person in *Kora in Hell, A Voyage to Pagany, Paterson,* and *Pictures from Brueghel;* of poetic agency in the short poems; of poetic purpose in "The Pink Church," "Russia," *The Embodiment of Knowledge,* and "The Desert Music;" and of poetic action as a whole tending alternately toward pathetic tragedy and toward comedy in his two plays, *Many Loves* and *A Dream of Love.*

The result is a willingness to take Williams's writing across its breadth of implication rather than confine it to any single linguistic, aesthetic, social, or psychological postulate. I use Burke's scheme, as he intended, pragmatically and not formulaically. What is sought is a reading of Williams that understands his writing as kinetic rather than static experience for the reader, as perceptions of a writer more engaged in expressing literary action than in forging literary objects.

Whatever of value may appear in this book owes much to the enlargement of Williams studies indicated more particularly in my list of Abbreviations. Such studies represent a fruitful process of opening Williams's poetry to reading in the light of its particular nature. The approach to Williams elaborated in this study was first formulated during tutorial sessions with John Timmerman Newcomb and Edward J. Ingebretsen, S.J., who were constructive doubters.

Frank Lentricchia and Edith Duffey have been generous with editorial suggestion. I have drawn repeatedly on their perceptions and am grateful to them without meaning to involve them in imperfections beyond their control. Similarly, I am grateful for the opportunity of conversation with Paul Mariani concerning my general sense of the relations between Williams's poetry, his character, and the course of his life.

Duke University has been generous with leave of absence and with financial support from the Duke University Research Council.

ABBREVIATIONS

Works by William Carlos Williams:

A   *The Autobiography of William Carlos Williams.*
          N.p.: New Directions, 1951.
Beinecke Beinecke Rare Book and Manuscript Library, Yale
          University Library.
BU   *The Build-Up.* New York: New Directions, 1952.
          Rpt. 1968.
CEP   *The Collected Earlier Poems of William Carlos
          Williams.* 1951. Rpt. n.p.: New Directions, 1966.
CLP   *The Collected Later Poems of William Carlos
          Williams.* 1950. Rev. ed. n.p.: New Directions,
          1963.
Contact   *Contact, 1920–1923* (New York). Rpt. New York:
          Kraus Reprint Corp., 1967.
CP   *Collected Poems, 1921–1931.* New York: Objectivist
          Press, 1934.
Direction "Dream of Love: A Play in Three Acts and Eight
          Scenes." *Direction Six.* N.p.: New Directions,
          1948.
EK   *The Embodiment of Knowledge.* Ed. Ron
          Loewinsohn. New York: New Directions, 1974.
FD   *The Farmers' Daughters.* New York: New
          Directions, 1961.
I   *Imaginations.* Ed. Webster Schott. New York: New
          Directions, 1970; Rpt. 1971.
IAG   *In the American Grain.* Norfolk, Conn.: New
          Directions, 1925.
IM   *In the Money.* Norfolk, Conn.: New Directions,
          1940.
Iowa   *Iowa Review,* 1970– (Iowa City)
IW   *I Wanted to Write a Poem.* Boston: Beacon Press,
          1958.
ML   *Many Loves and Other Plays.* New York: New
          Directions, 1961.

Others   *Others: A Magazine of the New Verse*, 1915–1919.
            Rpt. New York: Klaus Reprint Corp., 1967.

P   *Paterson*. New York: New Directions, 1958. Seventh
            paperbook printing.

PB   *Pictures from Breughel*. New York: New Directions,
            1962.

RI   *A Recognizable Image: William Carlos Williams on
            Art and Artists*. Ed. Bram Dijkstra, New York:
            New Directions, 1978.

SE   *Selected Essays of William Carlos Williams*. New
            York: New Directions, 1954.

SL   *The Selected Letters of William Carlos Williams*.
            New York: McDowell, Obolensky, 1957.

SP   *Selected Poems by William Carlos Williams*. 1949.
            Rev. ed. New York: New Directions, 1968.

VP   *A Voyage to Pagany*. New York: The Macaulay
            Company, 1928.

WM   White Mule. Norfolk, Conn.: New Directions, 1937.

Works by other authors:

Adams, Hazard, ed. *Critical Theory since Plato*. New York: Harcourt, Brace, Jovanovich, 1971.

Auden, W. H. *The Collected Poetry of W. H. Auden*. New York: Random House, 1945.

Barthes, Roland. *Writing Degree Zero*. Trans. Annette Lavers and Colin Smith. New York: Hill and Wang, 1968.

Blast: Review of the Great English Vortex, 1914–1915 (London).

Burke, Kenneth. *Attitudes toward History*. 2 vols. New York: New Republic, 1937.

Burke, Kenneth. *The Philosophy of Literary Form*. 1941. Rev. ed. New York: Vintage, 1957.

Burke, Kenneth. *A Grammar of Motives*. New York: Prentice-Hall, 1945.

Dijkstra, Bram. *The Hieroglyphics of a New Speech*. Princeton: Princeton University Press, 1969.

Eliot, T. S. *To Criticize the Critic*. New York: Farrar, Straus, and Giroux, 1965.

Ellmann, Richard, and Feidelson, Charles, Jr. *The Modern Tradition*. New York: Oxford, 1965.

Hartley, Marsden. *Adventures in the Arts.* New York: Boni and Liveright, 1921.

James, William. *Pragmatism.* 1908. Rpt. Cambridge: Harvard University Press, 1978.

Mariani, Paul. *William Carlos Williams: A New World Naked.* New York: McGraw-Hill, 1981.

Miller, J. Hillis. *Poets of Reality.* Cambridge: Harvard University Press, 1965.

Paul, Sherman. *The Music of Survival.* Urbana: University of Illinois Press, 1968.

Perloff, Marjorie G. *The Poetics of Indeterminacy.* Princeton: Princeton University Press, 1981.

Poetry: A Magazine of Verse, 1912– (Chicago).

Pound, Ezra. *The Spirit of Romance.* 1910. Rpt. New York: New Directions, 1968.

Pound, Ezra. *Literary Essays of Ezra Pound.* Ed. T. S. Eliot. 1935. Rpt. New York: New Directions, 1968.

Riddel, Joseph. *The Inverted Bell.* Baton Rouge: Louisiana State University Press, 1974.

Stevens, Wallace. *Opus Posthumous.* Ed. Samuel French Morse. 1957. Rpt. New York: Knopf, 1972.

Wagner, Linda Welshimer. *The Poems of William Carlos Williams.* Middletown, Conn.: Wesleyan University Press, 1964.

Wagner, Linda Welshimer. *The Prose of William Carlos Williams.* Middletown, Conn.: Wesleyan University Press, 1970.

Wallace, Emily. *A Bibliography of William Carlos Williams.* Middletown, Conn.: Wesleyan University Press, 1968.

Zukofsky, Louis. *Prepositions: The Collected Critical Essays.* New York: Horizon Press, 1967.

A POETRY OF PRESENCE

I   PREMISES

In outlining what he calls a "grammar of motives" in his book of that title, Kenneth Burke links the concept of "act" with four closely related and often interpenetrating components he designates as "scene," "agent," "agency," and "purpose," and he proposes this pentad of coordinates as especially useful to an understanding of human "action," itself an overarching term intended to separate willed motivation from reflexive or mechanical reaction. It is an inclusive plan, and one especially applicable for him in the realms of philosophy, social science, and politics. It has a link with the openness of William James's and G. H. Mead's pragmatism on its further side, and it moves toward spheres of rhetorical and expressive application in the nearer reach. The result is a view of human activity Burke calls "dramatism" (with its components: act, scene, agent, agency, and purpose), which is closely related to what he terms a "rhetoric" and a "symbolic."

This is the general outline of the theory I invoke for my approach to William Carlos Williams. It will be seen that my discussion of particulars of his work will be part of a larger consideration including not only such theoretical concerns as those Burke propounds but the variety of Williams's writing and of its literary relations as well. To speak of scene in Williams, for example, is to evoke his powerful commitment to the local, to the New Jersey urban and industrial milieu in which he lived his life, as the place from and within which he would define his writing. In this regard, scene carries clear spatial reference. But a temporal reference is equally plain. Scene may be regarded as existing now or then in Williams; it belongs to the present and more particularly to the new, to a present time in the making. Spatial scene often lacks determinative power for Williams. It is seldom more than open occasion for writing, and within writing open occasion for what writing may become. However, as Burke implies, concern with space leads to concern with time, the temporal potential made manifest in action. And action in turn is hardly to be considered without attention to agent—the actor of the drama or in this case the poet himself—to the agencies of expression he utilizes, and to the explicit or implicit purpose toward which the whole makes its gesture. Particulars of the spatial scene lie before the writer as possible but problematic occasions of poem, play, or story. The literary product is conditioned in turn by his election of newness of utterance as the defining agency of the temporal scene, and with the introduction of such temporality Williams brings the whole of Burke's pentad into play.

It is by way of temporal scene, also, that Williams shares most with those contemporary poets of whom he was most vividly and persistently aware: T. S. Eliot, Ezra Pound, and Wallace Stevens. (His election of the local left his creativity still free to seek its affinities.) T. S. Eliot, surveying his own development, noted of his youth that there was not "a single living poet, in either England or America, then at the height of his powers, whose work was capable of pointing the way to a young poet conscious of the desire for a new idiom" (Eliot, 58), and Wallace Stevens observed that in his day at Harvard, "it was commonplace to say that all the poetry had been written and all the paintings painted" (Stevens, 218). The sequel to such sentiment was to be the emergence of an avant-garde, a restless writing positioning itself outside of established community and, so, forced back on the literary power Williams was to celebrate as "invention." To him the impetus was plain. "Nothing is good save the new. If a thing have novelty it stands intrinsically beside every other work of artistic excellence. If it have not that, no loveliness or heroic proportion or grand manner will save it. It will not be saved above all by an attenuated intellectuality" (SE, 21).

In praising the poems of Marianne Moore he jauntily identified as her overriding virtue the fact that her reader will find "that his whole preconceived scheme of values has been ruined." And he added, "this is exactly what he should see, a break through all preconceptions of poetic form and mood and pace" (SE, 121). The result was a placement of literary value beyond determination by existing code. Instead there was the creation of an avant-garde and the beginnings of a movement to elevate its inherent maximizing and specializing of itself. Both the writer and his readers were thereby given a new character. If the valid poem must be innovative, it could only exist detached from preformed contexts. There was no other way in which "newness" could become the attainment Williams wanted to make of it. This in turn placed on the avant-garde and its readership (scarcely an "audience" in these conditions) the task of creating anew the contexts in which innovative poems could be read.

The results are generally familiar. Williams and his contemporaries must be not only poets but also theorists of poetry and its occasions. They had not only to write but also to create much of the milieu within which their efforts might be seen as writing. Pound's critical prose, thus, was aimed directly at both outlining and filling in a realm of knowledge, feeling, and thought that would be the ground on which his poetry rested. Eliot's early poems gained from the enlargement of context he supplied for them in his essays not because the essays explained the poems but because they contributed to a world of literary and intellectual remaking within which the poems took apposite place. Wallace Stevens's earliest work, that of *Harmonium* of 1923, was received with such condescension that he was not moved to attempt further book publication for eight years. He would withdraw his politically oriented *Owls Clover* of 1936 from his collected poems, and it was not until his writing began advancing its own problematics as its subject that a satisfactory context began to appear for it. Williams moved more generally and perhaps more crudely in stating his attachment to overall principles—those he called "invention" and "the local" in the prologue to *Kora in Hell: Improvisations* of 1920—and in continuing an emphasis on them. And somewhat like Stevens, he may be said never to have ceased building context within his work, as late poems like "The Desert Music" and *Paterson* 5 attest.

It is in such a situation that Burke's proposals take on particular value, directed as they are to the contexts of action, here of poetic action. Williams commented often on the spatial and temporal "scenes" he elected for his work. He was scarcely less voluble on the subject of "agent," of himself as actor and creator within those scenes, through a cluster of titles ranging from *Kora in Hell* to "Asphodel, That Greeny Flower." He may be said almost to have been obsessed with the question of "agency," with the special and demanding qualities of the poetry he was attempting to write. He devoted one major work, *The Embodiment of Knowledge*, wholly to the question of "purpose," his own purpose as writer and what he saw as the purpose of poetry in general. And the whole, his poems, plays, and stories, themselves constitute the "acts" in which the range of his creative grammar opens itself to view.

Little criticism of Williams has explored widely across this breadth. Apart from Linda Wagner's books it has been more usual to isolate Williams's poems in whole or part from the rest of his writing and to consider them as specifically vexing cases. The general drift of argument has ranged from insistence on his direct, nonmetamorphic use of the local, in earlier criticism, to a growing agreement that his poetry may best be regarded as a case of the "indeterminacy" sponsored by Jacques Derrida, as the case of a poet who, so to speak, himself wrote deconstructively. Much may be said for both the earlier and the later arguments. Williams clearly does make nonmetamorphic use of the local in his poems, and, especially if one somewhat neglects the late work of *The Desert Music* and *Journey to Love,* he does often seem to indulge in utterance whose "determination" is uncertain. It will not be my aim to differ radically with either of these judgments, but I will argue that we need not rest with either the too flatly journalistic implications of a poetics simply of the local or with the irresolvable ambiguities of a poetics of difference. I will, in short, be resorting to Kenneth Burke to argue that Williams is a poet of contexts and that the process or reading him is one of coming to recognize these contexts both in their own right and in their dynamic presence in the poetry and across all his writing.

Burke's pentad comes to hand in this task not because it lays any claim to finality. It is, in the jargon of our day, no more or less "privileged" a critical discourse than any other. Its value here will prove more pragmatic than otherwise as it serves particularly to address the breadth and variety in Williams's writing. In establishing his pentad Burke is at pains to stress the degree to which he is concerned with an interinanimating scheme of analysis rather than a simply referential one. His terms gain meaning along with each other rather than alone. None of his five components is offered as absolute either as principle or as pragmatic. We are not to suppose that literary action is constituted by blocks of "scene" or "agent" or "purpose" pieced somehow together. In the degree to which he relates all to the underlying concept of "substance," he in fact stresses the paradoxical nature of that concept. As substance, etymologically, is a quality discerned as "standing under" an entity, so, precisely, it is not that entity. To speak substantively or in substance, indeed, is to speak with a difference from the entity under consideration. In particular, I will be applying the pentad, seriatim, to Williams's writing and in each of my major chapters using one of its terms as a wedge with which to open a selected group of texts. But in each case my entering wedge will be no more than a device to unfold the texts in question to whatever may be relevant within them. Scene, for example, has particularly plain reference to the selection of Williams's prose writing dealt with in Chapter 2. At the same time, the featuring of scene in regard to these texts leads without pause to consideration also of agent, agency, and purpose in them—and especially to the configuration of all in regard to the text as an act of writing. Each of my chapters thus can be figured as a rearrangement of Burke's pentad, a different member serving as center in each case, but as a center functioning in relation to the constellation of other members grouped around it. So arranged, in an altering but also recurrent patterning, each case serves as one analytic model for consideration of the diversity that, all together, the cases comprise.

Although Burke's *Grammar of Motives* may be thus applied to a discussion of literature, its value, for my purposes, will be in the directions it opens rather than in conclusions it does not pretend to define. Burke's whole aim, in fact, is to stress the impregnability of action to reduction to any positive terminology, and this aim is no less true when utterance itself is considered as the act. At the same time, however, he does supply opulent means for talk about utterance as act and so delivers both himself and us from the protean skepticism into which deconstruction by itself so readily leads. If Burke can be said to bespeak any particular theory of knowledge, that theory shares more with a pragmatism such as William James's, in which idea finds its confirmation in action, than with skepticism or, certainly, any form of materialitic determinism. Ideas, thought, and discourse are endemic to human understanding, he suggests. Perhaps no one can prove that they ever lead ineluctably to conclusion. It is their presence rather than their finality that is significant, as it is by their means that we arrive at the quantity *we-think-we-may-know*, and so at critical measure. To discount them as the deconstructive skeptic does is only, in fact, to utilize them to the skeptic's elected end. That option is always open, of course, but Burke prefers other courses leading us instead to scrutinize human being in its dramatic reality, its undoubtable apparent presence.

If all knowledge is thus brought under the heading of Kant's practical reson, there is no real loss since critical knowledge at any rate has little discernible bearing other than the practical. In criticism such a bearing is clear in the degree to which talk about books becomes not definition but a means of reading, an act which falls under Burke's concept of "transformation" as it advances understanding toward its formation. Nor will Burke leave us unassisted in the effort to get beyond what he himself often identifies as a "Babel," a condition that to a degree applies to the breadth and discontinuity observable in Williams's writing, which speaks in altering and contrasting voices. Diversity of discourse, however, can exist only because it is shot through with discernible uniformities, its points of difference. We differ from each other and within ourselves, but just as certainly we do so in terms that themselves are open to further consideration and so again to transformation.

In the *Grammar* little will prove to be more central to my discussion than what I have called the "interinanimation" of its terms, their dependence on each other and on a common whole for meaning and application. In introducing his discussion of the pentad Burke makes this state of affairs explicit when he notes that what he wants, in his own italics, is *"not terms that avoid ambiguity, but terms that clearly reveal the strategic spots at which ambiguities necessarily arise"* (Burke 1945, xviii). These spots he designates also as the "ratios" derivable from the members of the pentad, the virtually ubiquitous occasions on which any one member of the group will assume meaning as it interacts with or gives rise to an-another. Scene in relation to act might be one such ratio as scene and act fit each other in implication or mood; or the appropriateness of agency in relation to the nature of agent; or agency, perhaps, as particular or part of scene. His approach in effect leads him to focus on the interactions existing in human motivation between and among the components of his pentad. He does not make such ratios sufficient in themselves; only the totality, action, hold that distinction; and action is the ambiguous substance possessing always that difference which allows it to generate such particular aspects as he proposes. He defines its particular fruitfulness in this way.

Since no two things or acts or situations are exactly alike, you cannot apply the same term to both of them without thereby introducing a certain margin of ambiguity, an ambiguity as great as the difference between the two subjects that are given the identical title. . . . Hence, instead of considering it our task to "dispose of" any ambiguity by merely disclosing the fact that it is an ambiguity, we rather consider it our task to study and clarify the *resources* of ambiguity. For in the course of this work, we shall deal with many kinds of *transformation*—and it is in the area of ambiguity that transformations take place; in fact without such areas, transformation would be impossible. (Burke 1945, xix)

Without transformation, we may add, both writing and reading would be as impossible as any other act.

The question, then, can be phrased as one of how to read William Carlos Williams, and restating Burke's argument leads me to form two initial principles: (1) Williams is to be read as a poet creating a literary substance that is ambiguous but not inherently more ambiguous than that of any other writer. My concern with him is first of all with the *kinds* of critical ambiguity that reading him generates. (2) Williams is a writer to be read as one whose utterance, insisting on particularly generated contexts as its distinguishing points, takes on the burden of persuading the reader to seek these contexts. Williams's reader is positioned by the author as coming to his texts, his stories, poems, or plays, for what they bespeak. The pleasure of Williams's writing is that of encounter. Its profit is discovery. He falls more plainly into that class of authors who hoped that their writing, as Ezra Pound's correspondent phrased it, would "give people new eyes" (Ellmann, 148) than among those who make their appeal to the "eyes" we already have. He would aim no lower than at a reframing of reading and its encounters. His aim is ambitious and prone to its own kinds of failures. Compensation is to be found in his successes as we are brought to some refashioning of our own readerly eye and, beyond that, to the use of such a refashioned eye toward and thence into the present contexts the writing implies.

There is a final appropriateness in associating Burke with Williams because the two men were for many years avant-garde comrades, antagonists in argument, friends, fellow residents of New Jersey, admirers, doubters, and sometimes critics of each other. They brought a temperamental and fruitful difference to their association, Burke's impulse toward intellectual sophistication contrasting with Williams's innate pull to the concrete and the local. Each in his way has left testimony of the other—Burke as essayist finding imaginative essence for Williams's poetry in its clinically immediate eye and touch: Williams as poet taking a stand on a present "earth under our feet" (*CLP*, 256) against Burke's interest in essentializing away from it. My book is not intended to allow Williams's concreteness to be swallowed into Burke's generality of thought. Rather, I see in Burke a theorist whose value today is immense precisely as his abstraction is so abundantly relatable to concreteness.

In addition, Burke and Williams joined forces in the wholesale drift of their thinking away from any sense of poetry as "romantic" in essence, as dependent upon metaphorical or what, adapting Roman Jakobson, I may call openly paradigmatic utterance for its existence. Burke's theory serves appropriately as a map for Williams's poetic. For both, writing exists in the statements it makes, provided that we read statement always as utterance within what Burke calls a "dramatistic" context and defines by means of his pentad. For both, poetry is discourse that requires a perception of references for its understanding, and both approach the problem of reference by pursuing a dramatistic line of thought about the art. Poetry, both might agree, comes to life most truly when it serves to intimate a speaker, a scene, purposiveness, and the like—when, in short, it is read as speech from an implicit play of which its utterance is the heart. It is speech which functions to establish the references upon which it depends. The play is unpredictable in character as it is no more than the sum total of context which poetic speech creates for itself. The romantic or metaphorical poem works by opening context to indefinite suggestion. Burke and Williams share an interest in valuing reference to context. Though their modes of reference differ, both are secular rather than transcendental in this regard. Together they resist, thus, any romantic diffusion of poetic scene into nature, say, and thence into spirit; of poetic agency into incantation and thence into symbol; of poetic purpose into apocalypse; or of poetic act beyond its own presence and thence into any kind of revelation.

The general progress of Williams criticism has been to move bit by bit toward a phrasing of whatever unity and poetic power may be claimed for the mass of largely tentative performance that is in fact his writing, and the purpose of this book is to advance that progress a further step. It will find its own frame in the multiplicity that the idea of poetry as a dealing with presence affords and in an effectually multicentered approach to that phenomenon. If a reader looks to poetry as words affording ritual symbolizing of the possible, then Williams must often seem to have been a weak poet. In recent poetic fact, however, Williams has been a force heralding a redirection of expression into the diverse avenues suggested by poets feeling something of a direct impact from him, like Allen Ginsberg and Robert Lowell, and more latterly and sophisticatedly by John Ashberry, all of whom make of poetry a facing of and dealing with presence. These three respectively exemplify Burke's claims for the drama of poetic agent, poetic scene, and poetic agency as focusing centers. Williams's own writing lacks such dominant centering and must be seen rather as a kinetic shifting among the points provided by the pentad. His writing in fact often emerges as an unsureness, but it nevertheless exploits the borders of a poetic region he felt the claims of strongly. As his frequent statements on the subject attest, he was aware of incompleteness in his work, but he was nevertheless compelled through a lifetime of effort toward what he felt to be that work's need—an utterance finding itself within a territory grounding him as poet and as individual.

II SCENE

PRESENT PLACE

Virtually everyone knows that what Williams called "things," what we shall here regard as components of "scene," of an adamant presence, take a large place in his poetry. He invoked and reinvoked as his own sense of writing his slogan "No ideas but in things," and he was largely faithful to the formula. His collected shorter poems can even be likened to a collection of snapshots of things, of unanticipated recordings of minutiae of the landscape, the environment, in which he lived his life. Trees, birds, buildings, parking lots, rocks, plants, animals, suspended moments of action jostle each other and are mingled with records of momentary feeling and occurrence. And such components of scene are regarded chiefly for what seems their own sake. Unlike Robert Frost, Williams is little interested in drawing scene out into subjective landscape. Unlike Carl Sandburg, he resists drawing scene itself into a whole of mood or feeling. He is a poet of locality as much as either of them, but Williams's locality seems to be apprehended by him as a spread of fragments or accidents without collective character. His poems seldom move far from the particulars of scene, but they also fall short of resolving scene into a controlling or shaping force. We are faced with the work of a poet for whom scene plays a crucial role, but it is a role which eludes easy characterization.

My first inquiry, then, is directed to the problem scene presents in Williams, a writer who relies on scene's presence but is unwilling to let his work diffuse into enfolding and proportioning breadth. To pursue the earlier likeness one step only, we note that a snapshot, like a poem by Williams, is randomly constituted by the scene it represents. Its interest is often its power to open itself to the kind of discourse scene generates.

In forming an arrangement for Williams's *Collected Earlier Poems*, Williams and John Thirlwall made choices that continue to appear mysteriously arbitrary. A substantial selection from *An*

12

Early Martyr, a volume of 1935, is placed early in the collected poems. It is preceded by a major grouping selected from *The Tempers* of 1913, followed by poems from *Al Que Quiere!* of 1917, and only then by selections from later volumes. Beyond such an intrusion of the 1935 poems into an early stage of his work, chronological order is further disturbed by poems from volumes of different dates placed separately and apparently at random in sections of their own between the groups identified with the published volumes. In the place of honor, at the head of the whole arrangment, stands the 1914 poem "The Wanderer," extracted from its original position as the final and hence summary work of *Al Que Quiere!*

The effect upon the reader is that of being jerked unpredictably back and forth between early and later writing. Most oddly, it seems, "The Wanderer" with its scenic declaration of the poet's baptism in the "filthy Passaic" offers not only the first but virtually the last word on that subject—the river and its environs—for the next twenty years, until the appearance of the short "Paterson." Instead, having declared his baptism in the Passaic, the poet then follows his avowal most immediately by selections from the early and decorated imagism prevailing in *The Tempers*; by two middle-length poems having to do with museum visits and the existence of art in history; by the 1951 montage of "Della Primavera Trasporte al Morale," alternating between images of a renewing Williamsian spring season and a panorama of the staccato humdrum of his own city life; and then, for the next eighty pages or so, by more controlled, more evenly measured poems selected from his work of the early thirties much dominated by the Objectivist thrust of that period toward what Zukofsky called a poem "at perfect rest" within itself (*Poetry* 36:274).

In an early letter to Williams, Wallace Stevens declared his conviction that "a book of poems is a damned serious affair" (*SE,* 13). In case Williams himself had such an attitude toward the forming of this definitive presentation of his own shorter poems, we will scrutinize its seeming irregularity for clues to purpose. One possibility is the current and widespread notion that baptism in the Passaic river of the opening "Wanderer" poem constitutes a determining presence for the poet's subsequent work. But the collected poems includes no more than small interest in determinate relation. The Passaic itself does not reappear in the volume for some time, and its environs are present in the poetry chiefly as generalized, often no more than assumed background to the varying thrusts of the poems. If indeed we return to the relevant passage in "The Wanderer," there seems clear reason to be doubtful of any simple identification between the poet's range of vision and the industrial New Jersey habitat despite his constant drawing upon it. Instead, something quite different is stressed.

Early in "The Wanderer" the poem's speaker reports that he has fallen into company with an old crone who appears to him and the reader as a bedraggled poetic Muse long since exiled from Helicon and subjected now to much indignity. Williams said later that he identified this figure with his admired and tutelary grandmother. Despite her reduced condition she remains loyal to her duty of inspiring the hopeful spirits who seek her and so undertakes a poetically educative séance with this aspirant, himself still in the process of fighting free of the imitative romanticism which had formed his earliest writing. She has much advice and disclosure to offer. Finally, well toward the end of the poem's approximately 350 lines, she moves toward the ceremonial act of baptism in a Pierian spring that has become the twentieth-century Passaic river of Paterson, Rutherford, and Newark: "Raising the water then in the cupped palm / She bathed our brows wailing and laughing." The "filthy Passaic," the poet notes, "consented," and he does indeed feel "the utter depth of its rottenness." The result, however, is far from being a whole identification with the polluted stream. The Muse herself seems more concerned with the river's "wandering" (*CEP*, 11) as the poem's title suggests, and the scene evoked by the stream is itself subjected to visible change. The kingdom into which the poet has been admitted is more emphatically one of restlessness and unpredictability than of "rottenness," and one which itself immediately undergoes a transformation at the Muse's will, though in still uncertainly formed lines.

> Here shall be a bird's paradise,
> They sing to you remembering my voice:
> Here the most secluded spaces
> For miles around, hallowed by a stench
> To be our joint solitude and temple:
> In memory of this clear marriage

And the child I have brought you in the late years.
Live, river, live in luxuriance
Remembering this our son,
In remembrance of me and my sorrow
And of the new wandering!
(*CEP, 12*)

The river's stench remains, but such offensiveness is also linked with natural "luxuriance," and the baptism is particularly commemorative of second birth into a wandering marked by mixed "sorrow" and redemptive beauty. The Passaic's gift to the poet is far from simple, and it is the opposite of binding. It is in fact a deliverance to mixture and uncertainty.

If Williams is indeed a poet of "indeterminacy," as Marjorie Perloff has claimed and Joseph Riddel has argued at more convincing length, we find a first anticipation of that end in the problematics of the local scene reflected in the collected poems. "Wandering," in the special sense defined by this opening poem, will be the keynote, the poet's disconnection from any prescriptive or determining sense of his world. From the beginning he asserts a double-mindedness about the value of that world for his own ends. His baptism has been definite but without clear implication. It is this sense of mixed poetic enablement rather than any clear identification with place that should govern our concern with Williams's lifelong attachment to what he called "the local."

The world present to the poet is of value not for itself but for what it opens to and within him. That gift, he contended, could be found in any scene, and it is for this essentially negative reason that he begins with an acceptance of "the local" as his own milieu. Considered as fullness, as terminus, the local could be a poetic death, as he thought it had become in Carl Sandburg. "Fatigue is the outstanding phenomenon as it affects [his] characters, they walk as if doped" (*SE, 278*), Williams wrote, and his long review of Sandburg's 1948 *Collected Poems* was a disquisition on the trap that the local could become if it was allowed to swallow up poetic freedom. Sandburg's virtue was that he refused to lie, but, equally, he "was incapable of taking his eyes away from what he saw" (*SE, 274*). As a result, "he fell into the facts themselves. He couldn't limit himself to being a mere poet, the facts were too overpowering, he himself was swept off his feet by their flood" (*SE*, 275). As "The Wanderer" indicates, the poet needs to use givenness, not regard it for purposes of dependence and record making.

In fact, Williams's largest creative concern with scene will be found in his prose: particularly the historical imagination of *In the American Grain*, the novels of the Stecher trilogy, and the short stories collected in *The Farmers' Daughters*, and it will be their nature also to divest the local of binding power over either the author or his characters. In the Stecher trilogy, to be sure, he will turn to what will pass as a literary realism, chiefly a rendering of the American scene known to his wife's parents during their lives and of their adventures in it. Here and elsewhere, however, narrative principle in fact will be that of a creative force making the world no more than a set of often-conflicting possibilities for individual action. The "naturalistic" story is commonly one of the world's impact on passive individuals. Williams's realism will be more the reverse, the narrative of individuals acting upon what the world presents, encountering and living among its givens but responding as idiosyncratic and independent powers taking the world to themselves and using it as far as they can in ways commensurate with their several wills. They are often odd, sometimes freakish, but they are seldom forecastable. The world affords them enough space and resource for their particular being.

From Williams's prose and poetry both, then, there emerges a very particular sense of the "scene" Kenneth Burke offers. Not scene as determinative of writing and its character; that could lead to no more than passive motion of the kind Williams thought he saw in Sandburg. Instead, scene as an enabling presence, as a resource of action. Having established this sense at the opening of his own collected poems, Williams immediately proceeded to a demonstration in that volume of the unpredictable variety scene, so considered, might yield. And such evoking presence would be repeated as the generalized scene of the historical essays, the novels, and the short stories. In itself, scene is potent but virtually void of definition. It is marked primarily by givenness and so becomes the ambiance but not the cause of event within it; it colors action but it leads to no delimited consequences. For Williams, as poet, it is certainly devoid of what Roland Barthes called "writing," an exigent world of literary practice. For the characters in his prose it is equally devoid of what might more generally be thought a "culture." The various outcomes it leads to become real only as they engender what Williams programmatically called "contact," transformational encounter with a scene which otherwise lies inert before the individual. It was such contact, the presence of agent, poetic person, within scene that would be efficient cause, not scene itself.

In initiating a magazine in 1920 (where concept now became title) he declared, "We, *Contact,* aim to emphasize the local side of the game of writing." But such a "local side" was to be found only in connection with an otherwise problematic scene. Where for Dreiser or for Sandburg scene had been determinant, for Williams it would be matter to wrestle with. "We want to give all our energy to the setting up of new vigors of artistic perception, invention, and expression in the United States" (*SE,* 29). Scene was indivisible from such engendering, but it could not supplant the act of engendering.

In the American Grain

His acceptance of local scene, then, opened something of possibility for Williams's writing, but his equal acceptance of innovation left open the question of what such localism might yield. Through the mid-twenties his publications provided a record of his own restlessness and uncertainty as they wandered between states of chaos and, increasingly, of sudden and sharp attainment. He had begun with clumsy imitations of Keats and Shelley in the 1909 *Poems* and proceeded through some half-dozen volumes, often of poetry mixed with prose, to reject such early mannerism including influence from the lush Pre-Raphaelite *Imagisme* that Ezra Pound was himself in the process of rejecting. Artfulness still played a large part in *The Tempers* of 1913, but there was increasing attention to immediacies of scene suggested by titles like "Man in a Room," "Chicory and Daisies," "Spring Strains," and "Overture to a Dance of Locomotives." The first of his "experimental" fictions, *The Great American Novel,* appeared in the course of the earlier volumes, a projecting of themes of love and creativity but only as being at war with assorted banalities of contemporary life.

In the late summer of 1923, he and his wife left Rutherford and settled in New York to begin a year of what he called "sabbatical leave," its first part to be spent in the city and its second in a number of European locations, in the poet's first extended devotion of himself wholly to writing, and for many decades the only such time. Concern with scene now dominated as he used his year chiefly for writing *In the American Grain,* a series of essays on the exploration and settlement of America, and his devotion to the task grew out of pressingly sensed interests. "Of mixed ancestry," he later wrote to Horace Gregory, "I felt that America was the only home I could ever possibly call my own." His father had been born in England and raised largely in Santo Domingo whence he emigrated to the United States. The mother's family, carrying the Sephardic name of Hoheb, blended Basque and Spanish blood with French and Jewish. She spoke both French and Spanish, the language that Williams largely used at home. Williams's own existence as newcomer in a nation of newcomers was thus immediate to him and one he bore close in consciousness. He wrote a variety of poems on his mother and father and on his English grandmother as well and devoted three novels to his wife's family, her parents especially, with their own combination of German and Norwegian stock. *In the American Grain* itself was to be largely a study in what may be called "immigration," ranging from the original onset of European voyagers and conquerors to later efforts at grasping the identity which such early thrusts predicated. Williams's approach would be, first, to discard any received or binding notion of American identity (no more than elsewhere would scene here prevail simply), and, second, to trace what he could individually and *ab novo* make of any American "grain." In his own case, at least, the American grain was the only possibility. "I felt that [America] was expressly founded for me, personally," he wrote to Gregory, and then, "that it must be my first business in life to possess it." To be native, to be local, was first to confront scene, but as a still-unoccupied territory, one requiring rather than offering statement.

> Nothing in the school histories interested me, so I decided as far as possible to go to whatever source material I could get at and start my own valuations there: to establish myself from my own reading, in my own way, in the locality which by birthright had become my own. (*SL,* 185)

The book was substantially complete by the end of 1924, and the whole was published in 1925. Williams was quite aware of D. H.

Lawrence's *Studies in Classic American Literature* which had appeared in 1923 and the content of which he in part overlapped. In fact, however, his aim was different from Lawrence's. The English writer had largely compiled a treatise against the withering effect of a continuing "Puritanism" in American letters. Given the loftiness of his own convictions in this regard, Lawrence could be heavily dismissory. Williams shared with Lawrence a 1920s revulsion from what they both called Puritanism, but for him the final purpose must be to find what might allow the best use of a national record that he also found to be appallingly damaging. His response, written at length, was the problem of scene—a facing of the given in an act combined of scenic presence and of intuition within it, his essential creative act of "invention."

The book may be said to have three loosely definable phases. The first, made up of his survey of early voyagers, considered the conglomerate of accident, venture, brutality, and even helplessness out of which America had been birthed. The second, and closest to Lawrence in its emphasis, explored what he saw as the blight of a generalized Puritan ascendancy over the nation, and especially over its literature, a blight he saw rooted in the *Mayflower* and Cotton Mather and yielding Benjamin Franklin as the hybrid fruit of Puritan and prudential impulse. In late sections of the book, then, he was drawn to a number of figures bent on absorbing the presence of wilderness that in Williams's view was always the substance. Père Sebastian Rasles, for example, a Jesuit missionary; Daniel Boone; Aaron Burr; and Sam Houston all shared the virtue of what Williams in the title of the Houston chapter called "descent," a process he was to be grappling with at length in *Paterson* and much of his poetry. The voyagers most often represented a randomness and inconsequentiality of encounter with the potent givenness of the wilderness scene. The Puritan, as far as he could, sought to shut out its presence in favor of his own world-denying zeal. The heroes of descent gave themselves to wilderness, in various ways yielding themselves to its reality, but also they found themselves swallowed up by it, or mere connoisseurs of it, or impotent in its presence, and hence largely without issue.

Houston's early life could stand as the emblem of all the figures of descent, reaching as it did toward wilderness for a sustenance he could not name but could not do without. Scandalously divorced from his wife, he "resigned the governorship of Tennessee, left everything behind him, and took the descent once more, to the ground," by joining the Cherokee tribe in Arkansas and identifying his life with theirs: "It is the saving gesture," Williams comments, "but a gesture of despair" (*IAG*, 213). Even so it was the gesture Williams also reached for, and as it was opposite to that of the Puritans so, even in its despair, it became the most natural gesture created by the scene that embraced them all. The Puritan did not descend, he arose—or set his aim in that direction—and in doing so generated a mentality resolute in its loyalty to abstract virtue. The choice was real, however. Descent moved toward contact, but it did so at real cost. Much had to be given up: "All things [the Puritans] explain, with clarity and distinction. It is firm, it is solid, it holds the understanding in its true position, not beneath the surface of the facts, where it will drown, but up, fearlessly into a clear air, like science at its best, in a certain few minds." And even, "There is vigor there—and by that, a beauty" (*IAG*, 110). The Puritan could not be simply dismissed. "Descent" could not be simply embraced.

Like the early voyagers in his history, Williams himself looked out upon an accidentally encountered landscape. A son of Spanish, English, French, and Jewish wanderers, now himself perched on a verge, he most naturally regarded America as potential rather than actual milieu. This first perception of scene remains basic in his writing. His book opens on the theme of exile with the voice of Eric the Red, driven from Iceland as retribution for a murder he regards as no murder but as vengeance consonant with pagan justice. Like Williams he is a wanderer, and the fruits of place will be only what he can make of them. "Greenland then," he meditates, "So be it. Start over again" (*IAG*, 3), sounding like a familiar passage in *Paterson 3*. In an image that will be made explicit in Williams's chapter on De Soto, Eric is the first tiny unit in the cloud of sperm that Europe will be releasing against the great egg of the new world, and he will be one of the many to fall short, go astray, to fail of conception and new birth. He himself will progress no further than Greenland. His son, Leif, by accident, becomes the discoverer of the new continent (in the account Williams is following), but the exploration he instigates will not proceed beyond battle with the Indians and a retreat to Greenland, there into further battle with his own clan.

The more effective beginning, Williams argued, would come from a wholly different if equally random encounter, and it would be not so much a begetting as an imposition or perhaps even a denial. His chapters on the *Mayflower* and on Cotton Mather (the latter made up wholly of excerpts from the *Wonders of the Invisible World*), along with a substantial digression in the chapter on Père Sebastian, all finding completion in the chapter on Franklin, sketched in Williams's sense of the centrality of Puritanism in American history. He recorded a visit with Valéry Larbaud in Paris, who was himself working on a study of Simón Bolívar, and noted the Frenchman's sense of the two European forces dominant in the American past. In their settlement, Larbaud maintained, the Spanish sought "in truth a New Spain, to build fine cathedrals, to found universities, to establish great estates. . . . They came as from the King himself to transport nobility, learning, refinement thither in one move." The English, he judged, "appraised the new world too meanly. It was to them a carcass from which to tear pieces for their belly's sake, a colony, a place to despise a little. They gave to it parsimoniously, in a slender Puritan fashion" (*IAG*, 108). Williams recorded no reaction to Larbaud's vision of the new Spain here, though in a later essay he would fault the Spanish also for failure to find contact (*SE*, 136). But he pondered at length the sense of a "slender Puritan" gift that the Frenchman outlined.

For D. H. Lawrence American Puritanism had been a case of small minds and souls stamping their imprint on what evolved into a national culture, this smallness compensated for only by little victories of personal prudence and gain. Williams did not quarrel with this view, but unlike Lawrence and such contemporary American critics of the Puritan heritage as Van Wyck Brooks and H. L. Mencken, he saw a dynamism at work that could not be denied. However perversely, the Puritan would at least act in a way close to Williams's concerns in founding a literary and intellectual culture, though it was doomed to rootlessness by its own necessary conditions. Transformation was beyond the Puritan as contact was unavailable to him. "Their courage," he conceded, "had they been gifted with a full knowledge of the New World they had hit upon, could not have stood against the mass of wilderness" (*IAG*, 111). It was present knowledge, consequently, that they sacrificed, and it was present knowledge that needed recovery.

The Indians, the American natives, lurk as much in the purlieus of Williams's writing as they did in the back country of the emerging land, reaching through its pages with tokens and symbols of what might have been gained if effort had been made to absorb rather than fence out the fact of wilderness. They offered an impetus that the Puritan ignored and that Williams would seek to rediscover, a life lived from the presence of physical world, of creative contact. The American would soon enough find a way to the physical, but it would be by a kind of blind "impersonation" of natural brutality only. If spirit was to separate itself from the physical, as it had with Puritanism, then the physical would survive only as brutality, in modern America "a panorama of murders, perversions, a terrific ungoverned strength, excusable only because of the horrid beauty of its great machines" (*IAG*, 68). This scene Williams, like all modern Americans, did indeed face. It could not be much altered, but his question would be how to generate a creative force within it.

A handful of further cases remained to illustrate the ambiguities of "descent" as alternative. Williams's image now was an almost biblical one of sowing, nurturing, and reaping. The mixed growth represented by Whitman's dedicated but underdeveloped verse, for example, was explicable in such terms; it had no choice but "to come from under. All have to come from under and through a dead layer." Poe, like Whitman, grew within these conditions. The seed had to descend in its planting. It could not rise to more than its nurturing allowed. "The quality of his flower will then be seen to be normal, in all its tortured spirituosity and paleness, a desert flower with roots under the sand of his day" (*IAG*, 213). Descent like scene itself was precondition only, an image of the uncertainty of a planting that was nonetheless indispensable.

Williams pictured Père Sebastian as the earliest of such planters. A seventeenth-century preacher to the Indians, he realized that his creed could find life among them only in the colors of their being. "TO MARRY, to *touch*—to *give* because one HAS, not because one has nothing. And to give to him who HAS, who will join, who will make. . . . It is the sun" (*IAG*, 121). The emphases bespeak urgency. Père Sebastian is no more a clear begetter than the voyager before him, but through descent into the alien he finds a way to begetting's first stage, that of contact. Williams's feeling for him and his kind is asserted by an obviously romantic turn of both sexual and vegetative imagery, but it also points at what he sees to be the inescapable poetic need. Scene must be attended to by both feeling and mind. Both must be able to give themselves up, or now, perhaps, down to its nature. Marriage can only be marriage of two who each yield much of themselves to what is alien. Valéry Larbaud was to laugh at his enthusiasm for Père Sebastian, for wanting Americans to take upon themselves such generosity of spirit: "Come to France," he joked, "and make us understand it." Williams would not be put off: "That *is* the moral source I speak of, one of the forces that has shaped America and must be recognized" (*IAG*, 122).

Père Sebastian's enfolding of scene in himself, his use of it in feeling and mind, finds parallel in Daniel Boone's openness to it, to a "new wedding," as he accepts the Indian as master of the world that Boone himself reached for. Underlying such awareness was the sense Williams conferred upon him of seeing that the essence of "descent" and hence of contact was moral and aesthetic rather than material; that and the political held nothing but failure. It was, Boone said, the speculator who had in fact won and despoiled the wilderness homestead he had opened. Descent predicated no success, least of all for the poet Williams himself was set on being. Scene was never more than possibility, and action would be what it was.

It is perhaps apparent by now that "scene" in Williams is especially bound up with act. In simplest terms, Williams makes the American scene the occasion either of act or of act's denial or perversion, and act in turn becomes the retroactive shaper of scene. He reverses Sandburg to propose that act makes scene what it will be, certainly in writing. Any discussion of the local in writing cannot help but invoke the scene-act ratio. The subject itself brings the scene into relation with act. The whole effort of *In the American Grain* is to restate that relationship such that scene-creating action will be possible.

Near the end of his book Williams turns his attention beyond voyagers, Puritans, or heroes of descent to regard a figure passing them in essence but complementary to them. This figure has brought his argument much obloquy, but such judgment may well reflect a misreading of the scene-act ratio in Williams's writing. Why, the argument goes, and apart from a pair of clearly inadequate pages on Lincoln tacked on at his publisher's request, end

such a study with Edgar Allan Poe? Why not, the ground now prepared, resolve all in such a satisfyingly native figure as Hawthorne
or Twain or Emily Dickinson? Williams will have some response to
each of these possibilities. He is uninterested, we may say, in finding
a "representative American writer," one who can most efficiently
be fitted into whatever native scene may be proposed for him. Such
a figure would be devoid of Burke's power of "transformation"
exactly to the degree he had become representative. The question is
one less of native voice than of native doing. William seeks the most
"active" or "generative" American writer, one who responds most
faithfully to the particular need for action toward which scene impels him. The American writer must first of all be an American
"agent," and in such terms Williams will unblushingly link American literature with those very pragmatic forces at work in American
culture which our literature has most often viewed as the enemy.
Puritan transcendence of mind was a vice, but a Puritan pragmatics
of action was indispensable provided it was radical to the present
scene.

It is clear that Williams joins with Lawrence in impugning the
post-Puritan American "classic," the New England ascendancy suggested by such figures as Lowell or Longfellow. Now, however, he
passes wholly beyond Lawrence's dismissory tone. The essay on
Poe completes Williams's volume by aligning it with his own positive commitment to avant-garde reconstruction. "He [Poe] counsels
writers to *borrow nothing* from the scene, but to put all the weight
of effort into the WRITING. Put aside the GRAND SCENE and get to
work to express yourself" (*IAG*, 227). The mere tinting of literary
conventionality with local color too clearly lacks what is necessary:
descent, contact, and from them engendering.

Poe stands apart from but also as addition to the other major
figures of Williams's book. He is an explorer, but explorer now of
his own ground of writing. He shares in the act of descent as he
isolates and redefines the very elements of his craft for whatever
may be newly generated there. He is even something of a Puritan,
like Williams himself, as he narrows his vision to essences requiring
abstract positioning and restructuring. At the same time, he passes
beyond the randomness of the voyagers and the Puritan's break
with contact. Clearly, he falls victim to the risk of dissipation and
waste inherent in descent, but that risk Williams would hold to be
inescapable.

Williams has greater regard for Poe as prose writer than as poet and will allow him only rare fulfillment in verse. He calls "To One in Paradise" the best of the poems and wants to add no more than three, he says, or possibly five other unspecified titles. All the rest are lost in the "tortured spirituosity and paleness" of an unavailing ideal. The stories carry the day as they most clearly embody structural concern. Williams had praised Poe for expressing "himself," but his essay divorces such self-expression from the expression of feeling for its own sake. Poe's self-expression was a dedication to method by which he sought to realize his sense of a writing done in truth to itself and its situation. Surely it is Poe's example that echoes in Williams's introduction to his own 1944 volume of poems, *The Wedge*. "Let the metaphysical take care of itself," he urges, "the arts must have nothing to do with it" (*CLP*, 4). Instead:

> When a man makes a poem, makes it, mind you, he takes words as he finds them interrelated about him and composes them—without distortion which would mar their exact significance—into an intense expression of his perceptions and ardors that they may constitute a revelation in the speech he uses. It isn't what he says that counts as a work of art, it's what he makes, with such intensity of perception that it lives with an intricate movement of its own to verify its authenticity. (*CLP*, 5)

It clearly was not Poe's effects that Williams valued, except as these are testaments to remaking, but his generating thence of ends from means, so that the poetic scene became available to him. His "originality," his crowning virtue in Williams's eyes, lay in that. Williams would restate the point in an essay of 1936.

> [Poe's] significance lies in his power to fix, recordize, reassert in cryptographic form (only vaguely sensed at the moment as greatness—but full of accurate meaning for all that) to make a cryptogram of his times, in form and content—with the passionate *regenerated force* of the artist underlying it. (*RI*, 106).

Williams cautions against seduction by the "popular, perfect" "Gold Bug" or "Murders in the Rue Morgue," though he might have found in them Poe's fertility of impact. Instead he directs attention to lesser stories like "The Business Man," "Loss of Breath," and "Hop Frog," where "humor is less certain" and "mood lighter" and where faults themselves are "allowed to become expressive" (*IAG*, 229) as they all the better embody scene. He proposes a short list of Poe's commitments which become index to his act: first, to "abstract" story material; second, to "a logical construction that clips away, in great part, the 'scenery' near at hand in order to let the real business of composition *show*"; finally, to a "primitive awkwardness of diction . . . especially in the dialogue, much in the vein of Mark Twain" (*IAG*, 230). Poe offers, clearly, values of structural address rather than of atmospherics. And this emphasis brings us back to the central issue. American writing will be true to its scene to the extent that it embodies scene in the conditions of the work's own literary making. *In the American Grain* thus finally delivers us to life in America, and to its literature as a process within scene to be valued as realization of such process within such scene. This is, then, "local" and hence "American" expression.

Emily Dickinson succumbed to a kind of denial, which led Williams to give her disappointingly short shrift. The only woman in our past, he said, whom "one can respect for her clarity" took upon herself the limits of "her father's garden" and so built a kind of defense against the potent void which in fact was milieu for them all (*IAG*, 179). Hawthorne was less vital than Poe because he accepted the format of the romantic tale as refuge from scene's demand and made his effort one essentially of a literary adaptation. Writing may find determination as it finds a place for itself in the scene of writing as such, as it becomes, perhaps, recognizably "romantic" or "classic," "tragic" or "comic." But the whole force of Williams's efforts from the beginning, of his operating in a poetically undetermined land, had been to hold on to local not literary context. He approaches along his own path the condition that Barthes designated as writing degree zero.

What has been felt to be "indeterminate" in Williams's poetry may thus be linked to the universality and unalterability of immediate presence that his whole approach postulates. The poem or story might have a freer if more suspect thrust at determinacy, at resolving into self-evident imaginations, the more it was allowed to digest scene or dimensional presence into its own malleable, non-dimensional literary being. Williams thought this had been the direction of Hawthorne, and he takes a counterview. If there really are no ideas but in things (that is what the necessity of descent implies), and things can only be present, then presence is the only source of ideas. However, writing cannot escape translating presence into thought, carrying it across into co-present language, just as the words and ideas of one language can be altered into the words and ideas of another. When translating things or scene, temporally ordered statements can be articulated with each other in ways that spatially ordered things cannot, and articulation itself implies design commanding at will the order of the things it invokes, if not the things themselves. Through all this, presence remains a problem just as in linguistic translation the original words and ideas may. Scene, like translation's original, is simultaneously resource, limit, and taskmaster. The American writer's task, Williams thought, could not be that of dissolving and hence resolving one state of being into another. Native scene could not be declared equal to native poem. The writer might, however, search the scene available to him as a translator does his original in the more promising hope of framing a presence within a presence, of newly ordering language to coexist with existing things so that, not otherwise determinative, they became the container and circle of reference. The poet could not help but write within his time and his place, and his work should bear that testimony. The poem of the local existed not about its scene but within and because of scene's generative potencies and counterpressures. Scene was present place. Scene was present time. And invention, a discovery within that place and time, was the task of a truly generative imagination.

The Stecher Trilogy

Our tentative formula then is that of scene fulfilled in action, of utterance within *this* scene. Scene itself, apart from its most general aspects, is hardly determinable without whatever language appears to confer aspect on it. The spatial scene, as such, is prior to the writer's language to be sure, and continues its own perdurable if brute existence beyond such occasion, but it has no image. To be a local writer is necessarily to create a locale, one of course that may be recreated by others in their turn. The only literary means available for such creation are those that words make available. This is the condition of Williams's praise of the language of Poe and of Gertrude Stein for its "side to side juxtaposition of the

words as the ideas." In contrast, the romantic "aroma" of Hawthorne's utterance (its often explicit evoking of presence undeclar-
able by language) in fact turns his writing away from real presence
to call up an abstract and hence wholly fictive reference to absent
literary or moral authority. If Poe would horrify or bemuse or reject
he must name horror or bemusement or rejection. Presence in him
is literal.

This is the principle that Williams would carry into his own most
ambitious effort at fiction, the three titles of the Stecher trilogy,
White Mule of 1937, *In the Money* of 1940, and *The Build-Up* of
1952. The three novels find one major focus of character in Joe
Stecher and a single predominant thrust of action in Joe's rise into
and absorption by the middle-class world. This progression is con-
tinuous to the whole but varyingly present within it. Each of the
individual novels exists as no more than a segment and with no
more independent structure of its own than a loosely chronological
order and the physical covers of each book impose. The total work
both qualifies as a "novel" and falls short of such traditional identity. Joe is indispensable to its action, but he is accompanied by his
wife, Gurlie, and by numerous relatives and acquaintances who
take significant part in the whole but who often find identities apart
from any question of his progress and hence from traditional novelistic "unity."

The trilogy, thus, offers to first glance a puzzling and even repellent seeming randomness and exteriority of structure. The reader
may seek relief, and to some extent find it, in the sharpness with
which the figures of Joe, Gurlie, and the infant Flossie, their
younger daughter, are rendered. And this is true in a degree of the
maturing children in the final volume. It is notable, however, that
the character for whom the first volume is named, Flossie, based
on Williams's wife, emerges chiefly in relation to the personage Williams makes of himself as the story nears its end. She is the "white
mule" of the first volume's title, so called for a rough but ready
moonshine whiskey, a local power. Her sister, Charlotte, has a
somewhat more integrated story. Their younger brother, Paul, dies
in a gunshot accident while still a boy. All, however, along with
Gurlie herself, are independent ramifications of Joe's and Gurlie's
union more than part of its pattern.

Lottie at first seems the more ardent spirit since she is the elder
and the focus of her mother's ambitions. She has displayed musical

talent from her early years, and when the trilogy opens upon her at the age of eleven she is already using her music as a weapon against Gurlie's managerial drive. At the same time that they struggle with each other, and despite Gurlie's own lack of feeling for her daughter's talent, it is Lottie's music that Gurlie seizes upon as the best hope of worldly distinction for her. Lottie devotes herself to her piano and its literature for the sake of escape and romance, while Gurlie values her devotion for what gain it promises, and the two are locked in uneasy and fundamentally hostile partnership. Lottie thus accomplishes the first of Williams's acts of engendering—descent into one fabric of art—but she finds it unavailing for achieving the sovereign virtue of invention or discovery. As a child she imagines her future childishly, but there is real warning concealed in her vision: "She could see herself bowing to a great audience at a concert hall. She could see the whole thing. There she stood with one hand just touching the top of the grand piano and bowing, bowing" (*BU*, 24). Her attachment to her music, and especially to Bach, who does not often please her suburban listeners, is intense. But she also shows something of Gurlie's direction of passion toward utility, and such a turn is the cessation of descent.

Though Williams was to marry Flossie, the younger daughter, it had been Lottie Herman who had first fascinated him and for some years continued to hold his feelings. He and his brother had both been her suitors, and in a passion-filled scene in the novel they decide between themselves that the younger, Fred, will propose to her. He returns with the news that he has been accepted, and Charlie Bishop, Williams's name for himself in the novel, feels the earth "dissolved under his feet." The wound is double. Not only has he lost his beloved, but his close bond with his brother is altered. "It was a deeper wound than he should ever thereafter in his life be able to sound. It was bottomless" (*BU*, 259). But Fred himself is scarcely the winner. Lottie will soon break her engagement to elope with an elegant and profligate painter whom in turn she will eventually divorce.

It is Flossie alone among the Stechers who is left to complete the use of scene that their stories had opened, to move or be moved to the point of casting herself wholly upon its reality, and thence to discover that such risk is in fact occasion. Despite her shadowy existence in much of the story, it is she who appears at those moments when the Stecher narrative runs most hardily against the circumstances that Williams makes determinative of scene and its activity. At the beginning there is birth. During childhood, and in contrast to Lottie, there is Flossie's contruction of a pattern that allows her to make a workable and self-nourishing place within her family. At its center is her love for her father, which enables her to discount her mother's continual fluster, to which she is helped by Gurlie's pragmatic decision that Lottie is the "genius" who must somehow be foisted into a career. Finally there is her acceptance of herself as unlike her sister and her need to fashion a place for herself from her own nature. The novel moves through two of its volumes before Flossie is brought even to school age. Her growing up in the third book is quickly encompassed and is attained in her acceptance of Charlie Bishop, Williams himself, and the birth of their son as the novel moves to its close. She is the "white mule," the native spirit bred out of scene and possessed of its flavor and dynamic. In substantial degree the stories of Joe, Gurlie, and Lottie are tales of misdirection and waste. The real Joe Stecher would end his life in apparent suicide. Flossie's story is one of absorption by the local and movement toward an engendering in keeping with its nature.

Williams was later to complain of feeling hurried in his writing of *The Build-Up* and restricted in what he could use in a novel closely related to living persons—Lottie and Flossie in particular as well perhaps as Ferdinand Earle, the American editor and painter with whom Lottie had in fact eloped. Even so, this third volume concentrates the indispensable matter of the story as a whole, its movement toward climax. The process comes to a head in Charlie Bishop's wooing and Flossie's acceptance of him, narrative that is so close to the bone of Williams's and the real Flossie's acceptance of each other that the author gives it the scantiest detail and places it, as it were, almost beyond the realm of novelistic analysis. But it is beyond that precisely as it had been encompassed in fact. And as fact it alone contains the seed of life that the novel's other characters search for fruitlessly. Charlie with other suitors has been attentive to the older sister. Flossie is too young and seemingly too characterless to attract his notice. She, however, has awakened to him. Her mother has no use for him. "He'll be poor, just a poor doctor—who writes poems. Poo!" Flossie takes comfort in the fact that her father likes Charlie, but she holds her own devotion close. "It was no one's business but her own; she never even mentioned his name aloud" (*BU*, 260).

Throughout this episode Williams gives himself fully to the claim out of which he was to attempt *Paterson*: "The province of the poem is the world" (*P*, 99). Perhaps more than at any other point the novel here indeed hews to world, relies upon presence to carry the moment's seminal opacity and force. To articulate more fully would be to endanger the primacy of fact, of the integrity of scene, upon which the whole event turns. Charlie, clearly, approaches Flossie on the rebound. Lottie has turned him down in favor of his brother. The fact cannot be altered. Whatever action he takes can assume shape only under its force. He moves to Flossie with no more ceremony than his request that she marry him. "You love my sister" is her answer. His own reply is true and exact. "'I don't love anyone,' he said, 'but I want to marry you. I think we can be happy'" (*BU*, 261). Now it is Flossie who is faced with the obduracy of scene—Charlie's willfulness and her own emotion. It is only the latter, of course, that she can really consult. Descent for her must be total, without circumstance or saving grace. She finds herself no place but where exactly she is. But a central condition does present itself: "If she said yes, it would be the end for her" (*BU*, 265). Acceptance would be final and an act of commitment willed by the only one who can make it—herself. The moment is existential in color, and, wittingly or unwittingly, Williams deepens that tone in the very slight commentary he appends.

> There is a sort of love, not romantic love, but a love that with daring can be made difficultly to blossom. It is founded on passion, a dark sort of passion, but it is founded on passion, a passion of despair, as all life is despair. (*BU* 262)

"Despair" here clearly functions as paraphrase of "descent." The ground truly engendering contact and invention is one necessarily bereft of solace or substitute, one that leaves no alternative but the act of invention. Flossie will accept the strange suit as her feeling for reality will allow no other choice. In accepting, she takes a stand on the rock of presence and in fact accepts what would become a devotion to making that rock bear flower.

Williams's feelings for and treatment of his wife during their lifelong marriage would pursue a tangled course. Her own choice once made, she would have no further comment except that implied by the patience, nurturing, and love which her life with him displayed. The union was the opposite of storybook except in its profundity. When in his "Prologue" to *Kora in Hell* Williams struggled to explain his feeling for poetic composition as an act rooted in fact and serving its necessity, it was to marriage that he reached for an analogue. He declared of his own union, "the best we have enjoyed of love together has come after the most thorough destruction or harvesting of that which has gone before" (*SE*, 19). Flossie's acceptance of him was itself born out of just such "harvesting" or, equally, "destruction." "It is in the continual and violent refreshing of the idea that love and good writing have their security" (*SE*, 20). Descent, contact, invention, renewal. For Williams here, as in *In the American Grain,* the terms dictated by scene struck deep. Whether the creativity they encompassed was that of poetry or of life, it was the essential, indeed the only gift that scene could offer. Flossie's genius was to grasp that fact. Charlie Bishop's was to act within its truth. More than any other of the novel's characters, it was they who had found what the American world could yield. Scene was a field of action. Its harvest was no more than what must be regenerated again and again from seeming indefinition.

The Farmers' Daughters

Williams had published a first novel, *A Voyage to Pagany,* in 1928, and his writing of poetry during the twenties had been dotted with other prose, some of it of "fictional" character. All of it, however, was marked by a high degree of experimental or avant-garde unconventionality. Then, about 1930, he found poetry drying up in him. Paul Mariani suggests that this was caused partly by the constant struggle he faced to achieve recognition and book publication (he himself had paid most of the publishing costs of his books to date) and partly by the onset of the Depression, which certainly was to force the poet to attend to the social and economic life he shared with his times. Whatever the exact reasons, he began the new decade with a flurry of attention to fiction. He had made some sort of beginning on *White Mule* after brief but abortive starts on other themes, and in 1930 Richard Johns offered to serialize its chapters in his newly founded *Pagany.* Johns's magazine would continue for three years or so, and it seems clear that this opportunity prompted a substantial part of the novel. After *Pagany* suspended publication, *White Mule* continued in the Berkeley, California, *Magazine,* where it came to the attention of James Laughlin who would seize upon it for his newly founded New Directions house in 1937.

Beginning about 1930 the short stories, also stretching out into three volumes, pointed a different way. The best signs suggest that many of his tales came to Williams out of his medical practice, which would carry him away from the upward mobility shaping so much of the trilogy. Upon completing his medical study at the University of Pennsylvania he had interned first at the Old French Hospital in New York and then in Child's Hospital for pediatric training. At the latter a clash with medical and financial corruption disillusioned him with the idea of a money-centered practice and in fact largely closed that door to him. When after postdoctoral study in Leipzig he decided to settle in Rutherford and practice there he succeeded a retiring physician who had made a career treating working-class patients, some in Rutherford, more in the adjoining mill town of Passaic in the hospital of which Williams became a lifelong staff member. To a great extent his medical life was bound up with a kind of immigrant different from the Stechers, often Italian or Middle European in origin, and with a variety of other patients who knew a life different from that of his own connection. In addition, he gravitated early toward obstetrics and pediatrics, though he also maintained general family practice. Many of his patients were women, and he was drawn into close and confiding relations with numbers of them. This caused a strain between his wife and himself as he perpetuated a series of emotional involvements, paralleled and enlarged in his literary friendships. Flossie remained at one center of his emotional life, but his two professions exerted strong individual attractions. He often said that medicine was a chore to him. He worked hard at it, however, and with emotional depth. It opened a breadth of elemental contact, sexual and otherwise, into which much of his writing would be reaching.

Nearly half of the forty-nine stories collected in *The Farmers' Daughters* are related directly to his life as a physician, and the group presents a useful sample of his fiction's exploratory directions. Common to all of them, and to his nonmedical stories as well, is his feel for the American scene, here as in the trilogy and in

In the American Grain open and potent but still often bare of individual resource and meager in present helps. Many of the stories can be said to be written in an awareness of double layering. At their base lies the process of life itself marked by little more than a duration through episode toward decay. Topping this layer, however, is a second, of willed action, with small resource, however, other than that of the individual himself. Enactment of will in such upper reaches is powerless radically to alter the lower layer. That continues on at its own level and in its own course. But the existence of the upper layer opens a variety of counterpoint in some stories, action emerging as a kind of inward and subjective resistance to the lower layer and its drift. Such tales, for example, as "Old Doc' Rivers" of "The Use of Force" are centered in characters who cannot alter the fate that has them in its power but who achieve dramatic assertion in their rejection of its right to hold them. They will be swept on but they will not go quietly. In a second group—perhaps "A Night in June" is a good example—the central character, following the route of descent, finds that the lower layer itself is a life impulse and so capable of sustaining endurance, which somehow makes his or her fate not happy but more bearable. Perhaps the darkest of the stories are those, finally, in which descent reveals no more than a blind directionlessness, the life process undoubtedly forging toward its own outcomes but in ways that remain beyond the characters' final ability to grasp.

Such distinctions are, of course, rough hewn at best, and to go outside the medical stories is to encounter greater range. Some of these stories, especially in the earliest volume, *The Knife of the Times* of 1932, reach toward what can be called human interest as their chief point of focus, character revealed simply in oddness, unpredictability, or even humor. Others fall back into the two-layer structure with varying degrees of offset between the inertia of circumstance and the push of individual will. Here as in the trilogy much rides on the interaction of these two, and imagination again will most succeed as it most manages an act of definition and choice within the blankness of which event so often consists. Flossie Stecher and Charlie Bishop had to find marriage, or make it, where scene seemed most alien. Marriage, it may be said, is itself not in nature but in imagination. The short stories are largely turned toward other considerations than courtship, but here too specific human gain is to be found only where vision can reach into the void of nature and return with its own invented, self-made fruits.

In the stories, then, the scene-act ratio prevailing elsewhere repeats itself. At one pole it is place-time as both resource and limit. At the other it is the eventfulness that fills and defines place-time. Place and time interact continuously. Williams's story at its most basic results not from sequence, order of procedure, or from other preframed structure but from the interaction. The result is what he described in a title for one story, and for a collection of them, as "Life along the Passaic River," so giving a preponderantly scenic emphasis to the whole. Event bodies forth eventfulness, and eventfulness bodies forth scene, all in such fashion that eventfulness and scene are often hard to distinguish from each other. The point is clearest, perhaps, in those stories where descent, on the character's part and on the author's, reveals little except a kinetic directionlessness. Bram Dijkstra and others have written of the impact on Williams's poetry of cubist painting, and something of this force can also be perceived in stories like "Life along the Passaic River" itself, or "The Accident," or "World's End" (other titles could be added), where the force of the tale is generated by scene-eventfulness existing vibrantly but virtually for its own sake. The force of such narrative is almost anonymous. Its voice is clear but hard to identify as either author's or character's. Its progress is willful or even arbitrary seeming. Passing beyond the interpretive thrust of *In the American Grain* or the evolutionary thrust of the Stecher trilogy, Williams now totally immerses himself and his tale in scene-event alone, but scene and event themselves as anonymous. Neither interpretation nor evolution is allowed shaping force. The story, as it were, generates itself out of its own elementals—eventfulness and scene—rather than out of what is shaped from their particulars.

"The Accident," carried forward to this volume from Williams's writing of the early 1920s, offers a workably brief example in its three and one-half pages. Its voice is that of the doctor to begin with, himself left without clear character. He has been struggling to keep life in a dying girl, but now must give up. "Death is difficult for the senses to light on," he begins. "There is no help from familiarity with the location," and this is a condition that will rule the very structure of the story itself. The girl's eyes are rolled back "until only the whites show," her mouth "is agape," her "tissues congeal." The doctor's confession is pressed out of him: "One is beaten." Then, in what can be likened to a cinematic quick-cut technique, these first three paragraphs are followed immediately by a jolting shift to a new opening: "It is spring" is the announcement, though a spring revealed in least lovely detail.

> Sunshine fills the out-of-doors, great basins of it dumped among factories standing beside open fields, into back lots, upon a rutted baseball field, into a sewage ditch running rainwater, down a red dirt path to four goats. (FD, 221)

In the midst of such a scene, juxtaposed with the dying that had preceded, a female presence suddenly troubles the speaker. Her hips brush against his, arousing him, but she herself is attracted by three boys making their way toward her with whom she plans a flirtation. Abruptly, again, the speaker is alarmed that the goats may harm a small child who is making his uncertain way toward them. Seeking to help the child, the speaker drags on him so that he falls on his face and breaks into loud crying. Shift again. In a nearby factory six women appear at two windows looking to see if the child is badly hurt. They are reassured and wave in reply. At a further distance a man and a boy bend over their work of planting in the fresh earth. The speaker gathers the child into a car, and the child, now soothed, waves good-bye to the scene, which vanishes as finally and abruptly for him as for the reader. The story is over.

Its title can be linked most obviously to "the accident" represented by the child's fall, but it also seems to apply to the whole contents. They, in turn, suggest an assemblage of many of the staple events to be found recurring in almost any embodiment of the life process. Their order is disjunctive and arbitrary, but they are there: dying, sexual attraction, nurture, the natural season and world, unforeseen happening, concern, recovery, new planting, departure. Brought together in this fashion they compose the accidentalness that Williams's sense of event so frequently makes out of life's underlying layer. The upper layer of his fiction is absent here except perhaps for the doctor's willed and enacted concern for the child. Even this, however, is subsumed in the whole, more the working out of instinctive feelings of nurture than of plan or choice. The story is most radical in its refusal to allow any one of its incidents to take on primary and hence shaping power. The story is no more "about" death than about sexual impulse, nurture, new planting, or any other of its concerns. It is about all of them, but only as together they assert both the arbitrariness and the perdurable recurrence that is life's own substratum.

We may say that the story's motive is one of "descent," even of despair, since it so totally falls short of any shaping or invention brought out of its descent. But descent is always central and inescapable to the act of Williams's writing. It is experienced, again, as the ground of invention. The author addresses scene in its rudiments, bent on foregrounding rudiments and the "accidental" or largely ungoverned process they body forth. The general similarity to descriptive painting drifting toward collage is worth dwelling on. We cannot really say that either the painter or Williams "remakes" nature. Nature remains existent, neither made nor remade. What is done, however, is to disassemble or disavow any preformed order, any preformed scene imposable upon nature. Time, space, and casual sequence are equally absent; none of them can be called on to supply the story's "meaning." Eventfulness is detached from any such ordering and made to exist for its own sake. The act of writing, then, becomes an acceptance, indeed a willed exploration, of this condition.

It is often the interposition of a cognate will within the story that adds the second and individuating layer to primary life process. The process itself is seldom lost sight of and equally seldom loses its hold over scene-event. It is in this sense that Williams comes closest, perhaps, to being classifiable as a "naturalistic" writer. But at most he is a naturalist without portfolio, without defined scheme or frame that would lead his stories into deterministic paths. To the contrary, his stories of the first or second kind, those in which character or author succeed in making contact within process, introduce an element of personal recognition and reaction that is alien to orthodox naturalism. Even in the stories of process alone event is "accidental" and hence unpredictable rather than determined. If his characters are more often reactors than actors, they are reactors according to an inner integrity (for better or for worse) rather than an inner or outer necessity.

An example is to be found in "A Night in June," one of several tales of his work as a doctor at childbirth. The life process, in full literalness, is in charge of event here. Seven times before, the doctor has delivered the Italian mother, Angelina, of her babies, and now he is called at three A.M. to assist with the eighth. It is a poor household he enters, but from the beginning he has a satisfied and peaceful sense of assisting process, of being humanely in relation with it. Both the mother and father know him as a friend, and through the poverty and disorder of the household he responds to them and their situation. Nothing is to be done immediately, and the doctor takes a short nap propped in a chair. He wakes "deliciously relaxed," and he repeats his sense of the situation. "Everything was quiet as before. The peace of the room was unchanged. Delicious" (FD, 140).

Neither mother nor doctor is any more in charge of event here than was the doctor-narrator of "The Accident." This time, however, characters interact in trust of each other and of the process that will go forward of its own accord no less than before. Process is slow, however, and the doctor debates with himself about using an injection of Pituitrin. He does not wish to hurry the birth, but equally he wants to spare the mother as much strain as possible. A debate forms within his mind between "science" and "an older school" (FD, 141), the school of acquaintance with and acceptance of the process he knows lies ultimately outside of his grasp. The balance must be struck, however. He injects a little of the drug and then, later, a little more, and the results are good. The baby begins to stir, and birth itself now gets under way.

The story has almost as little "climax" as does "The Accident." Here the baby is born as earlier the child had been delivered from the scene that had encased him. But on this occasion an additional element appears—clear and perceived "contact" with scene-event. It is stated plainly and artlessly, a recognized component of the scene as a whole. Whatever element of suspense and summary the story may attain is limited largely to the change in the direction from which the scene is registered.

This woman in her present condition would have seemed repulsive to me ten years ago—now, poor soul, I see her to be as clean as a cow that calves. The flesh of my arm lay against the flesh of her knee gratefully. It was I who was being comforted and soothed. (FD, 142)

The story thus moves at least to "recognition," and recognition is directed by experience to the sustaining powers of the process which catches up all the characters in it. It is a tale of harmony shared in. Individuals and process, alike incapable of leading to or "gaining" any end, find peace between themselves by dint of the individual's accepting participation in process, in scenic action, as the truth of his own nature. The role of character in Williams's stories is always bound up with that of the place by which the character is embodied. Although he had little good to say of Sherwood Anderson, there is much in his stories that recalls Anderson's open-ended studies of character-in-place. Conversely, Williams could at times express admiration for Hemingway, but his stories do not center in the detail of individual action and response as Hemingway's often do. It may be that he saw *Winesburg, Ohio* and Anderson's other tales as too formulaic, too much dependent, like Sandburg's work, on identification of character with scene: people in grotesque scenes act in grotesque ways. Certainly across the breadth of his own stories there is much individuality in scene-event, so that it is hard to give primacy to either pole of such a ratio. Unlike those of either Anderson or Hemingway, Williams's characters most often exist in a scene-event that they accept as fact and that thus takes on the quality of milieu to which they must suit themselves, or which they suit to themselves as far as that may be possible. Often both such suitings are present.

Within this generalization a variety of relationships prevails. Williams may project character strongly within scene-event (though still without overtones of personal rebellion or deep question) in such cases as those of Old Doc Rivers, the dashing, self-destructive, individualistic drug addict who is virtually canonized as a saint of healing by his superstitious patients; or Jack O'Brien, a combination of Thoreau and village bum, whom Williams extols as paragon of what local culture may engender; or the Italian patriarch who in courtly fashion offers the doctor attending his wife in their slum hovel a ceremonial pinch of snuff at the end of his call. I take examples here from each of the three volumes of stories, so together they span some twenty years of writing. It was a reaction that Williams liked to return to. Other characters, like the doctor in "A Morning in June," find their place by however unpredictable an act of accommodation, but the doctor's sense of having his hands on the process of nature itself, of sensing a holy of holies, may not be present at all. Often a rough-handed pragmatism takes its place. Again I take examples from each of the three volumes: There is the case of "Marge" who has sent her boyfriend Manuel out to work for a widowed farmer's wife. The farm wife agitatedly reports that he is maintaining a homosexual friendship with a visitor. Marge protests Manuel's firing on this account and hauls him away to find a job for him elsewhere. She takes what she finds and makes it her own. In "A Face of Stone" a pushing and insistent father repeatedly insists on the doctor's examining his child, with whom there is nothing wrong, and so manages his real aim, that the doctor attend to his ailing and abused wife whom he had been ashamed to thrust forward. Or, in "Lena," a provincial New Jersey woman can't get used to the strangeness of a Miami vacation. She is anxious to get back to her pig farm in the Jersey "medahs" where she had grown up. There is small overtone of any piety in such tales. In its place the power of scene-event to compel outcome is made both absolute and arbitrary, necessary to itself.

It is this quality in the stories that provides their surest link with both *In the American Grain* and the Stecher trilogy. Scene both engenders and is defined by action. In all three cases action is taken to be the reality governing the native scene and its literature alike. Williams is far from being any kind of heroic nativist. It is impossible to draw from him the rapturous identification of, say, a Thomas Wolfe. It is rare even to find the mixture of fondness and distaste that Mark Twain generated out of his own grappling with native scene. Equally, however, he is at a distance from Dreiser or Sinclair Lewis, and he differs explicitly from Ezra Pound who in one characteristic reaction in "Hugh Selwyn Mauberley" regretted being born "in a half savage country, out of date." Savagery is neither heaven nor hell for Williams. It is simply there, along with much variation, counterimpulse, and other complications to which he opened his nets of fiction as widely as possible. The result is, again, to identify story itself with scene-act. Pound could spend much effort seeking redefinition of poetry in relation to its past. Williams would be equally occupied in redefinition in accord with a present. Pound, we may say, sought precedents. Williams would seek no more than opportunities as they became apparent in scene-event itself. More rigorously than Stevens, he forced both subject and form to be expressions of what was there and then, his text both dealing with and becoming the cry of its occasion.

There was only occasional rebellion against occasion, or perhaps not even rebellion at all but, now and then, assertion. The compressed vitality of "The Use of Force" could pit the doctor's small patient against the whole fate that was both her illness and the doctor's intrusion into so secret and fearful a center. The assertive teenager of "The Girl with the Pimply Face" could both hold her poise against the doctor and, by following his directions, reduce her plague of acne. The doctor himself in "The Paid Nurse" could rise up against the systematic defrauding of a patient, injured on the job, by his employers and their medical satraps. But Williams's point in the short stories, as in both the trilogy and *In the American Grain,* was not to indict or redeem the land either directly or by his writing. Rather it was to scan it, as *In the American Grain* had made clear, for what of action, and hence of life and possibility, given its character, it could generate. The purpose of fiction as of poetry was immediate realization more than narrative construction, lyric expressiveness, or meditative exploration. The short stories drove the point home. As "The Wanderer" had indicated, the concern would be life along the Passaic river. What that life was, the stories would both seize upon and be.

The question will arise, finally, as to whether Williams's fiction and history is to be wholly "reduced" to such scene-act ratios as we have been concerned with here. The answer, of course, is no, but my argument has been conducted in the belief that the other members of the interinanimate pentad—act, agent, agency, and purpose—can well be approached in these texts with primary regard for scene-act and its implications. Perhaps I seem to have most neglected the question of purpose at this point. If this is a prose that completes its effort by returning to the purlieus of scene-act whence it has risen, what can be said of its substance and implication beyond such circularity? The answer lies in the realm of what Burke calls dramatism. Williams's prose acts out the process of what it is for this author to write essays and stories about and within this America. The purpose of the prose is not so much to reveal an American scene to its readers, though that, cumulatively, does take place. But scene alone will be inert unless we are as much aware of the writer writing within it as of what he writes about it. The act of writing is a part of his presence.

Williams himself was abundantly clear and emphatic in his acceptance of such a purpose for himself, especially in his vehement and repeated assertion of the alienness to him of almost any established writing. As he repeatedly centered the presence of "invention" in his own effort, so he took upon himself the need of inventing not just this or that utterance but utterance itself. Story, or essay, or poem for him would be not so much an entity within "literature" as an entity within the writing of William Carlos Williams. Invention in his sense would never be less than radical effort. The context of his prose, then, was greatly one of scene-act, act including the writer and his work as both were cases in point of life along the Passaic river.

I can add some resonance to my claim by including Williams in that broad group of American writers whose purpose was that of "interpreting" America. At one point, however, Williams added his own important codicil to that collective effort when he said that his aim was, rather than interpret, "to embody America and myself in it" (*EK*, 47). We may say that he creates for us his kind of American scene by virtue of his kind of participation in American literature. The result is stories both in connection with and within which world is well or badly used, or often simply used only as far as possible here and now. He leads thus not to slogans about life along the Passaic, or American life, but to present evidence of what kind of action, including his own, that life enables. The character his writing frames for itself is present and pragmatic. He is almost never a formal judge of his subject, but he never ceases to be, as citizen and as writer, witness within and to it. And the purpose from start to finish was poetic. Williams created a scene within which his writing alone must fashion place and event leading to its own form of literary being.

III AGENT

PRESENT PERSON
(FREEDOM AND FACT)

Williams's use of scene is a case in point of Burkian "transformation" or of what I have called "translation"—a whole metamorphosis of physical presence and its detail into literary action. The fact that "scene" in any story or poem is never anything less than a component of story or poem is of course common to all literature. What most distinguishes Williams's stories is his guiding of scene to a position of his own chosing, his freeing of scene very substantially from resonance or reference outside of the text. He works in effect toward freeing himself from any obligation to scene except that inherent in his authorship. Other kinds of scenic writers like Frost or Sandburg, or Wordsworth or Hardy perhaps, are more largely in debt to their scenes, respecting scene's potency and literarily depending upon it. Williams merely accepts it as presence. He does not impel us to make pilgrimages to the Passaic valley in order to understand what his writing is doing. In him, and in accord with Burke's stress on dramatism, scene is more like a warehouse of stage properties, items of background—in his term, "things"—than like landscape. Once seized, scene truly becomes his property in the more general sense, his poetically to hold, use, devise, transfer, or bequeath as he wills. Such freedom of use, of course, is inherent in Williams's stress upon "invention." Scene is important to him as it engenders literary action. And it is in relation to so marked a stress upon authorial freedom that I move on to consider the role of "agent" in his writing.

It will be helpful here to augment discussion again in terms of act, and so now of an act-agent ratio, a concept of agent or author present only in the act of writing. The author, we might say, enters writing as a second self, as *the self he can choose to act out*. His first self, like anyone's, is substantially a creature of bondage to the

whole complex of heredity and environment which pressses upon
him, to time and place. We have already seen Williams exploring
scene for its elements of poetic resource. In a parallel way we shall
find him translating self from bondage to freedom, to a state of
action, to become the second self, free to "pray" as Burke puts it in
his "Philosophy of Literary Form," to pray the self that is now the
author dramatistically realized by the action of authorship. The Dr.
Williams of 9 Ridge Road was in many ways a self who accepted
bondage. The William Carlos Williams of the poems and stories is
a self insofar as he fashions, and so exists for himself and us in
fictionalized clarity and freedom.

Underlying this whole line of emphasis is the mystery of what
makes writers write, of what impels and sustains them through the
undoubtedly dogged process of literary composition. I do not attempt a categorical answer here, but I do wish to indicate that a
central and little-considered motive in Williams's writing was to
gain a sense of regenerated and remade self. He was, we shall say,
an "expressive" as well as a "mimetic" poet, and what he chose to
express at length and in detail was his experience of and with a self
clear and free of demands not of its own accepting. To the extent
that he posed only those questions in his writing he wished to respond to, he surely is more like any other author than unlike. His
distinction in this regard will be found in the explicitness of his
commitment to such freedom and, as a result, a grounding of his
writing, as total act, within freedom.

The distinction I would make between bondage and freedom
does not impinge upon an author's native psychology, biology, or
sociology. These remain facts for him much as physical scene remains a fact. But in one case as in another the act of writing calls
for translation from objective to subjective realm. The writer writing, of course, has an inescapable identity with the same writer not
writing. But at the very least the act of writing is also its own case,
possessed of its peculiar resources and opportunities and open to
the possibilities of its own kind of transformation, that of translating the nonliterary into the literary. This set of possibilities most
strongly suggests itself as the one from which Williams the poet
drew nurture and fulfillment. As I have argued, Williams used act
or event to formulate scene. Life along the Passaic river was one of
immersion not so much in landscape as in "invention." By the same
sign, the poetic self found itself beyond its givens. Those doubtless

remained what they were, but poetic self lay in an invention of self in their terms. As poet, Williams would be of value to himself and his readers not to the extent that he remained himself but to the extent that he acted out a self.

In his "sabbatical year" in 1923 and 1924 he worked extensively on *In the American Grain* during the early months in New York, and he carried that work with him during his leave's second half in Europe. Once abroad he was kept busy with a wide variety and press of literary visits and activities and, eventually, with advanced medical study in Vienna. During his stay in Rome in early 1924, however, he was also to set to work on an opus he left unpublished during his lifetime which was not to see print until 1978 when it appeared in the *Iowa Review* under the title "Rome." Its form is that of an intense, informal journal or notebook, reflecting his brief stay in Rome but also echoing his Viennese visit and other locations. In general, it is testimony to Williams's wrestle with himself over the question of what he wanted his art, and himself as artist, to be, and it offers vivid testimony to his desire to tap sources within himself which had not yet found their counterpart in his writing. Sex takes an emphatic place in the document, but it is continually bound up there with questions of writing. The juncture, perhaps, is never clearer than at those points where Williams lights upon the idea of pleasure as the confluence of native impulse with the act of writing.

It will be tempting here to argue that Williams was in his way moving toward a reinvention of Friedrich Schiller's "play" theory of art as an explanation of poetry and the locus of the poetic self. In brief, Schiller had argued that poetry grew out of the interaction of common reason and reality on the one hand and subjective freedom on the other. The poet was a being who found his character in neither force alone but in their interplay and offset. He could not abandon reason and reality, but neither could he abandon freedom. Schiller did not make central use of the concept of pleasure, but as Williams drew on that term for his own thinking, he again and again veered toward Schiller's sense of poetry as a case (at best a productive case) of free invention within fact, or of fact stimulating the poetic mind toward freedom. Williams put the case most forcefully in postulating the centrality of pleasure to the act of thinking—the pleasure of pleasing oneself, which overlapped realms he called "knowledge," "work," and "morality."

All the facts of knowledge throng <u>all</u> its branches—taught
to young minds in a <u>few</u> lessons * *
THAT KNOWLEDGE IS ABSOLUTELY NOTHING <u>*</u> BUT
PLEASURE . An <u>ENDLESS</u>
                        pursuit   .   DIANA   ,   a chase,
a love pursuit.   It has an ENDLESS vista
                              leads to NOTHING but
the instant of its pleasure. There are no degrees. Plastered on
degrees mean nothing at all except interested lies. A low
scheme to trick pleasure out of work. Work is endless, all the
qualities of morality are accessories of pleasure and pleasure
alone.   And pleasure lost all morality is lost with
its consequences of
                  crookedness, lies, deceptions, disease,
perversions.

* *the fractures, are fractures of the whole, breaking down in
all branches, and that is medicine—this cull? It is subservient
detail—the ability to go free, deeply in and play infinitely upon
the pleasure of research.

Would be horrible, all these cadavers.

<u>Technique.</u>

Pleasure is in bits—turned to the whole—but it is in pieces the
organization of the material as a CLEAR ENJOYMENT   is the
end of the work.

Works of art are the type—standing over philosophy and science—the poet—holds his position by his clear composition
in which this principle is maintained—by the bits keeping his
work his understanding subjugated to his composition—there
are satisfying facts that give pleasure—clear and true.

it is when the <u>bits</u> of work are fully the <u>whole work too</u>
                       (*Iowa* 9,3:32–33)

The poetic self, he suggests, is a self existing in pleasure, and pleasure is composition—"keeping his work his understanding subju-

gated to his composition," organizing material, "as a CLEAR ENJOY-MENT." And finally, "it is when the <u>bits</u> of work are fully the <u>whole work too</u>." I shall need to return to the implications of this document in more detail when we come to consider the fertility of the act-agency ratio in Williams. For now, however, I want to emphasize the sense of poetic person it yields. The locus of that self is pleasure. Its fruit is the attainment of subjective freedom, freedom to find and dramatize its own nature as the bits of its work become "fully" the whole it would compose. As the Rome journal makes clear, pleasure is associated with a freedom and clarity of imagining. The Dr. Williams of 9 Ridge Road did not, of course, turn off or repress such impulses outside his writing. They were a constant and central aspect of his generic self. Writing, however, gave them liberation, exercise for their own sake, a degree and kind of self-fulfillment that other important presences and demands limited elsewhere.

The point is important as an aspect of the psychology of authorship, but critically it is even more important for Williams here stakes a claim to the literary territory that he would occupy and develop as his own. Literary freedom, especially in the avant-garde, veers readily toward the chaos of uncomposed self. Freedom was the ambiance, but what may be called difference was the manifestation. As poet Williams would work in freedom and would seek to energize his reader into freedom. But the result was not identical with freedom since it lay also in the given particulars with which the writer composed and the composition he made, and so inhered in the offset between the given and the free. As the poet filled the realm they made possible, so he would invite the reader to share that realm, to identify with it, with himself not as its guide but as its creator.

But freedom or pleasure, again, was thus in some way an aspect of "knowledge," "morality," and "work," all terms that combined to raise the specter of an antifreedom and that seem to reduce Williams's manifesto to nonsense unless we see in them the makings of a dialectical overlap of the general kind that Schiller had propounded. There is an interplay between "freedom" and "facts of knowledge," with the two finding their dual being under the more general head of "pleasure." Williams was to record his own experience of writing as one of "relaxation, relief" (I, 270) in contrast to many other activities. And in his *Autobiography* of 1951 he would add a little more detail to the concept. Speaking there "Of

Medicine and Poetry" he noted that much medicine could not help but be mechanical. It was a methodology of healing, but the healing itself seemed somehow without fruit. "The cured man," Williams noted, "is no different from any other" (*A,* 287), and by inference the process of curing was thus a repeated patching of the world, Williams's "scene," back into the same nondescript stage it had been in before the onset of illness or injury. At the same time, medicine made a path by which the poet could enter the world, penetrate to what he perceived as "secret gardens of the self" (*A,* 288). Once there the art of medicine might continue, but opportunity now existed to bring the second and poetic self more clearly into play. Unlike medicine, freedom of knowledge made the patient "somehow come alive to me" (*A,* 287).

In this way freedom of knowledge could reach beyond the pragmatics of medicine for the pleasure that was a substantial fruit. The most random or even repellent of individuals, seen freely and for his sake, was an occasion of freedom waiting for realization. Opportunity for life-giving contact was opened.

> The thing, the thing, of which I am in chase. The thing I cannot quite name was there then. My writing, the necessity for a continued assertion, the need for me to go on will not let me stop. To this day I am in pursuit of it, actually—not there, in the academies, nor even in the pursuit of a remote and different knowledge or skill. (*A,* 288)

Thus in both the Rome journal and the *Autobiography* the joy or even the obsession in seizing upon life as alive in its own right, and even as incomplete, the act of staying "in pursuit of it, actually—," is central. Paul Mariani has characterized Williams's effort as writer as that of seeing "a new world, naked," a formulation indispensable to any critical effort directed at the poet. But it seems not quite complete. No doubt Williams relished "nakedness," but he relished it as alternative to the "clothed" world of workaday role playing and self-protection. To strip the world was also to strip the poet's mind of its traditional clothing, to open it to what was in it and hence to its recovery of itself as generative force. Much of the time the mind has no choice but to be servile. In poetry the mind sought to strike off servility, escape from bondage, from use, self-assertion, "stature" of any kind not native to it, in order to return to its own local power. It could become a mind at play with whatever the world threw in its path and could thus be a mind engaged with world, but on its own and nativistic terms.

Kora in Hell: Improvisations

At the risk of sounding melodramatic, I will argue that the first of these terms is exile, a condition pondered by Williams, resisted, and even fulminated against, but nevertheless entered, in Burke's phraseology, dramatistically. Acting as author, he made it a ground of freedom for himself and one he could share with compeers like Pound and others who exiled themselves in geographic and cultural fact. But since the term "exile" carried unfavorable implications for him I might be fairer to his position and the testimony of his poetry if I settled instead for "outsider." Such a label will perhaps seem no less strange than "exile" for a poet who was so intent on finding a native voice, but because scene is so important in Williams's writing, and because it is generated by a poetic self as a product of its own freedom, the idea of "outsiderliness" is appropriate. In any case, no other position could be more natural for a writer to whom "descent," "contact," and "invention" were so reiteratedly central. They would hardly be so crucial to an insider.

We may recall that Williams discussed his historical essays of *In the American Grain* as an exercise in what he called the first business of his life, a rejection of the standard histories in order to possess an America which, thus, had to lie outside of present grasp and, as he later added, to generate a sense of "himself in it" (*EK*, 47). The first effort of the poetic self could hardly be other than to feel itself not yet included—more, to take a stand in such exclusion. Williams experimented with both painting and writing, and it was to the latter that he would be more drawn. Writing, he said, seemed to require less paraphernalia. But what should be done about his agreement with his parents to study medicine? In revelatory fashion he recorded a dividing but not quite a self-division of purpose. Medicine would be his practical profession, and it in turn would serve his self-enhancing profession, writing.

First, no one was ever going to be in a position to tell me what to write, and you can say that again. No one, and I meant

no one (for money) was ever (never) going to tell me how or
what I was going to write. That was number one.
Therefore I wasn't going to make any money by writing.
Therefore I had to have a means to support myself while I was
learning. For I didn't intend to die for art nor to be bedbug
food for it, nor to ask anyone for help, not my blessed father,
who didn't have it, nor anyone else. And to hell with them all.
I was going to work for it, with my hands, which I had been
told (I knew it anyhow) were stone-mason's hands. I also
looked at my more or less stumpy fingers and smiled. An esthete, huh? Some esthete. (*EK, 49*)

The fruit of medicine would be independence, the realm of the outsider. The fruit of independence would be poetry. But even poetry,
the passage suggests, would entail no bondage. The young poet,
committing himself to his career, was moved immediately to scoff
at the idea of being an "esthete." As his whole career would attest,
he would be a poet, but a poet outside of "poetry." In regard to
scene, Williams accepted the Passaic valley because that was where
he was. In similar fashion, self also would be found where he was.
The poetic self was resident in a pleasure generated out of the scene
and self that were natively its own.

His actual progress would be a good deal more tentative than
such summary suggests, however. His first and imitative volume of
1909 would be called simply, and quite conventionally, *Poems*. The
next two, *The Tempers* of 1913 and *Al que Quiere!* of 1917 moved
more aggressively toward an independence growingly reflected in
their titles. *The Tempers*, Williams said, was so called simply because he was aware that he was subject to such states, and he noted,
"I was budding, had no real confidence in my power, but I wanted
to make a poetry of my own and it began to come" (*IW, 16*). The
title *Al Que Quiere!* (an exclusion in itself of the untutored in outside languages) he translated as "To him who wants it," presumably
with a gesture of rebuff to those who did not. Here the poetic self
was somewhat clearer and more specific.

I was searching for some formal arrangement of the lines, perhaps a stanzaic form. I have always had something to say and
the sheer sense of what is spoken seemed to me all important,
yet I knew the poem must have shape. From this time on you
can see the struggle to get a form without deforming the lan-

guage. In theme, the poems of *Al Que Quiere!* reflect things around me. I was finding out about life. Rather late, I imagine. This was a quiet period, a pre-sex period, although I was married. The "Love Song" addressed to my wife is cryptic, shy. I was trying to tell of the power of love, how it can uproot whole oaks. (*IW,* 22–23)

By 1920 that same poetic self clearly emerged as an object of interest and pleasure to itself. Williams would be a Persephone, constrained from enjoying the things of this world but contrarily relishing the freedom that such outsideness generated.

Kora in Hell: Improvisations is a unique book, not like any other I have written. It is the one book I have enjoyed referring to more than any of the others. It reveals myself to me and perhaps that is why I have kept it to myself. (*IW,* 26).

The book was unabashedly a descent into the poetic self for its own isolate, self-pleasing sake. As Williams suggested, its scene had become the self alone.

He set a keynote in expressing his particular delight in its jacket design. He referred to the drawing a number of times in his writing and always with the same pleasure echoing a fascination with the biology of impregnation that had also figured in *In the American Grain.*

The cover design? It represents the ovum in the act of being impregnated, surrounded by spermatozoa, all trying to get in but only one successful. I myself improvised the idea, seeing symbolically, a design using sperm of various breeds, various races let's say, and directed the artist to vary the shadings of the drawing from white to gray to black. The cell accepts one sperm—that is the beginning of life. I was feeling fresh and I thought it was a beautiful thing and I wanted the world to see it. (*IW,* 28–29)

Williams's medical life would be largely given over to obstetrical and pediatric practice. *White Mule* finds its opening scene in birth. His short poems returned again and again to the theme of "the dignity of entrance" that figured in "Spring and All." *Paterson* was the record of a struggle to give birth to a long poem, itself mapping out a terrain that was the only kind of ground in which he found a hope of poetic pregnancy. It is a mark of his drive toward independence that he would so often return to the uterine drama that *Kora*'s jacket illustrated. The book's title recalled an exiled Persephone and, revealingly, offered nothing in itself or in the pages that followed showing interest in her rescue and return. Williams's Persephone—or Kora as he calls her, in fact naming herself as a "maiden"—, was in hell for the duration and possessed there of and by a demonic husband. What would come of her exile would be what she, or the poet who assumed her situation for himself, could bring to birth out of such Plutonic impregnation and her own gestative power.

It seems to be no accident that Williams recorded pleasure in the book because "it reveals myself to me." Following his earlier efforts, with their thrusts outward and away from any degree or kind of conventionality, its design most clearly revealed the locus to which the poet had come, not quite birth but birth's possibility, the freedom of the possible. From 1909 to 1920, thus, his writing was the record of a poet moving toward the act of conceiving himself. He would be white, black, or gray. He hadn't yet been decided.

The work's frontispiece, which Williams also selected, reproduced a drawing by Stuart Davis showing a pair of elderly and heavyset persons, perhaps clerics, walking soberly in a confused landscape made up of jostled houses, shops, and mills interspersed with gardens and suggestions of human activity and dominated by a giant structure that might be mansion, church, or even factory. The whole is completed by a pair of handsome borzois leaping gracefully over the confusion of the scene, to all of which the black-clad walkers pay no attention. This vision was certainly less schematic than the jacket design. But it could be read as portraying a "hell" constituted by the everyday world, a mixture of possibility and threat, to which the conventionalized walkers remain oblivious. All the figures in the drawing occupy this realm. No exit is shown, and within the scene nothing is given declarative identity, with two exceptions. The indifferent pair in the lower-right center of the drawing are offset by the white, leaping hounds of the upper-left center, who are the only figures acting their freedom. Taken by itself the drawing could easily be read as the scene out of which Williams's writing must grow, the freedom of the hounds as a suggestion of its own willful spirit, and the black-clad and heavy earth treaders as that spirit's contrary.

The volume's contents, preceded by the assertive "Prologue," moved immediately toward a structure and a texture that made them independent of reference and precedent alike. If Williams here was to be the free-leaping, free-coursing hound of his world (his first of many imagings of the poet as coursing dog), such ties could only be leases upon him. He borrowed only one detail, from a volume of Metastasio that Pound had chanced to leave with him years before in which the Italian had appended brief prose comments to his own poem. The combination of genres, in this case of a poetically formed prose with a more straightforward prose, was to be of perdurable value to Williams, and it appears to be in this volume that he began the pratice of interspersing poetry and prose not with an eye to their difference but with pleasure in their complementarity, their joint existence as explorations of writing. Beyond this detail, Williams's book was original conception, a new union of the sperm of invention with the ovum of "things," bursts or darts of poetic comment often but not invariably followed by what was scarely less freely conceived prose commentary. Perhaps its largest concern was with the person, the role, and the possibilities of the artist considered as a denizen of his world or scene but outside that scene's power to bind or loose.

Let us plunge into it. Sections 10 through 13 offer a particularly fertile field, keynoted in section 13's direct addressing of the question of the poetic self. Section 12 opens with the poet's meditation on the fact that it is his thirty-fourth birthday, and the commentary on its first part ends with a theme repeated elsewhere, the instability of the world.

> *Thinking to have brought all to one level the man finds his foot striking through where he had thought rock to be and stands firm where he had experienced only a bog hitherto. At a loss to free himself from bewilderment at this discovery he puts off the caress of the imagination.* (I, 52)

The uneasiness at a conflict between two uncertain worlds is apparent, and it is worth recalling here that the spermatozoa of Williams's design are far from sure of reaching their target, of escaping loss of themselves despite their effort. "Imagination" is as much a threat as a promise. The poet seeks to move forward, but the randomness of "forward" is impossible to escape. In part 2, however, he rallies his force. The horizontal line in the quotation is the division mark between the "poetic" and the "prose" bursts.

The trick is never to touch the world anywhere. Leave yourself at the door, walk in, admire the pictures, talk a few words with the master of the house, question his wife a little, rejoin yourself at the door—and go off arm in arm listening to last week's symphony played by angel hornsmen from the benches of a turned cloud. Or if dogs rub too close and the poor are too much out let your friend answer them.

The poet being sad at the misery he has beheld that morning and seeing several laughing fellows approaching puts himself in their way in order to hear what they are saying. Gathering from their remarks that it is of some sharp business by which they have all made an inordinate profit, he allows his thoughts to play back upon the current of his own life. And imagining himself to be two persons he eases his mind by putting his burdens upon one while the other takes what pleasure there is before him. (I, 53)

The piece ends by accepting division from scene—more than that, by embracing freedom as the very means by which the mind may retire to enjoy the "pleasure" that is simultaneously its freedom and the source of its poetry. So much has been made of Williams's stated attachment to "things" that this emphasis in *Kora* may strike one as atypical of his work. To the contrary, it is as central as the things, which unarguably take a large place in his writing. What is fruitful here in *Kora* is the relation things will have to the poet's poetic need. As we have noted in discussing scene in the poet's awareness of it, things are never more than occasions for imaginative "play," for what Williams in this volume and many later ones will refer to as "dance." Thing is inescapable, but dance is the equally essential mode or freedom of mind in which things are to be taken up. *Kora*'s prologue would give the matter crucial phrasing:

Bla! Bla! Bla! Heavy talk is talk that waits upon a deed. Talk is servile that is set to inform. Words with the bloom on them run before the imagination like the saeter girls before Peer Gynt. It is talk with the patina of whim upon it makes action a bootlicker. So nowadays poets spit upon rhyme and rhetoric.

The stream of things having composed itself into wiry strands that move in one fixed direction, the poet in desperation turns at right angles and cuts across current with startling results to his hangdog mood. *(I, 17)*

The result of such cutting "across current" becomes dramatistic, in Burke's terminology, in section 11. It is to be noted that the stimulus for such freedom of selection and composition is not drink but "some obscure wine of fancy."

When beldams dig clams their fat hams (it's always beldams) balanced near Tellus's hide, this rhinoceros pelt, these lumped stones—buffoonery of midges on a bull's thigh—invoke,— what you will: birth's glut, awe at God's craft, youth's poverty, evolution of a child's caper, man's poor inconsequence. Eclipse of all things; sun's self turned hen's rump.
Cross a knife and fork and listen to the church bells! It is the harvest moon's made wine of our blood. Up over the dark factory into the blue glare start the young poplars. They whisper: It is Sunday! It is Sunday! But the laws of the country have been stripped bare of leaves. Out over the marshes flickers our laughter. A lewd anecdote's the chase. On through the vapory heather. And there at banter's edge the city looks at us sidelong with great eyes—lifts to its lips heavenly milk! Lucina, O Lucina! beneficent cow, how have we offended thee?

Hilariously happy because of some obscure wine of the fancy which they have drunk four rollicking companions take delight in the thought that they have thus evaded the stringent laws of the country. Seeing the distant city bathed in moonlight and staring seriously at them they liken the moon to a cow and its light to milk. (I, 51–52)

Despite its stark title, *Kora in Hell* is one of the most joyous of all Williams's compositions, and the reason is not far to seek as the work displays so clearly a full acceptance of limit with enactment of a freedom within it. Like Kora herself, Williams is sequestered from any attractive "absence" he might well waste time in repining for. Instead, he will take his stand where he is, in the local that is present to him, to seize upon it for descent into the freedom that a self stripped for its own action makes possible. In concluding his own discussion of "agent" in *A Grammar of Motives*, Kenneth Burke moves toward the conclusion that thought rooted in the sense of agent, of the independence or outsiderliness of the thinker, may well drift toward an imagining of alienation, a point that much postromantic poetry might seem to attest to and that Burke develops with particular regard for Wallace Stevens. Burke would not make Stevens a poet of alienation, but he would stress the degree to which Stevens, to avoid such an end, must resort to a theory of poetry as knowledge. He quotes from Stevens's essay "The Figure of the Youth as Virile Poet": "There are in us, as in a flint, seeds of knowledge. Philosophers adduce them through the reason; poets strike them out from the imagination, and these are the brighter" (Burke 1945, 225). It is of course an opinion far older than Stevens's phrasing of it, and as such it serves all the more weightily here to phrase exactly the conclusion which Williams's practice seeks to avoid. Burke ends with the difficulty he sees facing Stevens, the conversion of poetry into a means of knowledge, an impasse with which Stevens indeed wrestled at length.

Precisely at the time when the term "imagination" gained greatly in prestige (in contrast with its low rating in writers as diverse as St. Teresa, Spinoza, and Pascal) theories of art took a momentous step away from the understanding of art as action and towards a lame attempt to pit art against science as a "truer kind of truth." The correct controversy here should not have been at all a pitting of art against science; it should have been a pitting of one view of science against another. (Burke 1945, 226)

Williams's *Kora* is certainly no less absorbed in "agent" than are Stevens and Burke, but in an endeavor that would undergird the whole enterprise of his writing, it seeks to relocate poetic agent from the realm of "knowledge" to that of action. For Williams, the poet may indeed strike sparks from his flint, but he will be poet not because of the sparks but because of the contact his striking achieves. If there is contact, sparks ensue as they will. He extends his sense of agent in a direction that Burke's total argument will allow for, but Burke's agent at this point is stalled in epistemological impasse. Neither Williams nor Burke invokes Schiller, but Williams's position seems clarified by him, and Burke's pro-tem conclusion is elaborated. What Schiller advocates in effect is a dialectic between what he calls a "sense-drive" (*Stofftrieb*) and a "form-drive" (*Formtrieb*) always at work within the creative consciousness. Their dynamic interplay resolves Kant's "purposiveness without purpose" as action, but remains itelf. Each realizes itself in action, in enactment of itself by means of the other. There is no standoff for Schiller between a "self" and a "world." The ambiguity in question, rather, is one kinetically operative within consciousness and attaining its end, which is never a final end, only in such interplay. I quote from his Fourteenth Letter in *Letters on the Aesthetic Education of Man:*

> The sense-drive demands that there shall be change and that time shall have a content; the form-drive demands that time shall be annulled and that there shall be no change. [In Williams's case we may read "scene" for "time."] That drive, therefore, in which both the others work in concert (permit me for the time being, until I have justified the term, to call it the play-drive), the play-drive, therefore, would be directed towards annulling time within time, reconciling becoming with absolute being and change with identity.
>
> The sense-drive wants to be determined, wants to receive its object; the form-drive wants itself to determine, wants to bring forth its object. *The play-drive, therefore, will endeavor so to receive as if it had itself brought forth, and to bring forth as the intuitive sense aspires to receive.* (Adams, 423–24; italics added)

As I have noted earlier, Williams would maintain a lifelong attachment to the idea of poetry as a "dance." Perhaps in Schiller we begin a little to see the dancers as well, to move a step beyond the impasse of Yeats's famous riddle.

At the same time, Schiller in his day and Williams in our own may seem to be hopelessly trapped in subjectivity. A "play" theory of art inescapably suggests some degree of trivializing, some reduction of art to personal gratification. There is no easy answer to this charge, but it does raise the question of where what we must call "freedom" finds its locus if not in just such a dance as Schiller and Williams aspire to. Our concern with freedom is ordinarily, and with good reason, attentive to pragmatics: we must continually address the question of restraints on the one hand and purpose on the other—freedom "from" and freedom "for" what? and how? Williams's poetic answer is based on one claim. Pragmatics are means; freedom of act is the end. Art, thus, whatever else it is, is freedom's enactment within scene.

As we shall see later and in more detail, Williams will propose the precedence of poetry over both science and philosophy to the degree that art, attained, represents a terminal state of being while science and philosophy exist as means. They may indeed include play of mind and even depend upon it, but they are not fully themselves until play is harnessed. There is a deep commitment involved in Williams's "play." He himself would earn his living by the practice of medicine, and the extent of that practice as well as his devotion to it is beyond question. Self, however, would not thereby be fulfilled. Science for him was literally a means: toward living and toward poetry. Nor was poetry a realm any more substantive than his persistent attachment to freedom of self would allow. Williams's art, in a word, would escape subjectivity exactly to the degree that any act would escape subjectivity, by becoming the self's self-chosen but objective end—art, thus, for self's sake. But art's existence as play did not insulate it. Poetry was not a transcendent state, but a state of freedom interactive with limit. To be in it was to know oneself as actor, a realization that might be more or less complete. Freedom was the consummation of action itself for its own sake. Ezra Pound once noted that literature could be compared to medicine in that it contained attention to diagnosis (injury, illness) and attention to healing (health). Williams's *Kora* would be a case especially devoted to the latter condition. Other texts would alter the ground.

Neither health nor freedom came with any guarantee attached, and freedom in particular had to face and accept the possibility of errancy as a necessary concomitant. Freedom, we may say, could never be relied on as sufficient cause for good poetry, only as indispensable to it. Williams's aim would never be less than that of valid writing, but even in the joyous mood of *Kora*'s composition he would often enough see the poet tumbled into the ridiculous, or worse, mocked by his own high-vaulting efforts, as in section 16.

Per le pillole d'Ercole! I should write a happy poem tonight. It would have to do with a bare, upstanding fellow whose thighs bulge with a zest for—say, a zest! He tries his arm. Flings a stone over the river. Scratches his bare back. Twirls his beard, laughs softly and stretches up his arms in a yawn.— stops in the midst—looking! A white flash over aginst the oak stems! Draws in his belly. Looks again. In three motions is near the stream's middle, swinging forward, hugh, hugh, hugh, hugh, blinking his eyes against the lapping wavelets! Out! and the sting of the thicket!

The poet transforms himself into a satyr and goes in pursuit of a white skinned dryad. The gaiety of his mood full of lustihood, even so, turns back with a mocking jibe. (I, 60)

Such comeuppances ranged from the comic, as in this case, to the somber, but even at their darkest they could not finally distract from this poet's essential sense of himself as outsider, as inventor, as indeed therefore the only begetter of his poetic self. My discussion of scene in Williams turned quickly into an examination of scene as dramatic "property," and therefore as poetic resource and limit both, and my examination of agent will tend in much the same way. The idea of freedom was central to Williams's idea of himself as writer, and it finds focus in his sense of poetic person as enactor of the poetic.

Self utilizing its resources toward poetic personhood stands as base to all his assorted and various writings. The combination of self and resources marked the spot where writing began. And as soon as agent was put back into conjoint existence with scene, agency, and purpose, the complexity of the poetic act reasserted itself. Self was by no means lost in the process. Its impulse was given even clearer focus. *Kora* presupposed a creative scene, described by Williams most immediately, as a year during which he would write something every day and, at the year's end, select and arrange what he wanted for a book. It found its agency, most generically, in the prose poetry of its literary texture and its resolution of structure in circular or gyral movement around a center. Its purpose may be described as exploration, examination of what the poet could find as a result of his self-imposed schedule. At the center of all these considerations, however, lay the self which delimited its own scene, discovered its agencies, and accepted its purpose, the self which had put itself into so arbitrary a box.

The result was a triumph of lyric writing, even of what might be called "dithyramb," a Dionysian revel of the poet in that god's spiritual-physical sphere. As such, it was sufficient to itself and climactic to earlier effort. But no more than any other dithyramb was it terminal. Agent, poetic person, had still other turns to pose for itself from its now freely accepted nature. It had discovered that to be in hell was still to be conscious, was necessarily to be oneself there, and to draw upon that resource. Self in such circumstances was the only source of the possible. In other works, consenting to face and include its world, this Kora would find other dimensionalities.

The Great American Novel and A Voyage to Pagany

Various kinds of exception have been taken to Williams's *Autobiography* not the least of which is that it devotes five chapters to his six months' stay in Europe in 1924 (greater length than he devoted to most such spans in his life) and so much distorts the record of his earlier years. However, it was during the twenties especially that he was going through a process of self-consideration which found expression in a manifold burst of experiment, initiated by *Kora* at the beginning of the decade. The decade opened with the commitment of himself to himself enacted in *Kora*, his definition and acceptance of himself as outside of common bounds and as a sufficient realm of "descent" and "contact" for that poem. This led to the exploration of what such commitment entailed. But his "sabbatical leave" of 1923 and 1924 had been immediately preceded in *The Great American Novel* with a burst of uneasiness. The "Improvisations" of *Kora* had been a revel in the joys of independence and a gratifyingly productive test of its ability to sustain expression. Pound thought the pieces the best writing Williams had yet done, even though he also found it appropriate to compare them to Rimbaud. The dilemma they posed was dramatized by such judgment. Was Williams's best work to be seemingly removed from contact with a recognizable local, and so available for comparison with writing already accomplished? His judgment on himself was harsh as he accepted Pound's phrasing. "What the French reader would say is: *Oui, ça; j'ai déjà vu ça; ça c'est de Rimbaud. Finis.*" *Kora* was "Rimbaud" as an enactment not only of immersion in self but of a season in hell, within which, however, this poet would seek his new note of self-realization. Williams clung to the alternative: "Representative American verse will be that which will appear new to the French. . . . prose the same" (*I*, 167).

From the freedom of self expressed in *Kora*, Williams thus turned in *The Great American Novel* toward rejecting the very independence he had so hardily won in favor, not of bondage, but of new conquests. To be free within the self, as on a kind of holiday, would be one desirable kind of attainment, and as far as it went indispensable. The *Novel* now raised a further and harder case, that of being free to "compose" an existent world. The drive toward "invention" would have to test itself against fact accepted as fact and so to enhance and complicate the idea of dance between contraries to which it had won. The immediate result was to stage the drama of authorship as an agon—as Wallace Stevens would put it, to Williams's discomfiture—"the constant interaction of two opposites," realistic fact and romantic freedom (*CP*, 2). Stevens had added, "the anti-poetic is his spirit's cure" (*CP*, 3). *The Great American Novel* was in its way abjuration of the free poetic person he had so latterly won in doubt, presumably, of its authenticity.

The *Novel* itself, along with *Spring and All*, a collection of poems and commentary, would be published in 1923, in Paris, symptomatic of Williams's immediate wandering both in the spirit and the flesh. *Kora* had been testimony to self unified in expression of itself as a dance of impulse. *The Great American Novel* was testimonial to the cost of such independence as the writer turned to look at himself in the scene he had chosen, in his own locale. Williams made jokes about the book in his comments on it in *I Wanted to Write a Poem*, but there can be no mistaking the seriousness to him at the time of the question on which it turned. For his title he accepted the cliché that both embodied and ridiculed his aim as a writer—to write greatly, and within the local. By increasingly freeing himself he had moved through the tentative steps of his early volumes, but what would he write if he now altered his range to frame that self as not free, as contingent being?

Something like half the work was given over to a survey of the American scene that would be elaborated by *In the American Grain*. There was a chapter on Columbus and Eric the Red and another on the Mormons, who played a role here resembling that of the Puritans in the later work. George Washington and the Dutch settlers of New York made brief appearances in contrast to the character of a contemporary Greenwich Village, and the whole was studded with varied glimpses of a contemporary American existence reflecting partly the authorial voice and partly the voice of rudimentary characters. The word "novel" in the title was, of course, ironic. The work had nothing resembling a plot and indeed addresses the reader as something more like a phantasmagoria—of too great and unsure a length—than any kind of realized composition. The bits no doubt added up but they exceeded a whole. There are many more parts than the reader knows what to do with once he perceives that they all converge on a central issue, and the work's form dissolves in repetition. Insofar as it had a center at all, it lay in the chapters portraying the writer's awareness of himself contending with uncertainty. On one side he sees a hope of art, but that hope cannot here be made to extend across the facts that engulf it.

The author considers the value to him of Joyce's example, but he concludes that Joyce offers nothing but secondhand assistance. "His art is words," Williams complains. "His failure is when he considers his art to be something else" (I, 169), a failure touching the very effort Williams himself is making. He considers the example of painting, but again finds it falling short of the demand facing him. Kandinsky and expressionism are rooted in "the seething reactions of the contemporary European consciousness" (I, 173). He moves on to consider Dada, but leaves it punctuated by a question mark. He turns to more conventional possibilities in European music: Kreisler and Ysaye are mentioned, as are Wagner and Strauss. Collectively, all such figures add up to a "swarming European consciousness" (I, 174) of no direct use because of its remoteness. The fact remains, however, that so far as art is concerned there is nowhere else to turn. "Every word we get must be broken off from the European mass" (I, 175). The only approach to a solution is to make a distinction: "We must imitate the motivation and shun the result" (I, 175). Only so may the poet, the inventing self, be called into action.

The work as a whole finds no resolution to the author's problem; whatever degree, finally, of composition it attains is evidenced in concentration on a distraught poetic self. It leaves such distress in raw form. Its chief claim to artistic success lies in its pointed parodyings of unity and attainment, in its dramatizing of conflict suggesting the "Expressionism" its author considers—perhaps here, in a way, transferred to an American base. Its theme is an unresolved "wandering." It does, however, succeed in outlining the scene within which that wandering happens, one that Williams would return to after his European trip in 1926 and 1927 in *A Voyage To*

Pagany. Published in 1928, this was a somewhat more coherent if still less than fully realized attempt at a novel on the theme of a personal American reality set off against a world of art largely European and alien.

That work was indeed to provide a far-reaching pattern of the ground of Williams's "wandering." It is the story of a character named Dev Evans, but framed so closely in accord with Williams's own character and situation that only the smallest degree of dramatic detachment is evident. It follows him through stays in Paris, Carcassonne and the Riviera, Italy and Rome in particular, a period of medical study in Vienna, a brief return to Paris, and then a final return to the United States. The itinerary was the one that Williams and his wife had followed, but in *A Voyage to Pagany* Flossie largely disappeared as a character in her own right to be replaced with a variety of companions for the hero. These include an ardent and liberated sister, Bess; a more domestic and cautious friend named Lou; and, in Vienna, a sophisticated mistress, thoroughly naturalized to the Viennese world. The "voyage" then which forms the work's narrative is made to spread widely across Williams's concerns: his own provincialism, the complexity of an artistic and scientific Europe, and his desires and dreams of completing himself in a female anima. It is of the essence that he ends by rejecting all three women of the story, as well as Europe, for what he sees as a bleak but unavoidble relocation in America.

The work has a progress and a unity unknown to *The Great American Novel,* but the power of its testament works against its success as a novel. Just as in the Stecher trilogy Williams would be willing to develop his narrative by having the characters both build and react to scene, *Voyage* is equally willing to reduce itself to the self as poetic agency for its substance. It is a latter-day *Werther,* leading its protagonist not to commit suicide but to face the inescapability of sustaining a self constituted by its own independence. The hero rejects the anima that has variously masked itself in the story, knowing that he must accept the loneliness of self-definition as his fate. The book's mood lies somewhere between the self-pleasuring freedom of *Kora* and the self-tormenting impasse of *The Great American Novel.* Neither pleasure nor torment is its fruit. Instead it finds the Puritan virtues—decision, resolution, and will—to be its hero's personal lot.

Despite its general adherence to the course of Williams's European trip, it makes little effort to incorporate more than a tiny part of actual events. After an ocean crossing in which he rejoices in the sense of his ship's "strong run against the sea" (*VP,* 12), and a stormy sea at that, Dev lands in France, there to be most enchanted by a sense of spiritual kinship with his sister. They agree in fretting against whatever seems to smack of the habitual in European life in favor of the moments it offers of isolated and superior vantage, as in a climb to the spires of Notre Dame after the darkness of the church's interior. As cultural entity, Paris is a mixed quantity for Dev. He is shown in only one detailed relationship with a fellow American writer, here called Jack but closely suggesting Williams's friend Robert McAlmon, and the encounter is far from strengthening. He admires the "freshness" of his friend's work but has to admit that in fact Jack has accomplished little as yet—a nutshell summary, the book makes clear, of Dev's sense of his own writing at the moment. Jack is too much himself to offer any fruitful union. "If you love a girl," Dev thinks, "you want to have a baby. If you love a man, you want to have—what?" (*VP,* 39). The question is loaded with the kind of half-sensed psychological awareness with which the novel is filled. Dev's greatest sense of freedom and release in Paris comes from his consorting with his sister—a union that itself cannot bear any licit erotic or biological fruit. His friend threatens equal sterility, Dev thinks, except for as yet unfulfilled promise. The whole Paris interlude ends on a gritty and classically nightmarish note as, Dev feels, he makes a public fool of himself at a dinner that his literary friends have arranged for him. The Paris that Williams had worried about from afar in *The Great American Novel* had turned out to be confirmation of his own isolate condition even when he himself was present in the actual city.

He is relieved to leave for the South with his friend, Lou, a sharp contrast to all that he has encountered thus far. She is "blessed Lou, cool, caring" in his eyes, the person, he suddenly persuades himself, "for whom the whole trip to Europe had been arranged" (*VP,* 68). It is only in Lou that one can see very plain reflection of Williams's wife, who has been said to be the original for all three of the women with whom Dev consorts. And it is revealing that his journey with her is broken off because she turns out to be too much of a "wife." She wants Dev to marry her, and so forces the question of his freedom to a crisis. In the "pagany" of Paris, he felt, he would never be able to let himself go on in freedom. Freedom there, in such loneliness, would be disintegrating. "To go loose to him," he feels, "was to go totally ungoverned, drunken, syphilitic, starved, jailed, murderous" (VP, 70). He likes Lou because she is "strong and brave," so much so, however, that she would "not break her heart over anyone" (VP, 80). When he postpones decision, she in fact does accept the proposal of a wealthy Englishman (a contrary to hard-up, American Dev), and Dev, in much complexity of feeling, accuses her of giving up independence at too great a cost. He enjoys his union with her and feels both protected and nourished by it. In it he has a theoretical "independence," but he is able also to depend on the emotional support she confers. Marriage, however—explicitly linking oneself to interdependence—is wrong. Lou as a reflection of Florence Williams is one embodiment of the America about which both Dev and Williams himself have such chaotic feelings. He wants its familiarity, its protection against his own self-destructive or at least profligate tendencies, but he does not want it as tie. This is a repetition of Williams's attitude toward the native that has been played out in my discussion of "scene" in his writing, as we see in Dev's attack on Lou's decision to marry:

> By marriage you do not do a serious thing but a frivolous one—you shift responsibility back upon a crowd of instinctive, senseless—
> Whoa! cautioned Lou.
> Yes, you do, you lay off a burden—the necessity of invention. (VP, 112)

Lou cannot agree and she goes her way. Dev-Williams finds that some abrupt turnabout is again necessary. "Invention," it seems, is not for the realm of life. His journey will be carrying him to Florence and Rome, and the novel prepares for an altered view of his dilemma in those ancient capitals of art. "Impossible to live, impossible to live, impossible to live.—But impossible; therefore the arts have authenticity" (VP, 116). Independence is not to be fulfilled in Paris with the illicitly exotic Bess or on a more humdrum stretch of tourism with the home-grown Lou. It is located not in geography, eroticism, or even in Dev's consciousness of his deep self that the women suggest. It must, therefore, be in the differently situated world of the same "art" he had embarked for Europe to find. Life seems impossible; art still lies at a distance.

Florence and Rome carry him not only to art, but to a wrestling with the whole accumulation of the past. They present a scene unmatched in Williams's writing for its concern with the question to which he usually gave short shrift. Much of Florence's art, and Michelangelo in particular, upsets and distresses him. The sculptor's *David* exudes a "delicate torment" and his work in general a "false crudity" (*VP*, 136). Michelangelo, like himself, seems to be an artist wrestling with himself and his own art, and Dev cannot understand why the sculptor infuses "the Christian anguish" of self-consciousness into "the quiet, the perfect, the lovely" Greek tradition from which he descends (*VP*, 137). Dev's confusion in the face of such disharmony opens a significant window on Williams's rejection of the past. Michelangelo is incomplete to the extent that he accepts impulses already attained. Dev's nearest glimpse of harmony comes only in a visit to the church of San Marco. Here, as he sees it, the architectural lines of the interior have been allowed to rest in structural functionality without being twisted into decorative expansiveness, and the painting of the apse and its chapels by Giotto and Cimabue exudes a localized and integrated sense that "reaches back truly outside of church into a sunlight which he identified by his earliest uncaptured intincts—" (*VP*, 140). The art of San Marco is moving and satisfying precisely as it leads beyond any particular historical struggles, harmonizes inner and outer, to find identity in a union of nature and experience.

Dev's stay in Florence is brief, and he moves on to Rome, where he is confronted with a mass of past and present in indigestible confusion. Somewhat like Michelangelo's sculpture, the city seems to strangle its identity in a writhing and never-ending contest between pagan and Christian. Dev feels the attraction of the pagan, but again he doubts his ability to accept it for himself. The Christian seems merely perverse and grotesque, a religion the city expresses most often in images of death and decay. Rome seems to embody the self-divisiveness of all European effort. Its one clear moment of revelation for him lies in his encounter with the untrammeled paganism of a sculpture of Venus Anadyomene that moves him deeply, but on the whole he feels only that a "fictive Rome is undoing him" (*VP*, 146) and that he must move on.

Williams provides Dev with no companion during his visit to Rome, so that his aspiring person is denied the opening of self that the women provided in Paris, the south of France, and Vienna. His reaction is to close down upon himself, and as he says, "make a wife of his writing" in a desire "to free himself from his besetting reactions by transcribing them" (*VP*, 145). Elsewhere, with his companions, Dev talks and thinks much about writing or, in Vienna, during his study in the clinics, about medicine. It is only in Rome, when he is by himself, that he writes—and what he produces, presumably, is the "Rome" journal I have glanced at earlier. This writing has become a wife, he says, but it offers little comfortable help. Its thesis is that Dev must find his pleasure in his writing; it hardly exists elsewhere. "Rome will live again—" he thinks; "They'll push it flat, singing; take the stones for black-smith's shops or hovels—tear it apart and begin eating the church again—any church—." Home presents an even bleaker picture, and almost in the same breath. "Without money N.Y. doesn't exist, to think of the horror of N.Y. without cash is the end." The city cannot support mere living: "strain and horror and nothing to ease—no water to drink—no land to plant—no place to go—nowhere to lie down—no sun to be in—a horrid year—two too great arms of the sea that are called rivers" (*Iowa* 9:3, 46).

The picture that Williams sketches in the novel is a hard one. The world, wherever he goes, is disappointing, disturbing, frightening. The companions he seeks out attempt to relieve his feelings, to warm him in their various ways, to find union with him. The poet here, however, rejects them all, accepts his place in the repugnant turmoil that is life. Ever more fiercely he uses his writing, himself, as a way of maintaining his outsiderliness, relieving his feelings, and so asserting that he must remain in estranged fascination with the scene around him. His only solace is picking up bits as he is able (the manner in which scene presents itself) and moving such scraps toward whatever degree of "composition" they themselves will allow. Giotto, Cimabue, the Venus of Cyrene, and, later, the precision of the Viennese doctors—none is more than a moment lying in the rubble which is his general European experience and which it must be argued was also his experience of home, of the world of the Passaic.

The important theme of Williams's tentative and awkward novel was in fact that of "outsiderliness," and finally of etrangement and exile. Europe in general offers only its bits and pieces. The European artists and scientists he encounters are a remote help at best. The past is no service since it is as fragmented as the present. Love is attractive but in its demands on his independence it is also a threat, as is the alternative it suggests of a self freed to itself alone. It is impossible to say how nearly *A Voyage to Pagany* transcribed the feelings Williams actually experienced during his trip abroad, but it is not hard to see the poetic fable he was making for himself out of that experience. Toward the story's end, his sister-anima pleads with him to change his destiny. "I want to do some good with myself," she says. "Oh *good*, Dev, in the French sense, the moral sense. To use well what we have, that's all" (*VP*, 329). Dev cannot accept her pleas, and he rejects them in crass and bleak definition for himself. "Art is a country by itself—A matter of learning how" (*VP*, 329), and he casts his own fate in absolute terms. "I love you all right, Bess, but God damn it, I'm not going to stay over in this country if I don't want to, not for anybody" (*VP*, 331). He sails for home, and his first glimpse of that destination is the "Nantucket lightship, anchored, rocking lightly in the smooth sea and men out upon it painting it a metallic red." "What a life": it is, however, an image of the life he has chosen. The novel's final words, given the whole act of rejection it had effected, must be what they are: "So this is the beginning" (*VP*, 338). The life of art can be made only by the artist's will acting out what he knows is himself and his.

IV AGENT

PRESENT PERSON
(DANCE AS SELF-ENACTMENT)

Paterson

Chronologically and otherwise it seems a long leap from the publication of *A Voyage to Pagany* in 1928 to that of *Paterson* beginning in 1946, but there will prove to be a powerful link between the two works in the degree to which both were concerned with the theme of the poet in a now self-elected situation. The novel had ended with Dev-Williams redeposited in the United States and with all of Europe, a number of possible artistic kinships, and three possible mistresses left behind him. *Paterson* opens with an epigraph denoting it, among other things, "a local pride," "a confession," "a reply to Greek and Latin with the bare hands" (*P*, 2). All of them combine to focus on the commitment its author had made and given voice to at the end of the novel. The years intervening had united to confirm and enlarge that choice. Williams's writing during the thirties was much given over to fiction—the two volumes of short stories and two of the Stecher trilogy. But all of this effort plunged him deeply and extensively into the Passaic world— the world of *Paterson*—and, in fact, the prose piece "Life along the Passaic River" was drafted originally as a possible component of the long poem. There is a very real sense in which the poem is made incomplete without the kind of material that sketch and other stories provided, but any effort Williams might have considered to combine the two would perhaps have undercut what he was in fact driven to accomplish: the dramatizing of a poetic self that knows that "Europe"—the past and its culture—or the embracing of possible refuge-selves could not serve to capture the being of a city known to itself only as a place of processing raw material and dumping the by-products, material and human. He published two collections during the decade, largely of already written poetry, but his writing of new poems seemed much curtailed, and parts of what he did write were designed for the long work, on which he began in earnest in 1942.

There is a sense in which *Paterson* is misnamed unless we allow large leeway to the union the poet enacts between himself and the city by calling himself "Mr. Paterson," or to the fact that section after section deals with the city as container and image of his poetic awareness: "the city / the man an identity" (*P*, 3). Book 1 during the four years before its publication had indeed been thought of as an "Introduction" to the poem proper, and there is a very real sense in which Book 1 still functions in that capacity rather than as a poem about the city. What in any case interested him most persistently was the problem of writing a long poem on such a subject, to begin with, and doing so in such isolation of effort as he found inescapable for his purpose. Efforts to see the poem as an exercise in indeterminacy thus seem misdirected. Read as a poem about a city, *Paterson* may well arrive at a kind of deconstruction. Read, however, as a poem about the whole situation the poet felt he must accept as his own, *Paterson* faithfully enacts the occasions and demands of the outsiderliness that Williams had committed himself to as early as *Kora in Hell* and had been so much concerned with in other work.

In his own language, *Paterson* 1–4 is an act of descent into his own ambiguous concept of himself as poetic agent. That sense of self had found one brief fulfillment in the lyric pleasure of *Kora in Hell*. Another kind of success had been reached in the scenic emphasis of the short stories of *The Farmers' Daughters*, and to a degree in the Stecher triology where the poet's eye had turned outward to regard the conformity of act and scene in the Passaic world. *Paterson*, in contrast, found itself drawn into a rhetoric of problematics, too often clawing at the reader and the poet himself for resolution, but at its best searching the implications of the poetic agent's sense of disconformity between scene and his own act.

Dr. Williams of 9 Ridge Road lived in his world and found the "language" to cope with such pragmatics. He could find the terms required to translate that world into prose fiction without scanting or faking over the absence of conventional structure it presented. By his own sense, however, translation to poetry required the very freedom of the agent which that world massively combined to deny. What obtains in *Paterson* to give the work success, then, is its embodiment of poetry in progress toward itself, the moments of contract Williams makes along the way recording free invention or discovery. These momentary interactions with the world draw both the world and himself onto a ground where poetic action and scenic presence, often embodied in the prose passages, can in fact be used to measure each other. The moments of contact allowed not only for a turning of the poem forcefully in the direction he most wanted it to go but also reached out to touch the larger problem of the alienation of self from self or from the whole which the poet witnesses and which the industrial city creates. *Paterson* comes together as utterance wherever such contact bits combine to form a drama of poetry in the making, of agent marshaling scene, agency, and itself toward an end necessarily undefined but readable and statable as dramatistic event.

At least two of the prose passages, however, focus more particularly on the poet's concerns in *Paterson:* the lengthy complaint of the poet Cress against Williams's neglect of her personal difficulties in favor of her poetry in Book 2, and the buoyant greeting from Allen Ginsberg out of the prevailing shambles of Book 4. The two serve to underline the importance Williams attaches to his own poetic effort: It was necessary to glimpse and strive for the interplay of scene and agent if the city of Paterson was to be endured. It was necessary to seek, if scarcely define, "measure" or "dance," the only possibilities of attaining poetry or of living an existence within the city. Cress's letter records failure in this regard; Ginsberg's points toward possible success. The two poets thus stand as opposing markers.

Paul Mariani argues that Williams's serious work on *Paterson* may in fact be dated from his meeting with Marcia Nardi when she appeared in his office seeking medical help for her child and inviting Williams's interest in some poetry she had written. That meeting led to both kinds of concern from him and to a continued period of interest, in her writing particularly. This Cressida, abandoned by her natural guardians, would be taken in hand by a guide whom she sees finally as a betrayer. By the time of the writing of the "Cress" letters that appear in *Paterson,* she had come to the point of feeling that Williams, despite his active support of her writing and some small gifts of money, was guilty of spurning her need for close friendship. As time passed Williams himself became more and more uneasy about the often unbalanced ardor of her approaches to him, deposited her letters with his lawyer for safekeeping, and did his best to break off their connection.

So far as the poem is concerned, however, she appears most plainly as a suffering writer who mistakes both the power and the possibilities of poetry. Her complaint against "Dr. Paterson" is that he is blind to her needs as a person because he is willing to know and have to do with her only as an author of poetry he in part admires. Certainly Williams did not make light of Marcia Nardi's personal difficulties, but clearly he felt he could offer little except marginal help toward their solution. What he could do was make some substantial effort on behalf of her poetry, and this he did. Cress appears in *Paterson* as a poet who believes that poetry can hardly emerge if the poet lacks the position and repose which she imagines are enjoyed by Mr. Paterson, who in fact finds himself to be a beleaguered and most unself-assured author. In her life she enacts dramatically the toll which the city takes of its inhabitants. She is certainly more its victim than is Williams. However, she is half blind to the fact that poetry, in and of Paterson, can only be the fruit of Paterson itself. If "divorce" necessarily exists between the city and the word, her failure is that she does not recognize that fact. On the one hand her letter phrases a value which Williams doubtless saw reflected in work of hers he admired:

> Only my writing (when I write) is myself: only that is the real me in any essential way. Not because I bring to literature and to life two different inconsistent sets of value, as you do. No, *I* don't do that; and I feel that when anyone does do it, literature is turned into just so much intellectual excrement fit for the same stinking hole as any other kind. (*P,* 87)

Against such utterance, however, stands her awkward implication that writing can grow only from warmth and support. If this is the case, Williams's poetic plight is nearly as desperate as Cress's own. Paterson's poetry as evidenced in Williams's work can scarcely be said to have emerged from the city's prosperity. Her plight is a vivid example of the human cost the city exacts, but her response, both in her letter and in Williams's actual experience with Marcia Nardi, turns out finally to be misdirected: "In living, one's shaping of the externals involved there (of one's friendships, the structure of society, et cetera) is no longer entirely within one's own power but requires the cooperation and understanding and the humanity of others in order to bring out what is best and most real in one's self" (*P*, 87). This is quite true of "living." But she has found what strength she has in commitment of poetry to the hardness of its own occasion; retreat from such occasion in her life yields only dependent failure. She suffers the prevailing disorder of "divorce," and at the end of Book 2 expresses its cost in a climax of extended and wandering quotation. Williams, however, is unable to wave away divorce or pretend to overcome its ravages. It is his own problem. The best he can do is aid her to make literary use of the predicament she shares with many others.

Against Cress, and at a positive pole, stands "A. G." and his letter of Book 4. Whatever of personal difficulty and need for endurance exists for him is, by instinct and conviction both, transmuted directly into occasion of poetry:

> I envision for myself some kind of new speech—different at least from what I have been writing down—in that it has to be clear statement of fact about misery (and not misery itself), and splendor if there is any out of the subjective wanderings through Paterson. (*P*, 174)

The two letters, the only such identified in Williams's work as coming from poets in and of Paterson, suggest the guiding impulses of his own writing. How shall subjective wandering become new speech? The destructive power of the city against all persons including poets is most real. The value to the poet of struggle against it, however, is not in redemption but in enactment. Poetry lives, however persons may, to the degree that it can translate raw fact into utterance, act. Ginsberg puts it as the conversion of "misery itself" to "clear statement of fact about misery," a transition Cress cannot make, and this sense of poetic value has exactly the resonance to merit a prominent place in *Paterson*.

In short, the drama of the poem through its first four books emerges as an act of considering a poem about unalterable fact, about Paterson, New Jersey. Ezra Pound had declared that *The Divine Comedy* was more lyric than epic, and whether Williams remembered this dictum from *The Spirit of Romance* or not, it marked the kind of poetic suspension prevailing in his own work, strung between the poles of historical fact (the contemporary city) and a searching of the poet's consciousness of it. Beyond Pound's dictum, I would urge that *Paterson* may well be read as dramatic lyric, often as internal dialogue, and that it can even be divided in three acts: (1) uncertain awareness of the external world; (2) uncertain awareness of internal turmoil; and (3) occasional resolution formed by the interaction of the two. Or, poet meets Paterson, poet recoils into self, poet enacts a discovered oneness with the city. Regarded thus the work marks a considerable growth in Williams's sense of himself as poetic agent. *Kora* had been an indulgence that could not be built on. *The Great American Novel* and *Voyage to Pagany* had been frustrated efforts to bring the poetic self into subjection to its elected world. Together, they failed to get beyond a standoff. In them the poet clings to his freedom, his own fulfillment, as his emotional base. He adheres to his idea that out of such freedom the bits of the poem should be so seized upon and staged as to become themselves the whole, but in neither of these works could he pretend to attain that whole. In *Paterson* 1 through 4, however, the staging is more often achieved. Bits remain bits but they enter into dramatic relationships growing out of their ramified, variegated, and unpredictable assemblage. *Paterson* 5, to anticipate, would emerge out of a different concern, one of proclaiming and celebrating the earlier attainment, but not altering it.

Our drama then, has three acts, but instead of following each other they are broken into pieces and scattered across the first four books of the poem to form its lines of structure among themselves. The actions of external awareness, internal awareness, and of interweaving are recurrent in the whole and, despite a general logic linking the succession of the four books, constitute the underlying action. In doing so they display the poetic that Burke identifies as "repetitive form." The poet debarred from resolving his work in a single focus enacts his structure instead by finding, leaving, and refinding its shaping principle. In Book 1 the poet deals with the primeval powers, the "giants," that have made and continue to sustain his world. Book 2 reduces the gigantesque to more human proportions during the poet's walk in the park. Book 3 effects a further reduction to focus on the solitary poet glimpsing and losing the "Beautiful Thing" he seeks. Book 4 concludes with the giants still at large and the poet returned to the point of a beginning, the point where in fact he had begun. Each of the four books, however, contains segments of the poem's tripartite action. Even in Book 4, which so much confesses the giants' untamability, the final word is not the poet's dismissal of the pragmatic success of his effort but an affirmation of his own independence of that failure.

Book One

Williams's image of the gigantesque, contained in his title for Book 1, "The Delineaments of the Giants," is deeply organic to the poem's being. It is given physical existence in the inert masculinity of the contemporary city, in turn cradled by the female range of the hills, the natural landscape that surrounds it, and the stream flowing through it. His question is whether these brute powers can be raised to imaginative life. He had faced a similar scene in *Kora* but with different results, as in freedom he had discovered not giants but gods crushed to earth, a pagan pantheon living all about him, in disfiguring disguise, to be sure, but still pregnant with traditional powers, and himself, there, as their king.

> Giants in the dirt. The gods, the Greek gods, smothered in filth and ignorance. The race is scattered over the world. Where is its home? Find it if you've the genius. Here's no place for a brain to grow. Herakles rowing boats on Berry's Creek! Zeus is a country doctor without a taste for coin jingling. Supper is of a bastard nectar on rare nights for they will come—the rare nights! The ground lifts and out sally the heroes of Sophocles, of Aeschylus. They go seeping down into our hearts, they rain upon us and in the bog they sink again down through the white roots, down—to a saloon back of the rail-road switch where they have that girl, you know, the one that should have been Venus by the lust that's in her. They've got her down there among the railroad men. A crusade couldn't rescue her. Up to jail—or call it down to Limbo—the Chief of Police our Pluto. They are the same men they always were—but fallen. Do they dance now, they that danced beside Helicon? They dance much as they did then, only, few have an eye for it through the dirt and fumes. (*I, 61*)

If the gods are debased in *Kora*, they are more so in *Paterson*. Their poet-king, Zeus, shares their bondage, except as he can enact the drama of estrangement. The gods cannot overcome the force of the giants, according to the ancient myth, without the aid of a mortal, and Mr. Paterson, no Hercules, cannot generate that power. As a result, the primitive forces of time and space and of the giants' weapons of rock, wind, fire, and water prevail. The city lies amongst them and is subject to their force. The gods without Hercules' help are left in the disfigured shapes the poet discerns, where they are glimpsed at all.

Each of Book 1's three sections, however, contains at least one passage enacting the interplay of inner and outer that will prove to be the poem's goal, the "marriage" of the two as each becomes foil and sustainer of the other. In the first of these, Mr. Paterson's thoughts are seen as momentarily jostled, in the way the vital flow of the river is broken by its rocky course. The vision of the two overlaying each other—stream of thought and stream of water— makes a point of contact, of utterance realized as poetry about water and thought simultaneously.

> All lightness lost, weight regained in
> the repulse, a fury of
> escape driving them to rebound
> upon those coming after—
> keeping nevertheless to the stream, they
> retake their course, the air full
> of the tumult and of spray
> connotative of the equal air, coeval,
> filling the void.
> (P, 8)

In the second he repeats his opening complaint that "there is no direction" apparent in either town or mind, and that in this they share a being. He ends the third in a cumulative act of wrestling with his interwoven opposition by picturing thought as "clambering up" the falls which, as "chatterer," is the "father of all speech" (P, 39).

In each of these cases, central as they all are to the theme Book 1 deals with, the third act of the drama begins to appear as poetic realization, a dramatizing of the complex that is the writer's subject and object. If "Paterson" is both the town and the poet who is of the town, its end can be found only in the interaction of the two. That interaction will not occur in the flesh, or in any time or space at all except, occasionally, the time and space of the poem, which is simultaneously, then, that of the world. The first of the three passages finds cadence of sound and resonance of meaning as it is absorbed in the cataract's rush to make of it both an image and a model for poetic meaning. The second finds a parallel composition of movement and meaning as it first accepts directionlessness in assertive but various statement and then dissolves into a dominant if double-faced lyric celebrating "Two halfgrown girls hailing hallowed Easter" (*P*, 18). This vignette epitomizes a simultaneous confusion and realization of spiritual purpose only to turn, half mockingly, half fondly, on itself with the conclusion, "Aint they beautiful" (*P*, 19)! In fact, they both are and are not. The third passage ends Book 1 with a return to the falls, the poet this time picturing his thought as climbing up against its face to a "moist chamber" where dwells "the myth" that "holds up the rock" (*P*, 39) which sustains the waterfall. Thus the poet makes an identity of contact between the seat of the brain itself—the seat of language—and the natural image of the cave at the waterfall's brink.

These three cases, though all are in Book 1, mark the goal toward which the whole poem will be directed, and in doing so declare a structure for it. In what remains it will be Williams's task to restage the facts of external encounter, internal encounter, and realization of their interdependence so that, as here, the bits will indeed combine as a whole. That whole will not pass beyond the bits at any point. Neither as city nor as utterance can *Paterson* claim transcendence of the particulars from which it is "rolled up." Its purpose is not transcendence but rather the enactment of situation and response in order to turn differing sides of its nature to the light and thus drive home the question it raises for contemporary awareness: whether its own world can be made available to creative action. Williams's answer will be discouraging at his most somber and only qualifiedly encouraging at his highest moment in Book 5. However, he holds to his question as the gist of any humanizing possibility, given the local reality with which the poet must deal.

Book Two

The first two sections of Book 2 seem to move onto surer ground, as so much of their content is given to external awareness generated by Mr. Paterson's walk in the park on a Sunday afternoon. After the turbulence of Book 1, the poet catches himself up by the reminder "Outside / outside myself / there is a world" (*P*, 43), and he bends his attention its way. Self-consciousness cannot be wholly abandoned, however, as facing the populace and following the citation of a bit from what appears to be one of Cress's letters, he faces the hardness of his question: "How do I love you? These" (*P*, 45)—with denigrating emphasis on the final pronoun. The answer, but a distant one at best, is suggested by the cloud of grasshoppers stirred up by his walking and reminding him of a sculptured Aztec grasshopper exhibited at Chapultepec. The sculpture emerges out of rock with the same randomness that is Paterson, in a realized image of the contest between art and an amorphous world. If art triumphs in this case, however, it does so at cost: "the stone lives, the flesh dies" (*P*, 49). This poet can answer the challenge he has raised only in a switch, again, to internal awareness, a retreat to lecture himself and his reader on his perennial theme: "unless there is / a new mind there cannot be a new / line" (*P*, 50). He can meet, see, feel for the populace that is Paterson, but only such surface contact is available for sections 1 and 2 of Book 2.

What he encounters is a mixed and motley lot of picnickers, "guilty" lovers, and random loiterers. Their language like their presence is real but unrealizable except for the internal judgment "Minds beaten thin / by waste" (*P*, 51). "Come on! Wassa ma? You got / broken leg?" someone calls. The speeches voice squalor and randomness. "What a bunch of bums! Afraid somebody see / you? *Excrementi!* / —she spits. / Look a' me, Grandma! / Everybody too damn / lazy" (*P*, 57). There is brief suggestion of debased gods, like those of *Kora*, when the poet recalls the artistically conceived figure of a peon in an Eisenstein film, "Heavenly man" (*P*, 58), but such pagan overtones are swept away as in section 2 the scene is taken over by a preaching evangelist and the poet retreats into internal confusion: "Blocked. / (Make a song out of that: concretely)" (*P*, 62). His move toward exterior encounter is limited at best.

The evangelist, Klaus, of course, cannot redeem Paterson, but his presence here anticipates and overlays the brief appearance in Book 4 of the historical evangelist Billy Sunday, who takes a large fee from the mill owners for his efforts to divert the workers from their strike. Klaus, in contrast, is a good man and an honest one, but he is "Outworn," hence, "though he sweat for all his worth / no poet has come" (*P*, 79). Like Cress and the dramatic figures of Book 4 he appears here as something less than a redeemer. Even so, Mr.

Paterson's realizing in him of the interdependence of inner and outer encounter—Klaus as fellow striver for an eloquence of the unsayable and Klaus as one more of Paterson's depressing exhibits—builds him like them into dramatic reality, if only ironically. Klaus's message is plain. He testifies from experience that he has brought his own sense of failure and despair to his God and received from him the answer. He is to give away his money and rest in an abundant treasury of divine grace. For Mr. Paterson, his appearance is another case of double vision. Klaus is allowed full expression of his own honest feeling, but his message is broken up by the insertion of excerpts from Cress's loneliness, accounts of Alexander Hamilton's vision of Paterson as an industrial rather than a spiritual gold mine, and editorial matter directed against perceived evils in the Federal Reserve System. Klaus's religion has driven away whatever inklings of pagan fulfillment the crowd might have caught, but in turn it is wholly undercut by the reminders of the hard rock of money on which the city rests. Section 2 ends with the poet's retreat, again, to internal musing in an address to a force unnamed here except as an indefinite "You," but in early states of the manuscript identified as a deity. "If there is sublety, / you are subtle" (*P,* 74). Mr. Paterson's dramatization of his own confusion reveals him to be hardly less at sea than Klaus the evangelist and in far less buoyant a mood. He addresses his own cosmic power bitterly, "in your / composition and decomposition / I find my . . / despair" (*P,* 75).

Such internal retreat carries him directly into section 3 and to reassessment of his earlier advice to himself on the need for invention. What ensues is the moving and complex passage celebrating "descent," Williams's first extended use of the triadic line characterizing much of his late poetry. Here it leads from the confusions of afternoon in the park, where "Walking" had been a refrain word carrying him from one passing moment to the next, to night and the now-still image of the city at rest around the stream flowing through it. The directional word here will be "Listen" (*P,* 79). The result is a poetically sustained long passage weaving between inner and outer, dreams and reality, as the male city converses with the flowing stream, pictured as female; as the lovers in the park reach out for each other; and as Mr. Paterson reaches for a vision partly sensed but also enacts the uncertainty of his reaching. Night is the time for love even if love is as unsure as it is in Paterson. But just as the love is uncertain, so it occasions longing and a desire for deliverance, as can be heard clearly in the concluding six-and-a-half-page burst from Cress's anguished darkness as woman and poet, to which "listening" is Mr. Paterson's only response. The point is that for Williams Paterson is a prodigious emotional as well as social fact. His life is its life. Cress's failure is his failure as she fumbles for inventive response to her own plight, but in listening to her the reader and the poet hear the repetitive, suffering voice of the city's fallen condition and of Mr. Paterson's.

This last section of Book 2 makes a unique contribution to the poem as the city's profound ills thus find expression in a voice full of genuine hurt though at the same time sunk in self-pity, a voice that in its burden without end utters Mr. Paterson's own despair as citizen and as poet. He is naive to imagine that poetry can redeem his world, but he is implacable in demanding that that world be heard. Paterson is a city of defeat and loneliness, a city of worn-down, of wasted rather than dreadful night, and here at the end of Book 2 Williams lets its voice flow forth without internal poetic reshaping or answer.

Book Three

Book 1 had been dominated by the poet's own perplexities and actions. His inner encounters had dominated. Book 2 sought to turn outward and, though still much plagued by the poet's uncertainties, had captured the scene in the park and, penetrating more deeply, Cress's rambling embodiment of Paterson's degradation. There is a sense in which the two combine to establish the inner and outer aspects of the matter which fills Mr. Paterson's mind. Book 3 moves on to be concerned again with the doubleness of that mind in action as it wrestles now with three of the giant forces that are loosed to twist and ultimately level the inner and outer alike: wind, fire, and flood. Paterson is one of many "corrupt cities" where there are "no palaces, no secluded gardens, / no water among the stones" (P, 107); but the poem has changed direction by even raising such a question as beauty, the last possible virtue Paterson might be thought to yield. Beauty, however, has been an evanescent shimmer that has beckoned the poet from the beginning, not quite present until now in its own person but gracing the work here and there, as a by-product of the marriage of inner and outer reflected in occasional passages: the "beauty of holiness" faintly echoed in the evangelist's sermon; a melancholy absence haunting Cress's personal and poetic defeat. Book 3 will realize this latent image to the extent that it is possible in Paterson, linking it, however, with its "cost." Paterson's beauty is marked not only by strangeness but by degradation and even perversity. It is a beauty Williams will image in the book by evoking the figure of Toulouse-Lautrec who caught the underworld of Paris in such fashion as to make a strange form out of it, attractiveness and repulsiveness combined. Paterson has none of the metropolitan glamour of Paris, but the beauty it affords will be a condition of its own kind of decadence.

Mr. Paterson himself would have it otherwise if he could. Book 3 opens with a slender lyric celebrating the beauty of the locust which, despite its nature as a weed tree often crowded off to edges of streams or other back corners, brings forth a delicate and fragrant bloom out of its gnarled shape. To Williams it is "the sweet, white locust," but his immediate question is "How much does it cost / to love the locust tree / in bloom" (P, 95)? The cost of beauty in Paterson is the city's failure to see its possibilities. As the verve of Lautrec's painting could not have existed without the decadence in which he lived and from which he made his art, so Paterson's Beautiful Thing can find being only because of the city's squalor. It is a perverse beauty, the only real treasure the city affords, and its cost is precisely marked by the condition bringing it forth.

What he finds is by its nature no more than transient and uncertain, as divorced as possible from what Paterson or beauty "should be" but deeply at one with Paterson's double existence in the poem as exterior and interior reality. Section 1 of the third book moves from its opening in the locust-tree lyric to a perception of the library's volumes as agencies of a cool wind "echoing the life / there" and beginning the movement the whole of Book 3 will sustain of approach to the Beautiful Thing. Its appearance sets the keynote of its evanescence as it "fills the tubes / of the ear until we think we heard a wind / actual" (P, 95). It generates momentary potency as it reinvokes its first avatar, "and there grows in the mind / a scent, it may be, of locust blossoms / whose perfume is itself a wind moving / to lead the mind away " (P, 96). But the Beautiful Thing is not just the blossom and its charm, it is explicitly a mystery, a superimposing of outer and inner so that the presented beauty, itself combined out of "wind" (exterior) and "scent" (interior), combines "to lead the mind away." Paterson's beauty, in short, is more than a matter of attractive objects somehow rescued from the city's squalor. It is the city, rather, exhibiting aspects of its outer self that catch and activate poetic consciousness in their union with inner perceptual and emotional activity. It is a case of the city's awakening the poet to become "Mr. Paterson"—now collecting his perceptions and his thoughts, at least momentarily, into unitary expression of his identity with his sad town—without losing its poetic power over him, unpredictable as it may be. In *Kora* poetic mind had been made sufficient to itself. In *The Great American Novel* it had been hopelessly estranged from the scene which was so unshakably its own. *Paterson 3* advances the dialectic more forcibly, perhaps, than any other of Williams's writing to date as its stumbles upon, is ever fleetingly entranced by the city's ability to turn itself now and then toward the light, always slantwise and unpredictable, of the kind of beauty the poet can generate from it.

The revelation is enthralling, so much so that it can easily lead to clumsy, brutal efforts to possess it. As section 1 proceeds, the enraptured poet slips and falls to become would-be raptor, rapist, seizing upon the vision that teases him so, but only to turn destroyer as his violence strips beauty to its flesh and bones and so, of course, reveals the degradation that is its substance.

> Haunted by your beauty (I said),
> exalted and not easily to be attained, the
> whole scene is haunted:
>   Take off your clothes.
> (I said)
> Haunted, the quietness of your face
> is a quietness, real
>   out of no book.
> ....
> (then, my anger rising) TAKE OFF YOUR
> CLOTHES! I didn't ask you
> to take off your skin   .   I said your
> clothes, your clothes. You smell
> like a whore. I ask you to bathe in my
> opinions, the astonishing virtue of your
> lost body (I said)   .

> —that you might
> send me hurtling to the moon
> . . let me look at you (I
> said, weeping).
> (*P*, 104–5).

The peculiar-sounding bath afforded by the poet's "opinions" is essential to recover the "astonishing virtue" that the Beautiful Thing possesses. Book 3, thus, is a study not of virtue found by a subjective will, urbanely gleaned from the dump as in Wallace Stevens, or even of love among the ruins as in Browning, the superseding of a lesser state of decayed worldliness by better fulfillment. In Williams the Beautiful Thing coexists with and is part of the fallen state by virtue of its own fall and by virtue of the poet's now interwoven and poetically intricate participation in fallenness, a participation that can in no way be forced or grasped beyond its uncertain existence in world and mind.

The force and power of this double vision increase in section 2 as wind gives way to fire, and the mystery of transforming squalor into beauty is now embodied by a new storm, the fire that had, historically, seized upon Paterson in the past. Here, true to double vision, it is reenacted both as itself and as the image and vessel of the poet's own desire for transformation. The fire motif of section 2 is again united with the poet's action, made one with it. As storm, indeed as rape, it seizes upon the city to lift it for the moment into a holocaust of transformation but only, of course, at the cost of destroying whatever it grasps. At first, it is the vision of transformation that seizes the poet's eye, for the moment, in a rapture of pleasure.

> An old bottle, mauled by the fire
> gets a new glaze, the glass warped
> to a new distinction, reclaiming the
> undefined. A hot stone, reached
> by the tide, crackled over by fine
> lines, the glaze unspoiled .
> Annihilation ameliorated: Hottest
> lips lifted till no shape but a vast
> molt of the news flows. Drink
> of the news, fluid to the breath.

Shouts its laughter, crying out—by
an investment of grace in the sand
—or stone: oasis water. The glass
splotched with concentric rainbows
of cold fire that the fire has bequeathed
there as it cools, its flame
defied—the flame that wrapped the glass
deflowered, reflowered there by
the flame: a second time, surpassing
heat.
(*P,* 118)

And as the section proceeds, caught up by the exuberance of the
fire, the poet extends his sight to grasp another image of "fire" as
instigator of another kind of beauty. He calls upon an image from
the Pacific war then raging—a soldier driving a bulldozer, that war-
like implement of peace, through the debris of a barrage on Iwo
Jima, making a path for his companions. "Beauty" again, in the
world that is the poet's, is the fruit of a literal burst of devastation.
At another moment, his eyes returned to the city, he is again caught
up by the flaming spectacle it presents as a "shriek" of fire whirls
away the room where he reads to reveal a tin roof, half a block
long.

. . . held by the fire—to rise at last,
almost with a sigh, rise and float, float
upon the flames as upon a sweet breeze,
and majestically drift off, riding the air
            sliding
            (*P,* 121)

And it is not at all clear whether we are looking at transformation
only as a mere "wonder" of the fire, or at a transformation from
squalor to beauty, or at a transformation from form to hopeless
formlessness.

It is this kind of polyvalence that carries into the climactic ending
of section 2 and Williams's several pages on the Beautiful Thing
now incarnate as an abused and injured girl, one he had actually
been called upon to treat medically, housed in a basement room at
her employer's house. Either she, or another figure again superim-

posed upon her, further identifies the Beautiful Thing as a "whore" of the town, consort of "the guys from Paterson" who in their fight with "the guys from Newark" was "socked one" in the nose (*P*, 127). The scene, having the same relative importance here as Cress's long letter in Book 2, yanks the poet violently back to external vision, as the Beautiful Thing that has so far been chiefly a set of visions evoked from the "library" is suddenly present before him in the flesh. This piece of waste, victim of Paterson and its life, appears before him, but in doing so it breaks his double vision to collapse the high pitch of section 2 with its actuality. The poet's voice can find relief only in subjectivity, a stammering out of his helplessness (beyond emotion-fraught description of her) in the face of such a presence. The scene might have set poetic vision into action. Instead, as in Book 2, it carries the poem to a kind of awestruck stammering.

> I can't be half gentle enough,
> half tender enough
> > toward you, toward you,
> inarticulate, not half loving enough
> BRIGHTen
> > > the cor
> > > > ner
> where   you   are!
> > —a flame,
> black plush, a dark flame.
> > (*P*, 128)

The outer world is the ultimate presence, darkening flame.

External force continues to dominate in section 3 as flood succeeds wind and fire, most obviously to reduce Mr. Paterson to the state of the drowned dog that appears early in it. The phrase "Beautiful Thing" now disappears from the poem. The giants' force triumphs, and the section is dominated by a spate of verbal debris, the leavings of the flood. Mr. Paterson begins by giving himself doubtful-sounding advice, "write carelessly so that nothing that is not green will survive" (*P*, 129). Then comes the third "so be it" passage in which he accepts flood as he had accepted wind and flame, but his human effort in behalf of the gods against the giants' weapons can persist now only as a kind of holding action.

In the midst of the scattered observations that follow he is led at
one point to exclaim, "Why do I bother with this / rubbish" (*P*,
134)? And he will come to no answer until the section's very end.
Instead huge gobbets of verbal drift pile up on him: one whole page
of broken and slanted lines jumbles together talk about everything
and nothing from cooking eggs to Antonin Artaud (whom Pound
had been urging him to read) to wedding bouquets. A second page
is given over to Pound's whining answer to Williams's protest that
he didn't like Artaud and didn't want to bother with him. Pound
writes in the incoherent fake-folksy gibberish characteristic of the
correspondence of his late years. A third page is filled with meaningless technical detail recording a futile drilling for fresh water in
Paterson at an earlier date concluding that no fit water is to be
found but suggesting that rock salt might be reached instead. The
remainder of the section retreats into subjective despair. The Beautiful Thing has slid back into the rubbish which is its home leaving
Mr. Paterson a desperate course: "Let the words / fall any way at
all—that they may / hit love aslant" (*P*, 142). The poem is not yet
ended, though Williams is approaching the passage he at one time
designed as an ending, but it is falling heavily onto one only of its
bases, the external chaos that will largely predominate through the
whole of Book 4. When he does conclude it is only to seek an exit
for himself and, doing so, make a kind of apology for his collapse:
"Let / me out! (Well, go!) this rhetoric / is real!" (*P*, 145).

Book Four

Book 4 does move "out" in its first section as Williams turns now
to the dramatic passage made up of the relationship of a nurse
dubbed "Phyllis" to two would-be lovers: an aging lesbian for
whom she serves as masseuse, who pictures herself as "Corydon,"
and Mr. Paterson himself, who actually plays a heavy-handed Corydon in a quest for physical union with her that had led to a kind
of rape in Book 3. The whole section appears to have been blocked
out as a unit during Williams's stay at Yaddo in 1950 and without
wholly clear thought as to its relationship to the longer poem. Paul
Mariani, indeed, identifies it as one aspect of a "confessional"
mood that was to seize intermittently upon Williams in his later
years and that had already surfaced in work on his play *A Dream
of Love*, but he notes that once the section was finished Williams

was satisfied that it would indeed fit into his broader pattern. There is a sense in which the whole of Book 4 hangs from the thread at the end of Book 3, "Let me out." Books 1 through 3 had moved to a crescendo of interaction between poet and town that ends in the leveling of both by the flood. "Out" was the only way left to go, whether in the mock idyll of Corydon and Phyllis, moved now to New York's fashionable East Side, or in the two sections of fragments that follow it. Williams for some time felt that he had in fact ended his poem with Book 4, and in particular would write Marianne Moore a defense of what he regarded as that ending. But that decision would of course change with Book 5 some years later.

The work that he finally completed includes the fifth book, and despite its appearance as coda to the whole, it was unhesitatingly added. It seems a misdirection, thus, to regard Book 4 as anything except a temporary close. In this light it becomes more an interval in the poem, a pause, an act of detachment from the poetic intensity of the first three books. It is preceded by the flood debris of Book 3, and it rests in that image throughout its own course. Little is left of the double vision informing the earlier books; the Beautiful Thing has disappeared for good, and even the poet's own restlessness finds only momentary poise in the dramatic detachment of his mock idyll. When mind reasserts itself as subject in the book's later section it is still with an air of emotional detachment from the city as it scans the debris the flood has left. In Book 5, the earlier poetic will resume in a new voice as, now satisfied that Paterson's debris cannot be lifted up, it returns to its habitual double vision proclaiming the "identity" of the virgin and the whore that, as Beautiful Thing, had underlain the early books. Paterson, surely, was "whorish" enough to satisfy the most demanding of slummers. Book 5 would, then, reassert the doubleness that had held much of Book 3 in its power—the dialectic at work in the city obliquely matching that in the poet—a "whorishness" surely, but rooted in an innocence of its own condition and so turning that complexity outward as its true face. The "nine months' wonder" the poem had hoped for at its outset had led to a kind of bastardy—and that bastardy is largely the substance of Book 4. But the bastard child was no less inherently innocent than his legitimate brother or sister. Bastardy was not so much of his essence as of an external condition in whose making he had had no share.

It is the human being of Phyllis, of Allen Ginsberg, and of Mr.

Paterson himself that serves as example. The nurse-masseuse states that her home town is Ramapo but that she "trained" in Paterson, a training reflected in the streetwise self-possession with which she, as present and contemporary, faces the coquettish advances of her patient, the direct sexuality of Mr. Paterson's wooing, and, in the background, the importunities of a drunken father to return home. She measures each of the three with a cool eye. When Corydon presses her for details of her private life, she responds bluntly that her father is a drunk. Corydon, with lifted eyebrow, chides her. "That's more humility than the situation demands. / Never be ashamed of your origins." Phyllis's response is direct and to the point, "I'm not. It's just the truth" (P, 157). She likes her life in the big city: "Believe me there's plenty of money here" (P, 150). She cuts her employer's fancifulness down to a present size:

> But she's a nut, of the worst kind. Today she was telling me about some rocks in the river here she calls her three sheep. If they're sheep I'm the Queen of England. They're white all right but it's from the gulls that crap them up all day long. (P, 152)

And she responds forthrightly to her father's plea to come home from New York:

> I don't care what you say. Unless Mother writes me, herself, that you've stopped drinking—and I mean *stopped drinking*— I won't come home. (P, 157)

She accepts her employer's invitation to accompany her on a yachting trip, and proceeds to enjoy the luxury it affords. Whether she is seduced or not, she is whore enough to seize upon such luxury as comes her way. She enjoys her séances with Mr. Paterson as they gradually lead to sexual union. He is in a fever of excitement over his conquest and its fruits (an aspect of acknowledging his own participation in Paterson's whorishness), but her attitude toward both her lovers is summed up at the end. Corydon, again, is probing into her private life:

> Have any of these men
> you speak of .   ?
> —and has he?
> No   [she lies].

Good.
What's good about it?
Then you're still a virgin!
What's it to *you?*
    (P, 169–70)

Phyllis, in short, is given existence in the poem in her own right. She is neither swept up into a vision of the Beautiful Thing nor allowed to sink to the level of one of the city's "automatons." She is like a character out of one of Williams's stories. She is a vastly limited being, low visioned and venal enough, but she has taken a measure of her world and found it usable.

In section 2 it is Allen Ginsberg's letter which most clearly strikes a parallel note. He too is unabashed about his own mixed past. He has studied "off and on" at Columbia, worked as a copyboy, spent a year in a mental hospital, hopes to find a newspaper job, and writes poems. He has returned to Paterson for the first time in seven years. He is casual about his situation, which aligns him with Williams as a poet of and in Paterson. "I hope you will welcome this from me, an unknown young poet, to you, an unknown old poet, who lives in the same rusty county of the world" (P, 173). Like Phyllis, he takes himself as found, is the "local" which is also Williams. Neither of the two is very radiant a "gist" as they present themselves to Mr. Paterson, but together they bespeak a residual toughness of fiber. That, at least, exists in the city's lumpishness. Ginsberg's poetic hopes, he says, carry him also to a doubleness of vision, not exactly the same as Williams's but like it projecting a tension between himself and the world around him as substance for his writing. He speaks discerningly of Williams's work, in contrast to other citizens imaged in the poem who are mystified by his efforts. Williams, he feels, has made him see Paterson, "an accomplishment you almost cannot have hoped to achieve. It is a misery I see (like a tide out of my own fantasy) but mainly the splendor which I carry within me and which all free men do" (P, 174). In Book 5 Ginsberg will amplify his response out of his freedom to deal with the town as he will. "Paterson is only a big sad poppa who needs compassion. In any case Beauty is where I hang my hat" (P, 213). Such declaration was certainly heartening to Williams, and whatever doubts he would later develop about the value of

Ginsberg's poetry, here was as good evidence as he could hope for of at least incipient radiance in the scene with which he had struggled and that had occasioned such struggle within himself. Section 3 reechoes this mixture of feeling in its passage centered on the idea that "virtue" in Paterson is equivalent with "effort." It is "a complex reward in all / language, achieved slowly" (*P*, 188), and the sentiment leads consistently to the book's close. After finishing his survey of Paterson as an innocent-corrupt village, Mr. Paterson is momentarily but forcefully seized by a desire to lose himself in the sea, the flood, just as Paterson's river, now rotten with accumulated pollution, finds its own ending there. Its appeal is strong.

> Listen!
> Thalassa! Thalassa!
> Drink of it, be drunk!
> Thalassa
> immaculata: our home, our nostalgic
> mother in whom the dead, enwombed again
> cry out to us to return   .
> the blood dark sea!
> nicked by the light alone, diamonded
> by the light   .   from which the sun
> alone lifts undamped his wings
> of fire!
> (*P*, 202)

To accept such primeval urges echoing both Homer and Whitman, however, would be to accept regression and so abandon the whole effort at "gist" which occupies Book 4. Consequently, he reverses direction in the book's final passage to picture himself, the swimmer he has been all along, emerged from the sea. He naps briefly on the beach, a necessary moment of recovery, and then reassumes his station ashore, Paterson's "shore." He dresses, calls to the dog that had figured in all books of the poem as an image of the sniffing, seeking poet, and turns "inland." Book 4 itself ends in a brief, violent envoi: "This is the blast / the eternal close / the spiral / the final somersault / the end" (*P*, 204), but Mr. Paterson, whatever the condition of his poem at this moment, is free of that abrupt dismissal as he moves to an interior that will emerge in its time as his work's true close—insofar as closure was possible.

Book Five

Movement would be marked by the recoil of Book 5 from outward to inward, but to an inner consciousness now substantially complicated by the poetic struggle acted out through the first four books and by the events befalling Williams in the intervening seven years. *Paterson* 1–4 had been an epochal contest with the doubleness of vision occasioned by Mr. Paterson's effort to embrace both the depressed condition of the city and his own willingness to take it as such while seeking the Beautiful Thing. His effort had tended to flop between the poles created by Schiller's play theory, so that the city stood outside of play, estranged in fact, impervious to poetic translation. At times he could perceive it as though he were "inventing," as in the lyric passages where poetic idea served to release "thing" from its inherent deadness. At other times, notably in the walk in the park, the vision of the gang girl, or in much of Book 4, he was driven to little more than direct witnessing, to descent alone. *Kora* had achieved its own lyric freedom apart from any demands of scene—in it scene was for the taking or the leaving. *Paterson,* however, was rooted in an act of identification: the poet as the city, or the two, rather, as inseparable.

Book 5 does not let go of the dialectic; but as coda to the first four books, as restatement and new development of them, it seizes upon a different locus for its poetic energy. The city as such drops out of sight—into the uncertain limbo of Book 4, where it existed in fact. That lump was disposed of, but its mark is retained as poetic self continues to feel the force of the dialectic which Books 1 to 4 had generated. Mr. Paterson is no longer in the city in Book 5, but he is still as fully of it as ever. His effort will be the one he had begun with—to find a language—but now it will be turned to contemplate itself in the realm of poetic action where Schiller had placed it and where it was now spoken for by clouds of witnesses of Williams's own choosing. The local, the present to him, will remain as poetic authority. In Williams's own terms, Book 5 will be concerned with "idea" and "thing," with virgin and whore, dancing and lunging, the ceaseless interaction that his whole search for art as a descent completed by invention had predicated from the beginning. Such a process had no room for simple fixity. All must be motion, interaction, translation.

The Mr. Paterson of Book 5 becomes wholly and explicitly the poetic self, shaped and moved by Paterson still but also its own theater of action, which to a large degree it had been all along. Now, however, that theater was affirmed by cognate parallel, by Williams's creation of a museum populated by artists from past and present whom he could see as sharing with himself the sense of double vision for which his linking of idea and fact made a center. The book was largely to be built on two interpenetrant dualities: that of the virgin and the whore, which runs throughout its length, and that implied by the phrase "satyrs dance," a figure taken up in section 2 and continued intermittently to the end to link the grotesque and the beautiful. In addition the book was strongly marked by his feeling for the Unicorn tapestries displayed at the Cloisters Museum in New York; but this actual museum, like Williams's self-constructed temple of art in Book 5, would still be marked by a dialectic: the unicorn, itself a mythical beast, is hunted in a bloody contest resolved only when a virgin is put forward to lure the creature to its capacity. This was defeat and victory both, for when the intact unicorn is shown, in the final panel, in an idealized pen surrounded by banks of entwined flowers, it is hard to say whether it is in captivity to the hunt or ensconced in glory. As a figure traditionally associated with Christ, it would at this stage, perhaps, have to be seen in both conditions at once. Williams will make much of this image, identifying it with art and the imagination.

But the book's first reference is to a play of García Lorca's, the second to a novel of Philippe Soupault's which Williams and his mother had translated in 1929. Lorca's play invokes the simultaneous reawakening to love and the entrapment of an old man by a young maiden. The novel, in Williams's own words, was about a "little French whore, very intellectual, exotic, strange . . . contradictory, amusing" (IW, 48). Double awareness in the complexity of each tale is thus established as the theme of Book 5, raw fact and imaginative translation of it interfused and pointing, immediately, to "A WORLD OF ART / THAT THROUGH THE YEARS HAS / SURVIVED / —the museum become real" (P, 209). "Art" was no longer the suspect and alien presence it had been for Williams in earlier days. His own experience and broadening acquaintance with it had made firm a kinship—at least with what he would select from it. If the museum had become real, it could as well be said now that the real had equally given way to the imaginative. Section 1 moves on to celebrate such "identity" as that of the virgin and the whore evoked in his texts. Lorca's Don Perlimplin and his maiden, Belisa, in their garden and Soupault's temptress were no doubt worlds apart in fact alone. And in fact alone each woman could be seen as either tempting to wantonness or as source of vitality. What was "real" in them, however, was not their fact alone but that fact translated and invigorated by co-present "idea": the recurrence of emotional fascination, stimulation, and reawakening. Such identity of contraries leads Williams on to ponder the painter Audubon at work in the American wilderness fascinated by the creatures of the New World and following their lead to sight a "horned beast among the trees" (P, 211), a glimpse, perhaps, of the fictive unicorn prepared for and led to by the very reality he painted. The interplay of real and ideal is summed up quickly: "—the virgin and the whore, which / most endures? The world / of the imagination most endures" (P, 213).

It is this world that had been Audubon's care in all his heroic effort to record in art the fact of his birds, and Williams moves into it immediately by extending his museum to embrace the two contemporary painters Jackson Pollock and Ben Shahn. "Things" for the former were the materials of his art, "blobs of paint squeezed out," but "with design" (P, 213). Ben Shahn had presented Williams with a painting he called *Tribute to Paterson* about which the poet had some reservations but which he hung in his house because he admired the pattern made by the windows shown in its buildings. The section ends with an evocation of brutish-delicate elements existing pell-mell in the tapestries' picturing of the unicorn hunt, themselves interspersed with prose derived from Gilbert Sorrentino and an unnamed writer, both given over to plainly whorish detail. Which of the two elements was more "real"? Williams suggests that for the artist they contribute equally to a "measure" of thing and idea and recommends openness to both, "'Loose your love to flow' / while you are yet young / male and female" (P, 216).

It is at this point that Williams moves ahead to the great central lyric informing all of Book 5 beginning "Satyrs dance," but not before he has interpolated a prose passage from the jazz musician Mezz Mezzrow, recording Mezzrow's own fascination with Bessie

Smith records he had heard by chance. "Inspirations mammy was with me," he says. "Every note that woman wailed vibrated on the tight strings of my nervous system: every word she sang answered a question I was asking" (*P*, 221). Not only did satyrs dance, they danced unpredictably and from out of nowhere, just as the Beautiful Thing had done in its appearances. The satyrs' lyric itself was a virtual litany of artists who had, in their work, simultaneously evoked "fact" and "idea" as they worked with the material that surrounded and pressed in on them. Gertrude Stein had, in Williams's view, moved toward art through a "rout of the vocables." Paul Klee's abstractions "fill the canvas" (*P*, 222), the famous task challenging every painter. Dürer's *Melancholy* had amassed its identity out of a tumult of unrelated detail. Leonardo had seen the dream of art to inform its object and simultaneously satirized that dream in *La Gioconda*. Hieronymus Bosch had pursued what Williams saw as unified vision through all the phantasmagoria of his painting. Freud is included among the artists along with Picasso, Juan Gris, and Beethoven, all these, like the last, stamping their "heavy feet" (*P*, 223) but making dance of their stomp. All, finally, are spoken for by the grisly, haunting detail of a Jew comforting his fellow captives while all are being shot to death by machine guns. Art was real, and earnest, but always it made its way by feeling creative action to be most alive in the very obduracy of things. Mr. Paterson is still of Paterson and its world, but he is now more concerned with the duality of counterpressure attested by his own world of art. The section ends with the citing of an interview Williams had had with a television reporter who does his best to make the poet declare his writing is nonsense. Williams pleads hard against Mike Wallace's singleness of vision. Wallace maintains that a poetic passage sounding like a grocery list must therefore be only a grocery list. Williams tries to spell out for him the heart of his own message, and that of Book 5.

> In prose, an English word means what it says. In poetry, you're listening to two things . . . you're listening to the sense, the common sense of what it says. But it says more. That is the difficulty. (*P*, 225)

Section 3 opens without interruption on the doubleness theme and continues to develop it to the end of the poem. Its first two and a half pages continue the furnishing of Williams's private museum with extended attention to Brueghel the Elder's painting of the adoration of the Magi. The scene may, in fact, be described as threefold in its interest to Mr. Paterson since at its center is the visible, adorable fact of new birth. That fact, however, is momentarily scanted in favor of attention to the Magi, their adoration and their gifts and, contrasted with them, the "savagely armed men" who accompany them as they converse with a "potbellied greybeard" in their midst, all looking like "the more stupid / German soldiers of the late / war" (P, 226). The fact of birth which brings all together is treated by Williams immediately following the Brueghel section as he refers to Saint Matthew's narrative of the incarnation and uses it to reevoke his own theme of the identity of the virgin and the whore. This virgin has been deflowered by the Holy Ghost himself in a miracle that preserves her virginity but nonetheless fazes Joseph, her husband, in a supernal case of reality as doubleness. As Joseph inclines "to put her away privily," an angel appears to him revealing the miracle that has taken place in the infusion of spirit into fact. He gives way, yields primacy to the mystery that has occurred and the birth that will ensue. His role is much like Mr. Paterson's own.

Within such a complex, Williams asserts, Brueghel has above all been faithful to "the two sides." On one side are the soldiers, to whom the birth is suspect, and who are inattentive to anything except presence.

> mouths open,
> their knees and feet
> broken from 30 years of
> war, hard campaigns, their mouths
> watering for the feast which
> had been provided
> (P, 228)

On the other side are the Magi who divine the miracle.

> —they had eyes for visions
> in those days—and saw,
> saw with their proper eyes,
> these things
> to the envy of the vulgar soldiery
> (P, 227)

The passage as a whole, with Brueghel as its creator and therefore in fact its chief actor, summarizes Williams's final sense of himself as poetic agent. He had in his own poetic life, now drawing to its end, been both impelled and tormented by vision, but by vision that had much eluded him. His most extensive poetic concern with it, *Paterson* itself, had failed to find a permanent bonding between thing and idea. The Brueghel passage appears then as his best restatement of his concern. Neither thing nor idea could be made with any certainty to contain the other. The literal eyes of the soldiers and the visionary eyes of the Magi saw two different ideas of the single thing which, of and to itself, as certainty, continued to evade both. Faced with the equivocalness of her own situation, says the gospel writer, "Mary kept all these things, and pondered them in her heart" (*P,* 229). What then of the hoped-for vision? The answer Williams spins out in Book 5 is a subtle one and amounts to a widening of the centrality consequent on his whole sense of poetry as action rather than vision, as acting within presence. In a sense his thought can be said to advance little beyond the freedom of creative agent he had asserted and enacted in *Kora* nearly forty years earlier.

In fact, however, a small but immensely useful point has been gained as this book moves on to frame the artist's freedom not *from* the world but *in* it. Williams's free-leaping hounds of *Kora's* frontispiece must become the sniffing dogs of Paterson's park. The central Christian mystery upon which he so unexpectedly draws here is one of incarnation, of the entering of the spiritual into the mortal. Neither Brueghel nor Williams is concerned with the theology of the act. What holds the attention of both is its presence as rough fact and visionary insight alike. The artist is of the wide world, and he is misdirected unless he can in one way or another—as attested by the whole variety of the museum Williams has assembled in Book 5—reach out to the inclusiveness that is the world and poetry's substance, and indeed the substance of any right seeing. Brueghel may seem to treat the traditionally august theme of the Nativity as a muddle. In fact, however, he is assembling and juxtaposing the elements out of which birth will be the issue.

Book 5 will continue to echo this theme throughout its long and lyrically sustained conclusion, as Mr. Paterson now withdraws himself into a scene much evoked from the hunt tapestries, himself within them "an aging body" but, in his doubleness of being, creative spirit and caged animal in one:

among the thronging flowers of that field
    where the Unicorn
        is penned by a low
wooden fence
    in April!
      (*P*, 232)

The hunt has swept much bloody fact into its course, most notably
the hounds, poetic dogs, torn and wounded by the unicorn in their
struggle. The virgin herself, the instrument of his capture and the
Beautiful Thing, is glimpsed only for a moment:

    through the rough woods
      outside the palace walls
among the stench of sweating horses
    and gored hounds
        yelping with pain.
      (*P*, 234)

Then toward the conclusion the poet's thoughts draw away from
the tapestry to reenter the world of their own kind of fact as Williams recalls his English grandmother, who he suspects may have
borne his father out of wedlock, whose venturesome life he had
celebrated in other poems, and who had been the battered muse of
his original self-dedication in his early "The Wanderer." The world
was the world; the imagination was the imagination. The human
condition and therefore the condition of poetry was existence
within the ceaseless interplay of subjective and objective will that
both together enacted. What was needed was participation in that
condition as it stood, and such participation could be nothing other
than action.

We know nothing and can know nothing
           but
the dance, to dance to a measure
contrapuntally,
      Satyrically, the tragic foot.
      (*P*, 239)

It is Mr. Paterson's final word in this book. It places him as denizen
of his city and as his own poet at the center of the ceaseless, costly,

revivifying mortal process that is life itself. The word "measure" would often have a stricter meaning for Williams as a gesture toward the sense of prosody he sought. Here, clearly, it is stretched to identify the whole process of poetry as a self-enactment within scene, the common doom, the common calling. The dance is sure as it is both inescapable and of the only essence our nature and situation allow.

Pictures from Brueghel

In fact all of Williams's late poetry, including *Paterson* 5 as its last major exhibit, perpetuates his concern with poetic agent, and in addition extends that concern in a number of ways that draw directly on the intimate detail of the poet's private life during his last years. It is heavily a poetry of private person and poetic person mixed and related. For that reason, perhaps, Book 5 has won the reputation of somehow belonging more to the late work in general—that brought together in the posthumous volume *Pictures from Brueghel and Other Poems* in 1962—than to its parent work. Such a view has its merit, but it does less than whole justice to the degree in which Book 5 is linked to the thematic center created by the earlier *Paterson*'s dramatizing of an agential or poet's concern. *Paterson* 1–4 is inextricably rooted in Mr. Paterson's double existence as individual and communal voice. There he is himself, but that self must take on the whole burden of a brute world. Book 5 renews and somewhat reduces this concern in its final image of the dance, of measure, but it is still opposed to any transcendence into self free from brutishness. The measure exists between given world and given self in creative interaction, thus reasserting Mr. Paterson's claim to at least a generative milieu and an occasion for the art that is his own.

The additional question, however, haunting all of Williams's late writing of the nineteen fifties and early sixties is the degree to which he experienced a deep if never quite definitive change of personality as a result of illness and aging combining to undercut the radical self-dependence which had made the base of his earlier work. During the writing of *Paterson* he had undergone an operation for hernia, which had to be repeated before it was successful, and this experience was followed by a mild heart attack. *Paterson* 4 was completed in 1950, immediately after which he and Flossie undertook an extensive trip across the country that included his strenuous and stressful participation in a poet's conference at the University of Washington. This conference was all the more demanding in that it marked his most major acceptance to date by contemporaries whom in past years he had often regarded, and they him, with doubt and distrust. Immediately upon his return to Rutherford he plunged into work on his *Autobiography*. During all this eventfulness he still kept an active hand in his medical practice with which his son now assisted him. Then, in early 1951, he suffered the first of three strokes that would befall him over the next four years before the onset of his final decline. A period of recovery followed during which he turned to composition of "The Desert Music" in response to Phi Beta Kappa's invitation to compose a work for their annual meeting. A second and much severer stroke occurred in 1952 and plunged him into a period of deep depression that righted itself only after extended treatment and hospitalization.

Certainly these events took a toll. In particular they threw him into a long, perhaps never quite to be resolved reassessment of the theme of marriage. This had also been a theme in *Paterson*, but now he reflected on his own marriage with Flossie who, independent as she was, had stood by him as loving wife, friend, critic, sympathizer, and, in all domestic matters, as caretaker. This last service would grow ever larger with the years and their manifold illnesses. All the while he had been striving with the difficulty of "marriage" between language and fact in Paterson, he had been living within and depending on a marriage which now seemed to have been sustained far more by his wife's dedication than his own. During and following his depressive spell Williams was smitten with guilt feelings about his numerous if always unenduring infidelities, and this sense deeply colors his late poetry, as is indicated by the title he gave the second of its three volumes, *Journey to Love*. It is consumed with feeling for the intricacy and dependence of love between man and wife, and for man's affection for and dependence on women in general. The buoyant lyric agent of *Kora*, the embroiled lyric agent of *The Great American Novel* and *Voyage to Pagany*, and even the celebrative if sobered lyric agent of *Paterson* 5 were, in much of the late poetry, set aside in favor of a fourth avatar of Williams's poetic self—a wounded, shaken, more patient and acquiescing seeker after feeling and knowledge rather than, as in the short poems particularly, a knower.

His own journey to love with Flossie had indeed been a long trek from the act of will he made of their commitment to marriage in *The Build-Up;* he was not even yet in secure grasp of its end; and for perhaps the first time Williams's poetry had become largely one of the uncertainty or unpredictability of personal self, of groping exploration, though still committed to the centrality of poetic self to its own being. Now, however (in an image which would finally dominate the writing), being had become the precariousness of the poetic self's power to generate the light needed to reveal and humanize its world. The aging poetic self was still possessed of light, but its light like any other dispelled only parts of the darkness which surrounded it. The late poetry was greatly a loving consideration of such parts for all the virtue they could be made to yield. If the doubleness of will of *Paterson* had combined to pose a dance within the duality of idea and thing, the final phase would more often be concerned with a duality between the self's knowledge and its experience, and even a doubt of its knowledge if also a willing participation in the limits of that knowledge. The poetry emerged sustainedly but with a sense of its own limit qualified by its technical exploration of the poet's lately won "triadic line."

The late poetry, of course, does not cancel out the earlier. It stands rather as evidence of what the creative power of invention central to all of Williams's writing could attain with the scene and the sense of self now at hand. I find it unnecessary to judge whether an "earlier" or "later" style is to be given the critical palm. The underlying formula of idea generated by fact is hewed to in the late work as fully as ever, but the late work would also attest the specific poetic ability of shaping rather than being tied by such a formula. Presence here was still that of what was present to the poet accepted in the light of imagination needed to bring such a self-centered realm into clear and sharp relief.

"The Desert Music," composed in 1951, was as Paul Mariani makes clear written in part out of Williams's effort to prove to himself that he was indeed recovering from the effects of his first stroke, that he was again a whole man and, as the poem insists, still a poet. In its way, it returns to a version of the *Paterson* theme (that poem was still suspended at its fourth book) as the poet labors his conviction that the most desertlike factuality, the rawest rawness of things themselves, are the source of the truest poetry. During this period also he was to be pouring energy into the third volume of the Stecher trilogy and so finally completing that extensive survey of home ground. Late in that year, however, he came under consideration for the post of consultant in poetry at the Library of Congress. His ultimate humiliating rejection, on grounds of supposedly radical political activity, coincided with the impact of his second and heavy stroke, and his hospitalization for depression in 1952 and early 1953. The two volumes most visibly affected by these shattering events would be *The Desert Music* of 1954 (excluding its title poem) and *Journey to Love* of 1955. The publication of *Paterson, Book Five* in 1958 would then come as a full delineation of the ground that had been held. It is with the two earlier of these volumes that I shall be concerned here, the latter especially, since it is in them that the growth of Williams's final sense of himself as poetic agent would most clearly be displayed.

Given the sad sequence of events that had befallen him, what could this now-constrained poetic agent hope to accomplish other than facing of consequences and a disciplining of his utterance to their presence? The facts, as always, were unalterable; poetry's task now as in 1920 was to lift "to the imagination those things which lie under the direct scrutiny of the senses" (*I*, 14). A generally defined progress may be discerned leading through *The Desert Music* and *Journey to Love* marking out development toward the imaginative embracing of the new presence. In particular, *The Desert Music* delineates what may be called the problem, while *Journey to Love* is concerned with the approach to what Williams variously called "light," "imagination," and "love" as the problem's resolution. Finally, the great testimony of "Asphodel, That Greeny Flower," at the end of the second volume, opens itself to full exploration of a translating process which, reversing the cynicism of a poet Williams refers to as his opposite, can be called "Love Alchemy," to make of Donne's blackness of mood a restorative essence of poetry, one recaptured and used to open and enlighten the world in which this later lover finds himself. Williams had turned from the scene of *Paterson* but only to face another kind of presence as essence. As a consequence the poetic problem of finding self in focus upon presence had to be reapproached in keeping with the new situation.

Let us begin with the opening poem of *The Desert Music*, for which Williams reached back into the second book of *Paterson* to reprint the "descent beckons" lyric where he had first found prosodic fulfillment in his triadic or stepped-down line. In *Paterson* it had also served to open a section of the poem much concerned with the failure of love as creative force and culminating in Cress's sustained wail of incompleteness and misery. As we have seen, the idea of "descent" as an essential part of the poetic process had occurred early in Williams's writing, and later, in *Paterson* as well, it had served the double purpose of delineating one phase of the imagination's work, albeit one that could prove overwhelming were it not finally transmuted or escaped. Williams's revival of the passage here in *The Desert Music* was certainly in part a celebration of the triadic lines in which many of the poems in the book would be written. But also, placed as opening of this volume of 1954, it could not have failed to appeal to him as an essential statement of his own pressing condition. The passage moved to a dark ending.

> For what we cannot accomplish, what
> is denied to love,
>   what we have lost in the anticipation
>   a descent follows,
> endless and indestructible.
>   (*PB*, 74)

He would open, thus, with the theme of love's failure, and in a curiously Eliotic tone. But as the combined titles of a desert "music" and a "journey" to love suggested, his bleak opening would prove to be only an opening. It surely stood as powerful summary of the complex of feelings he was to deal with in the two volumes, his awareness of a simultaneous imploding of emotional buoyancy and imaginative vigor occasioned by his manifold afflictions and recognitions. He had once again to begin from a bottom, albeit one now secured to him by a verse form in which he felt confidence and which promised opportunity for the discursive tentativeness his new state would demand. If the descent had to be experienced one more time, at least it could be entered with a verse measure limber and adaptable to uncertain demands.

Williams's triadic line was clearly of importance to him for its form—a line of variable length and accentuation—and also for its power to serve as a verse unit. Enjambment between the lines was common, but at the same time their typographical arrangement enforced a sense of minor pause twice within each line and impelled the reader toward a major pause at its end. Often the logic of the lines might strive against this major pause and so create a hesitation that might or might not be overcome by the thrust of the poem's meaning. Such a sense of approaching statement rather than asserting it was ideal for Williams's purpose in many of these later poems. For example in a second case from *The Desert Music*, "To a Dog Injured in the Street," he returned to his recurrent image of the poet as dog, one now injured and yelping with pain. The triads proceed quickly to invoke "the bomb," an image which hangs over a number of the late poems and takes a major place in "Asphodel." The "bomb" had exploded in the world, at Hiroshima, but another bomb has exploded inside the injured poet's own head laming him and for the moment driving him back to an ironic recall of his fledgling love for John Keats: "A drowsy numbness drowns my sense / as if of hemlock / I had drunk" (*PB*, 86). He thinks of the contemporary French poet René Char, who out of the horror of war and destruction has wrought poems of great and delicate beauty, but then he reverts to his own memories—of a boyhood pet he had kicked one night thinking that her suckling pups were eating her, and of seeing an unnamed hunter stab his knife into a dead rabbit's private parts. "I almost fainted," (*PB*, 87) he recalls. Such images of a wounding and brutal essence in nature cluster within the title image of the injured dog to which he returns, and the poet hangs on the verge of collapse into them until he rouses himself.

> Why should I think of that now?
>   The cries of a dying dog
>   are to be blotted out
> as best I can.
>   (*PB*, 88)

Williams's "problem" still dominates here. The agglutinative force of the triadic verses has allowed an act of descent, even of "wandering" into the despair of his own condition and its obsessive power. He knows he must overcome its effects and leans heavily at the end on René Char's example to free himself.

With invention and courage
  we shall surpass
    the pitiful dumb beasts,
let all men believe it,
  as you have taught me also
    to believe it.
    (PB, 88)

The poem cannot yet pass far beyond a call for the resolution necessary to address the problem's presence, but it contains a gesture
at least of leaving the image of injured, yelping animal behind it.
A third *Desert Music* poem, "Deep Religious Faith," pushes a
little further into the vitalizing power of invention, thus again linking the thrust of the late work with Williams's earliest poetic impulse. Invention is pictured as a force impelling the mind past
"death," past beauty, past even "the remote borders / of poetry
itself" (PB, 95), and it holds within itself the light of creativity, of
love, and even, now, of patience.

                Yet it is
that which made El Greco
  paint his green and distorted saints
    and live
lean.
  It is what in life drives us
    to praise music
and the old
  or sit by a friend
    in his last hours.
    (PB, 95)

Without it, "the paralytic is confirmed / in his paralysis" which
(echoing Pound) is a "half-savage country" where

  The rose
    may not be worshipped
or the poet look to it
  for benefit.
  (PB, 96)

The poem goes on to celebrate such vitality, though as a power he must find, or refind now, rather than as one at hand. In addition to such "problem" poems as I have cited, *The Desert Music* also contains ventures into a more generative tone of verse, although they are often touched with the melancholy out of which the problem poems grew. In "To Daphne and Virginia" Williams regards the youth and femininity of his two daughters-in-law, so distant from his aged and crippled condition, but comically settles upon the image of an old goose, "slopping / noisily in the mud of / his pool" (*PB*, 79)as something nearer his own state. In another poem the sound of a music-camp orchestra rehearsing near the cabin where he and Flossie are vacationing brings a momentary sense of harmony and fulfillment. A poem addressed to two Catholic friends celebrates their devotion to the Virgin Mary, but his sympathy for their feelings swings out to reassert his own dedication to a natural female principle in the world, "to which I have come / O *clemens! O pia! O dolcis! / Maria*" (*PB*, 86). It is the virgin-whore paradox of *Paterson* 5, here for the moment resolved in a sense of sharing a religious impulse he cannot escape, although he recasts it in his own wholly secular and earthy feelings about women.

But it is not until the appearance of *Journey to Love* in 1955 that it is possible to perceive a body of writing that moves systematically beyond definition or glimpse of poetic "light" toward generation, organization, and harmonization of feeling. The note is struck in "The Sparrow" where, with feeling and humor both, Williams returns to animal imagery not to lament his damaged condition but to assert it as his perennial essence. The sparrow is a tramp among birds, but he is also embodied vigor and undefeatability. In his unsubtle courtship he "drags his wings / waltzing, / throws back his head / and simply—/ yells" (*PB*, 131). He bathes vigorously in street dust to rid himself of lice. His mundane image even suggests "the aristocratic unicorn." His smallness and truculence plus the color of his eyebrows "give him the air / of being always / a winner" (*PB*, 131) despite his mate's eventual triumph over him in their union. When in time's course he dies, perhaps "flattened to the pavement," his mashed effigy still proclaims his identity. "This was I / a sparrow. / I did my best; / farewell" (*PB*, 132). Such a mode is far from the elegiac tone prevailing in *The Desert Music*. The aged poet has redefined his poem in relation to the realities of his total scene, and with wry humor picks up the double-vision device of *Paterson* to write entirely and perceptively of his admired urchin among birds while also writing detachedly and encompassingly about his own nature and even his own end.

The same kind of voice prevails when he comes to write of the locust tree in "A Pink Locust," that same variety of tree which had been a haunting and evanescent presence in *Paterson*. Now it has become a fact containing both itself and the poet in an image of weedy vitality. If Williams had seen the sparrow through his own sense of himself, now, as a local product of mixed quality, he discerns himself in the locust's propensity to take over wholesale whatever ground it can get a root into—a clear emblem of his poetic effort from first to last. He recalls Gertrude Stein, whose experiments he had admired, in declaring that "A rose *is* a rose," but he insists on his own behalf that "the poem equals it / if it be well made." Beyond poetry, "Life affirms / no greater reward," and here is the much-damaged poet still finding that reward. He is no rose among poets, he concedes, but "like this flower [the locust] / I persist" (*PB,* 141). He has refound under altered circumstances the truth of Mr. Paterson's discovery of Book 4 that the value of poetry is inseparable from the effort. The poem is act, and Williams despite his limitations is, like the locust, still there and still acting, thankfully.

The poem is act because life is act, and poetry must be poetic life, the fact of idea, or nothing. In the course of his own general argument Kenneth Burke develops his sense of idea as that which is mentally detachable from experience. Williams's poetry implied an opposite course; its art was repeatedly that of attaching idea to unreducible experience, indeed of finding idea unreal and incomprehensible unless it was so attached. This line of movement characterizes his late poems as it had his earlier work and of course describes the "effort" which *Paterson* 4 had found to be the requisite of poetry. The leading idea of *Journey to Love* was love itself, concurrent with what Williams also called "light" and "imagination" (*PB,* 180). Whichever of these terms was invoked by a poem, or whatever combination of them, they could mean little until they were brought into conjunction with fact as image and so were given their body. Again, the idea was an old one in Williams's writing.

Love and poetry were either of imageable fact or they were without reality. This direct relationship between poetry and fact was given a tentative statement in the short poem "Address," as the poet is caught by a look in his grown son's eyes and recognizes it as the token of a state of mind inclining indeterminately to love and to art both, or even to a less graspable process that is no more than incipient creation. It has a little the look of "agony," but perhaps, Williams thinks, "it was only a dreamy look / not an unhappy one / but absent from the world—" (PB, 144). It is a poet's look, perhaps, a lover's look opening a path into the wholly uncertain but exceedingly present world from which the late poetry emerges. In this case, Williams cannot do a great deal with it except take note. His gambit is to recall Robert Burns, lover and poet both, and to leave open the question of whether "Flow Gently, Sweet Afton" is a poem of love actually felt. For Williams, in any case, the ideas of "love" and "poetry" have taken on reality in the look on his son's face which in turn leads him to such rumination as he pursues. It is not the idea of love that can resolve the presence of that look or Burns's lines. It is rather the presence of that look or those lines that engender a possible idea only. In this late writing Williams often speaks as an older and uncertain man. His poetic quest, however, now carries him close to the heart of his matter—descent, the human incarnation of abstract power—light, imagination or love, and to his cherishing of its presence when thus it is met.

Such persistence is the informing theme of "Asphodel, That Greeny Flower"—love, light, and imagination now known as incarnate and as a grace creating an island in darkness upon which life and poetry persist. The asphodel is a flower of modest bloom at best. It lacks vivid color, but the poet remembers having collected and pressed it when he was a boy; and the ancient myth that has made of it the one blossom in hell captures his imagination with its suggestion of continued life. Williams's asphodel blooms in old age and decrepitude, not only in the presence of debility and death but in the face of the threat of outliving one's generative powers—a direr threat, as of death within life. But in fact love like the asphodel casts its verdant hue now in the midst of such desolation, and with it blooms still the memory and imagination it evokes. It is hardly surprising that the earlier sections of "Asphodel" return often to the image of a garden, which is the fact of cultivation wrested from the tangle and waste that would exist without cultivation. The love the poet celebrates is far from being mere sentiment. As marriage, it is rather a garden to be inhabited yielding the fruits of the effort that has brought it into existence. This love is a conversion of earlier senses of both love and poetry as impulse into "marriage," the established support upon which this poetic agent depends. He has become a husbandman of love and of poetry both.

Book 1 will enact their celebration again in a kind of dance figure, the poet envisioning himself and his wife finding measure in relation to each other across often-troubling spans of event not spelled out in the poem but serving it as a kind of continuo against which the dance pattern seeks to define itself. The force of this pattern is felt at the opening as the poet recalls his discovery that a flower could indeed bloom in the netherworld and that such blooming persists. "I was cheered," he notes, "when I came first to know / that there were flowers also / in hell." The image of hell, scene of his earliest effort at realizing poetic person and within which the poet must take his salvation in *Kora*, returns in this late testament. And one aspect of this "hell" is what the process of marriage has enforced upon his wandering ways, though this aspect now is seen to have possessed its own blooms. "Today / I'm filled with the fading memory of those flowers / that we both loved" (*PB*, 153). The asphodel, "Of love, abiding love / it will be telling / though too weak a wash of crimson / colors it / to make it wholly credible" (*PB*, 153–54). The poem centers on a vision of marriage as a process finding its way across uncertain ground. The measure of the dance that marriage enforces is a serving and not a denying force. The doubts expressed years before in *The Build-Up* and *A Voyage to Pagany* have been dispelled. Williams now knows that marriage is source of the invention needed to create a way upon which life itself has come to depend. The lesson has been sharp at times.

> I cannot say
>   that I have gone to hell
>   for your love
>   but often
>   found myself there

            in your pursuit
I do not like it
    and wanted to be
       in heaven.
    (*PB*, 156)

Heaven for this poet, however, is unreal. Marriage is reality; it is the presence of love and now the begetter of reality.

    Death,
            is not the end of it.
There is a hierarchy
    which can be attained
            I think
in its service.
    (*PB*, 157)

The journey to love is a journey not quite toward the love of a person, though for Williams it certainly was that also. But it was maximally a journey toward what the images of marriage, garden, and dance implied—a state of being, of learning what it was in the beloved that acted as a magnet, as though the beloved were the container of a treasure in which the lover might share. Sharing, indeed, was the essence of this dance, as participation is necessarily the essence of any dance.

It was the love of love,
    the love that swallows up all else,
        a grateful love
a love of nature, of people,
    animals,
        a love engendering
gentleness and goodness
    that moved me
    and *that* I saw in you.
        (*PB*, 160)

It was by an inclusive thing-contained that the lover, errant as he may be, has been held. Marriage is education in how to take the world, what to do with it. One tried to learn through extended rehearsal but at all points grasped the lesson by almost accidental disclosures. Much like the education that poetry made possible, marriage presented itself as open demand and fulfilled itself only in specific, discovered response. In *Paterson* 5 Williams had declared that the dance was "sure." The dance, seen closely now in its precariousness, could not quite be called sure, but as it had taken place it was certainly inescapable. It was, as love or as poetry the dance of response, a creation of being out of nonbeing invoking the two as measure and countermeasure. To refuse it or falter in its demands, as Book 2 will go on to say, would be to collapse into countermeasure alone.

Rather like *Paterson* 5, the second book of "Asphodel" spends much time building not quite a museum but at least a catalogue of instances by which love and poetry have over the years asserted their power to enforce the dance. Against them stands "the bomb," testifying to Williams's appalled reaction to Hiroshima and to the cost of suppressing the forces he feels so powerfully have made the only presence on which he in his present weakness can rely and on which all relies. The bomb contains as synecdoche "all suppressions" from Salem "to the latest / book burnings" (*PB*, 168). Williams had felt the impact of such ironfistedness when he was refused the Library of Congress consultantship, but his knowledge of death so entering and overpowering life was more than personal. He pictures the modern oil rig, ever seeking more and more energy to be used up, as a drill entering his side also. It is not only a gathering to himself again that he feels, but the gathering of public eventfulness. "Waste, waste! dominates the world," and waste is the opposite of husbandry, gardening, or the dance. Against waste and death stand only words. Their frailty is clearly attested by the fact that "there has come an end / to them," or at least to their former ebullience in this poet. But, the opposite of the bomb, poetry has been seed for planting and now for harvest.

> For in spite of it all
>   all that I have brought on myself
>   grew that single image
> that I adore
>   equally with you

and so
it brought us together.
(*PB,* 169)

Now, death drawing near, "All appears / as if seen / wavering through water" (*PB,* 162), and it is only by the twins of poetry and love that measure continues to assert itself. Williams cites a young artist who shrugs his shoulders at Cézanne, declaring an interest solely in the abstractive power of Hindu painting. The young artist's remark is a rejection of the dance of art that had helped to form the old poet, but, savingly, it is also an affirmation of the dance itself as continued search for self-measure. The young artist praises one or two of Williams's poems, and the old writer feels gratitude at such recognition. He recalls moments from his past, a glimpse of the Jungfrau after days of fog and a chance meeting with Gypsy women in Granada. Such presences are of course memories, but more than that they are seeds now become fruit to furnish the attained garden his life must be. He returns again to the sea, that image which was rejected in *Paterson* and then accepted in Book 1 of "Asphodel." But now, cumulatively, he sets the image more precisely within bounds created by measure.

The poem
    if it reflects the sea
        reflects only
its dance
    upon that profound depth
        where
it seems to triumph.
        (*PB,* 165)

No ideas but in things had been *Paterson*'s claim. Now, by virtue of the dance, the garden, the marriage that his life has become and depends on, the original idea is amplified. No ideas but in the fruit of things. Fruitlessness, the failure of contact and invention, is the bomb, waste, and death. Against them poetic agent has only one recourse, that of poetic action, the refocusing of presence as actuality, the translation of scene from inertness to resource in a manner compatible with its own nature.

The image of the garden dominant in Books 1 and 2 of "Asphodel" yields in Book 3 to that of husbandry itself, the art of saving and being saved from waste by the power of "forgiveness" of all the error and misdirection which the world seems imperatively to breed. What else is to be done with waste? If it is saved and accumulated it will overpower life. If the final act of gardening is a harvest, all the chaff, the weediness, and the rakings must be let go with a blessing for what they have had a hand in producing. Book 3 turns almost pathetically to Flossie, imploring her forgiveness for Williams's own waywardness and shortcoming, but it also reaches beyond such poignant intimacy to continue the broad image embracing the whole poem—the husbanding of imagination and love.

Against forgiveness Williams briefly recalls his friend Marsden Hartley and himself in younger days both delighting in and recoiling from the brute force of an express train rushing past them, and Hartley's remark, "That's what we'd all like to be Bill" (*PB*, 171). The world of power is a world of might carelessly expended, like the train's splurge of weight and speed. The bomb, as it were, has its temptations, and Williams here again faces the question of the world's way. He and his artist friend both had been ambitious and driving men. Each pursued his own art with carelessness and intensity both. At any moment of their earlier lives it could well have seemed that power and intensity alone were the needful things. Williams appeals to his wife for forgiveness speaking as a repentant wastrel, but almost in the same breath he still half seeks to justify the occasions that have made forgiveness imperative. "It is the artist's failing / to seek and to yield / such forgiveness." He adds, equivocally, "It will cure us both" (*PB*, 175).

Love and marriage are, then, summed up by book 3 as forgiveness, and, in the "Coda" which ends the work, all together are swept into the single and resolving image of "light." It is a figure which Williams delineates very precisely in these lines, finding its embodiment in precarious relation to a destructive force that often generates and accompanies it. Light is most certainly a precarious and even transient blessing in this context. As in lightning, it may be inseparable from the "thunderstroke" that follows it and unable to "undo" the darkness that has preceded. It exists as flash and for the moment, but for those who have learned the nature of things it makes the capital on which they must draw "to avoid destruction"

(*PB*, 179). Like all else in the poem light must be harvested and used, and time's passage itself has to be watched "as we might watch / summer lightning / or fireflies, secure / by grace of the imagination" (*PB*, 179–80). It may be that the marriage which the whole poem celebrates is nothing more than the fruit of one such illuminated moment (standing against the account in *The Build-Up* of a suitor who had made himself groom by an act of will) when at the altar he was

> so moved by your presence
>   a girl so pale
> and ready to faint
> that I pitied
>   and wanted to protect you.
>   (*PB*, 181)

Into the darkness of feeling with which Williams surrounds the story of his courtship in the novel, enough emotional presence had made its way for it to turn out to be the illumination upon which the poem ends. Marriage for this pair was preceded by darkness, and the wedding itself is only fitfully illuminated. The years that follow will hold more darkness but now at least with the knowledge that the light may flash here and there, now and then, and so continue to be the power that makes a continuation of marriage possible. "Asphodel" is far from ending in any radiant flood. Instead, it is what has been saved and cultivated that now serves, whether that serving be thought of as light or, in the concluding lines, as light united with the title image of the frail and ephemeral flower itself.

> Asphodel
>   has no odor
>   save to the imagination
> but it too
>   celebrates the light.
>   It is late
> but an odor
>   as from our wedding
>   has revived for me

and begun again to penetrate
　　into all crevices
　　　　of my world.
　　　　(*PB*, 182)

Poetic agent, by virtue of imagination, has at the last become husbandman, gleaning from presence whatever is still available to
compose it into an image of poetic and hence usable actuality.

V   AGENCY

PRESENT IMAGE

In speaking of the primacy of "agency" in certain of the philosophical schools in which he is interested, Kenneth Burke not surprisingly lays a particular stress on pragmatism and on the pragmatics of empirical thinking which combine in denying or undercutting the role of preestablished guide in thought or action. The pragmatist, or even more so the empiricist, he argues, rests officially in means and more particularly in the power of means to shape whatever end may emerge from action. It is the means, in every case, which will determine what end is possible; the end does not work back to enforce a selection of means proper to itself. One familiar result of this ordering of things is that pragmatism can collapse quickly into an easy cynicism, in which any means may be seized upon without extensive thought for the range of their consequences. If a thing can be done, such reasoning would run, it may well be done: a logic leading again and again to the conversion of technical means themselves into unforeseeable and often wayward ends. William James himself seemed to give sanction to such a view in the stress he put upon the idea of an immediate "cash value" as his test for the propriety of means, suggesting thus that his own philosophy recommended a no more than shortsighted expedience. If some given course of action could be shown to be feasible, then there seemed no categorical reason why it should not be pursued provided that it promised any sort of "profit."

James of course would not finally accept any such reduction of his phrase. In the popular lecture series represented by his *Pragmatism* volume he was reaching out for widely understood terminology, and here no doubt he overreached. His own defense of pragmatism, in fact, was quick to seize upon, if never to develop fully, a sense of outcome that was inherent in means themselves. Certainly many of his own statements of the problem ran beyond any quick resort to mere "cash value" to imply, rather, an inevitable inherence of value. For example: "If there be any life that it is really better we should lead, and if there be any idea which, if believed in, would help us to lead that life, then it would be really *better for us to believe in that idea, unless, indeed, belief in it clashed with other greater vital benefits*" (James, 42).

Burke is quick to seize upon the complex opening in pragmatist thought that James's syllogism here effects, and especially the re-shuffling of more familiar ideas of outcome that he is proposing. End in effect becomes an element emergent in experience rather than its determinant, its emergence is an "if—then" possibility rather than a declarative proposal. Purpose is not denied. Indeed, it is plainly enough indicated here by James in the vitalistic terms that are perhaps implied by any notion of human action, though he is less than clear as to how the vitality to which he gives primacy is exactly to be understood. Burke is particularly concerned with James's argument in favor of the "will to believe" that belief is vital to action, and that action leads to benefits felt by the subject as an exercise of will, the enjoyment of freedom, and the advancement of his own being. The outcome of belief for James was the enabling of action rather than the assertion of goal. There is no inherent reason, of course, why disbelief might not also serve such a mediate purpose, and James in fact would make no clear distinction be-tween the two in this regard. He would maintain only that the fruits of belief itself were, in Burke's terminology, those of "agency" and that they should be judged in this light rather than another.

This centering in agency evident in James's thought moves Burke, then, to a brief comment that will prove useful in my own discus-sion of the role of agency—of language and technique—in Wil-liams's poetry, a matter on which the poet himself commented ex-tensively. Much of the difficulty which that comment attempted to face may be located in the interplay of two emotional loyalties commanding Williams's writing both explicitly and implicitly from beginning to end, and indeed seen by him as vital to his art. Both may be said to imply, in Burke's terms, a strong "scenic" content. To be loyal to the local was for the poet to accept himself, his sur-roundings, and his direct experience as sufficient to his poetry. It was to see such loyalty as adequate to the generation of whatever poetry he would accomplish. "Newness," while declaring some-thing about the quality of that poetry itself, posed no quarrel with scene, and indeed, as I have argued, may even be taken as the temporal aspect of scene itself. It led, however, to the addition of agent to scene; newness of utterance as such had to be something that only the poetic agent could accomplish. Williams's poetry, then, may be seen as growing from these principles of immediate scene and immediate agent, principles not inconsistent with each other but depending on agencies of composition for their transformation into art. The two loyalties could coexist, but they had no necessary connection. There was nothing inherently local about newness. Pound and Eliot, indeed—much to Williams's displeasure—had seemed to assert that to attain newness it might be best to flee the local. Equally, there was nothing productively new in mere locale, as Williams's criticism of Whitman or Sandburg attested. Everything depended upon the generation of poetic agencies which would by their action prove the poetic possibilities of the local and the new.

Similarly, Burke allows for the inherence of outcome in agency; he finds poetry in the agencies of poetry as in fact they mediated between scene and agent, the local and the new.

> James's pragmatism, with its stress upon the act of belief, stands midway between the ethical or dramatist sense of act and the positivist-scientist reduction of the act to terms of sheer events (a behavioristically observed scene). And this midway position is fittingly manifested in terms of *agency*, the function that is essentially mediatory. (Burke 1945, 283)

What is thus mediated? On the one hand there is the "ethical or dramatist sense of act," of the poetic agent purposively formulating and composing poetry. On the other the "sheer events" implied by the acceptance of presence as sufficient occasion for composition. We are accustomed to think of art as a "medium," and Burke shortly picks up on these terms: "Since art is a medium, the Art for Art's Sake formula would embody the grammatical form: Agency its own Purpose" (Burke 1945, 289). He would move thus to include an element of what he called the "mystical" in such pragmatism, such willingness to discover purpose in whatever means had been accepted.

My discussion of both scene and agent in Williams's writing has had a certain circularity; each tended toward the proposition that in Williams's sense of poetic action, present scene or agent was generative of poetic scene or agent. In either case, the local was bent toward poetic translation. On the other hand, poetic scene or agent was limited by present scene or agent. Thus, scene or person becomes both resource and limit, which generate vitality and validity of utterance respectively. Much the same will hold true of agency. Poetry will be the realization of technique as immediate to the local. If we follow Williams's own numerous efforts in his essays to formulate his sense of his writing, a chaos may seem to emerge, largely composed of half-thought-out and half-stated stabs at what he hoped he was trying to do. To the extent that his aim was "newness," such confusion may in fact have been inescapable. But understanding of his poetic effort, I argue, has much to gain from a close look at his sense of agency, of poetic being, as it is indirectly manifested in his criticism. Following Burke's formulation, "agency" for Williams was the poetically mediating power newly embodying the local and so driving toward regeneration. It was the means by which Williams defined to himself his sense of acting as poetic agent while clinging to the local, and it is the force shaping his identification of poetic outcome with poetic means.

It is with the last of these three aims that I may best start, by noting that while Williams turned his attention to extended discussion of purpose in only one case—the posthumously published *The Embodiment of Knowledge*—he in fact began early to develop his poetry under the aegis of stylistic options he took over largely from Ezra Pound. Pound's poetic theater of reference impressed upon Williams a powerful and permanent sense that poetic means generate outcome, that purpose is not a priori: in Burke's formulation, "agency its own purpose," or even "art for art's sake." Poetic agency in Williams may be seen most plainly first as an entity that was independent of binding attachment to either scene or self, and second as an entity that would mediate scene and self, retain them both at hand but also bend them toward outcomes inherent in agency. This was Pound's greatest legacy to him. Scene and self as such might be merely given in the local; agency was active in regard to both.

Williams's connection with Pound was a long and mixed affair, too complex in its entirety to be more than sketched at this point. But the drift of the evidence reflecting upon the earlier and more formative years of their friendship seems generally clear. During their college days, about 1902 to 1906 in all, including Pound's two years at Hamilton, Williams regarded Pound as an exotic, even irritating companion, but also as an indispensable friend. He was by no means inclined to accept him as a poetic master at this stage, continuing in fact in the vein of mixed Keatsian and Shelleyan imitation that filled his 1909 *Poems,* published three years after Williams had left Pennsylvania and one year after Pound had left the United States to begin his long European residence. What he would have seen in Pound's developing interests, however (it was enough still in 1908 to make him uneasy, even apprehensive in his reaction to Pound's *A Lume Spento*), was a theater of poetic concern which during the continued correspondence and friendship of the two Williams would gradually in effect and in part come to make his own. Williams's own publication, indeed, suggests that Pound functioned more closely as guide during the years of their now-rare face-to-face meetings than while they were together in their university years. The notable instance, of course, is the publication in 1913 of Williams's second volume, *The Tempers,* in London by Elkin Matthews, Pound's publisher, with Pound serving both as publisher's mediator and as critic of Williams's now-altered mode. He praised only one or two poems and found the others less satisfactory. Williams's poems in *The Tempers,* even so, were largely free now of Keats and Shelley and were in the business, as Williams himself said, of exploring a poetic realm that was still one of experiment for him.

The poetic theater Williams had now entered was somewhat indistinct, but it was in part that of Pound's earliest volumes: the general late Victorian sphere of "Pre-Raphaelitism" or "aestheticism." What Pound certainly found in it, and what in his early poems forms the basis of his own sense of poetic agency, included Browning's dramatic, often fragmentary moments of revelation; Pater's doctrine rooting all art in a wholly materialistic and empirical world out of which intense experience might be gleaned (what Pound in an early essay referred to as the "luminous moment"); Rossetti's linking of emotion with the sensuous; and finally, to some degree, Wilde's insistence on art as an entity made up by the artist and sustained by his will and skill against any mere givenness of the aesthetic in a natural universe. Neither Pound nor Williams was to make a strict program of this or any other configuration, but it is wholly consistent with much of Pound's early writing and Williams's now-developing poetry. These tenets, it may be said, were Williams's earliest guides toward a remade poetic agency of his own. They consorted easily with his shift, finally, to "free" and unrhymed verse as his predominant style. Poetry existed in important part as dramatic selection or even fragment rather than discursive mimesis. It was concerned with an intensified rather than an ordinary aspect of things existing in material circumstances. It grew out of the whole sensuous involvement of the artist in that kind of experience, but at the same time it would find embodiment only by such means as his own creative wit and discipline brought to it.

The point emerges most clearly, perhaps, in an examination of Williams's contributions to the magazine *Others* between 1915 and 1919, a period during which he was both rehearsing the elements he had assembled from Pound and at the same time beginning the process of knocking them into agreement with his own growing sense of the centrality of the local and the new. And it was during these years also that Williams would receive a second important creative impulse from the Armory Show and later exhibitions of the new European and American painting, though his exact early relationship to the emergent and generally "expressionist" or "cubist" avant-garde remains cloudy. In somewhat later years he plainly expressed admiration for Picasso, Braque, and Gris. He responded to the expressionist painting of Marsden Hartley in New York during the World War I years and came to know Marcel Duchamp— at the time evading the French draft in New York—and so was directly exposed to Dada. Bram Dijkstra has argued that Williams was close to Alfred Stieglitz and his Photo-Secession Gallery—with its emphasis on the new French and American painting—perhaps as early as about 1911 (when Stieglitz gave Picasso his first American exhibition), despite the fact that Williams's few comments on Stieglitz were grudging and indicated little response to him or his efforts before the middle 1920s. Williams's own commentary on painting and painters, collected and scrupulously edited by Dijkstra, demonstrates a continued and living interest in the art, but one not really getting under way until the late 1920s.

Despite such mixed and slender evidence, however, there is at least one document which Dijkstra dates 1915 that offers significant suggestion of what Williams felt the visual arts had to offer him as a poet. It records his reaction to a manifesto that the sculptor Henri Gaudier-Brzeska contributed to *Blast,* the organ of the London vorticists, and thus still attests the vitality of Pound's influence upon him. Gaudier had contributed one manifesto to *Blast's*

1914 issue in which he revealed a generally cubist or at least post-Cézanne drive toward the reshaping of nature in abstract volumes and planes as the center of his own sculpture.

And WE the moderns: Epstein, Brancusi, Archipenko, Dunikowski, Modigliani, and myself, through the incessant struggle in the complex city, have likewise to spend much energy. . . .

We have been influenced by what we like most, each according to his own individuality, we have crystallized the sphere into the cube, we have made a combination of all the possible shaped masses—concentrating them to express our abstract thoughts of conscious superiority. (*Blast* 1914, 158)

Gaudier had volunteered for wartime service and enthusiastically joined the fighting in France, whence he wrote in early 1915 that his experience of combat had left his attachment to vorticist principles undamaged, indeed strengthened and increased. His words appeared in capitalized letters in the manifesto of that year.

MY VIEWS ON SCULPTURE REMAIN ABSOLUTELY THE SAME. IT IS THE VORTEX OF WILL, OF DECISION, THAT BEGINS. I SHALL DERIVE MY EMOTIONS SOLELY FROM THE ARRANGEMENT OF SURFACES, I shall present my emotions by the ARRANGEMENT OF MY SURFACES, THE PLANES AND LINES BY WHICH THEY ARE JOINED. (*Blast* 1915, 33–34)

It was apparently this latter document that in 1915 moved Williams to thought about the problems of structure which his emergent new verse presented to him and from which he drew principles that are the clearest early indication of his willingness to find answers in the visual arts to the questions of poetic agency he faced as a now avant-garde poet. Gaudier was near the source of cubist practice emerging in Paris after about 1907, and he drew Williams toward wholly innovative, wholly rethought ideas about what poetic technique could be and how it could be made to work—how in particular, as agency, it could mediate between the impulses already moving him powerfully toward both the local and the original. Gaudier, of course, had written as a sculptor concerned with the agencies of his own art. In turning to that argument, Williams continues in its terminology but clearly seeks to use it analogically for the poetic agencies with which he is concerned.

First he announces the centrality to himself of his own self-defined poetic purpose, at the same time declaring his intention to give form to such subjectivity by means of whatever objectivity he encountered (I quote from Dijkstra's conflated text of Williams's "Vortex" essay):

> Furthermore by this acceptance I deny—affirm my independence from—the accident of time and place that brought the particular phrases to me, in that, now as always, I express my freedom from necessity and from accident by using whatever I find in my view without effort to avoid or to find. Thus I am free to take whatever appearance fits my purpose.
>
> I meet in agreement the force that will express its emotional content by an arrangement of appearances, of planes, for by appearances I know my emotions. (*RI, 57*)

Williams here, no doubt, is partly at play with a document that had come accidentally to hand. His reaction to it, indeed, may well be taken as a case of the "independent" use of such "appearances" as those with which he is concerned. At the same time, his preservation of his essay (despite his never having published it) and indeed the signs of revision and amplification it shows indicate a concern with the problems Gaudier had given him to wrestle with.

His argument continues to assert his simultaneous commitment to place (the local) and to his independence of it; and it proceeds to cast his own means—language—in Gaudier's terms.

> Thus in using words instead of stone I accept "plane" to be the affirmation of existence, the meeting of substances, whether it be stone meeting light or perfume striking mountain air or a sound of certain quality against one of another or against silence.
>
> The affirmation of existences and freedom in the quality of the sound or the perfume or the stone. (*RI, 58*)

But if the local is thus both accepted as occasion for his writing and rejected as any kind of sufficiency for it, so equally is the counter-force of self, or self-expression. Like the local, the poetic self is no more than occasion for the "force" that, originating there, gathers both the local scene and the originating self into a newly mediated relationship made possible by the agency of "planes" in Gaudier and of "words" in Williams. "Emotion" behind or around his poems will count for no more in itself than will the local scene, he implies, though both are indispensably among the resources of poetic agency.

I seek my emotions for the reasons given above: to put them beside others by which I affirm and recognize both my existence and that of others which again react confirming mine. And thus in the same way by expressing whatever emotion may occur, taking it without choice and putting it surface against surface, I affirm my independence of all emotions and my denial in time and place of the accident of their appearance. (*RI*, 58–59)

Although it has been common to see Williams's early poetry as struggling to free itself from the romantic and aesthetic trammels of his youthful fondness for Keats and the example of Pound's earliest work, I am suggesting that in fact Williams's moves from romantic to Pre-Raphaelite to his own kind of modernism are more importantly acts of opening and adapting a center which Pound had delineated and which some elements in the contemporary visual arts suggested. In effect he was a poet who enlarged and somewhat altered his aesthetic inheritance but who never abandoned its most basic commitment to a remaking of agency. He was, doubtless, a "vitalist" in much of his thought and emotion. At times his writing moved toward democratic and populistic sentiment, but it more often and perhaps more vehemently veered toward emotional reaction against the democracy—the Passaic region—in which he lived except as that scene served poetic purpose. "I will express my emotions in the appearances: surfaces, sounds, smells, touch of the place I happen to be," he wrote in "Vortex"; "I will not make an effort to leave that place for I deny that I am dependent on any place" (*RI*, 58). The "I" in question was the poetic self, and Williams's declaration was in effect a commitment of poetic self to self-determination. If "foregrounding" is a common aspect of all poetic practice, Williams's foreground would be the poet in action manifested in the poetic agencies he would be grappling with again and again. His commitment to an aestheticized center for his work thus turned out to be an enduring one, and, as Burke argued, such functional aestheticism was no more at bottom than a poetic pragmatism—a willingness to seek the essence and end of poetry in its means.

Shorter Poems, 1913–1923

Williams's "Vortex" essay did not draw any binding blue-print from Gaudier, but it can be used to follow out a loosely defin-able three-fold intentionality in the poetry. The first impulse was toward images that made a self-sufficient presentation of scene or self (in keeping with Pound's rules for imagism) as a poem's sub-stance—"that sense of freedom from time limits and space limits" (Pound: 1935, 4) Pound had recommended in the use of scene or self as a poetic concern. Scene thus may be brought forward as present fact available for its own sake. Similarly, the self in Wil-liams's writing is affirmatively present existing in scene, but it knows itself as free in regard to that scene within poetic action. It is able to seize upon it and make it subject to self-inclination and so also to self-presentation. This ability underlies all his poetry, but also it is given prominence in its own right as an express poetic agency when the poet's feelings or opinions serve explicitly to shape his work around his own kind of reaction to presence. Williams's presentation of self is most commonly self-dramatization only by virtue of self's shaping presence within the work. Self is more com-monly extrospective, so to speak, than introspective and so a par-ticipant in the poetic action that is going forward.

In a second direction the poem addresses itself to scene as meta-phorical in possibility, capable of being opened from itself to a sec-ond state of implication in an act of conversion so that the primary images of the poem, retaining their original sense, are at the same time metamorphosed across the course of the work to create a changed condition. In a third direction Williams would be espe-cially aware of the interposition of "appearances" or "emotions" as unresolvable poetic stuff, so that the individual poem found being in a kind of standoff; it affirmed the poetic self's freedom to translate scene into language without premise or conclusion, a mind-versus-facts phenomenon as in collage or cubist painting. The poem in this structuring of its images emerges more or less success-fully by virtue of an uncertainty among points of view and finds existence as an irresolution of images. These three directions: pre-sentation of scene or self in free-standing image for its own sake; the conversion of scene to a second state of presence; and unre-solved images of scene or self appear with great frequency. None of them necessarily excludes any of the others from any poem, but it is often possible to read a poem most successfully by approaching it with regard for the primacy of one or another of them. Williams had made an initial appearance in the emerging avant-garde scene in *Poetry* magazine, but Harriet Monroe's constraining hand had lain heavily upon him. In 1914, with Pound's rise to authority in the London *Egoist,* he found a second important outlet for poems, but one for the moment often dominated by a self-consciously declarative and nativistic tone. "The Wanderer" first appeared in its pages as did a number of the largely unreprinted poems of advice addressed to his "townspeople," many of them with a Whitmanian tone. Other contributions reflected a musing and observing emphasis like "In Harbor" with its image of moored ships murmuring to each other of their voyaging, and another, "Aux Imagistes," greeting Pound's own emergent school. A considerable portion of Williams's *Kora in Hell* along with a part of its "Prologue" appeared in Margaret Anderson's *Little Review* in 1917 and 1918 during Pound's ascendancy in its pages. But by far the best general sample of his emerging technique is to be found in *Others* magazine beginning in 1915 and continuing on and off until his own strong-tempered suspension of that journal in 1919. This spread of magazine publication following his volume *The Tempers* of 1913 is on the whole more revealing of the directions and variety of his concerns with agency than the poems partly gathered in miscellaneous order into his early volumes, or certainly the rearranged inclusions and exclusions of the various collected poems. His contributions to *Poetry* had been characterized by a delicacy amenable to Harriet Monroe's taste; to the *Egoist* by a down-to-earth, "American" kind of self-presentation; to the *Little Review* by his most concentrated iconoclasm to date, while *The Tempers* poems had been colored by Pre-Raphaelite echo. *Others,* with which he was closely involved as editor, displayed the widest variety of experiment.

It is to this last publication, then, that I turn to develop a threefold intentionality shifting among the aims of presentation, conversion, and irresolution of image, an intentionality powerfully controlled by commitment to a postimagist technique. The first subgroup of poems is heavily dependent on presented images of self as their agency. A variety of image structure in Williams has been noted and studied by both J. Hillis Miller and Linda Wagner. What I would do with the image of presentation here, beyond asserting its presence and its large importance, is to link it with Williams's drive toward functionality of utterance especially as it accepts and uses the poet's apartness without ever leaving home ground. Perhaps there is no more familiar case among these *Others* poems than "Danse Russe," the short presentation of the poet, naked, dancing before his mirror, asserting his loneliness, and half playfully and half seriously asserting still his claim to be the "happy genius" of his household. He is both a unique and a common man managing simultaneously to affirm and deny the mores of the world to which he belongs. He is a vaguely indecent yet a thoroughly decent fellow, a self taking himself as found and enjoying it.

Agency is that of image presenting self as an act of poetic play. If there is verbal play in the verse it is no more than the ease of phrase suggested, perhaps, by "happy genius," faintly echoing the shopworn and so too readily classifiable notion of unhappy genius. But any such resonance falls largely to one side as the merely present force of self dominates the poem. Among the *Others* group there are eight or ten additional poems that depend heavily upon the self though often more circumstantially than "Danse Russe." Williams's brief fling at issuing personal advice to his fellow "townspeople" is echoed in "Tract," for example, in his directions on how to conduct a funeral—advice clearly emanating from a personally detached and heterodox vantage. In "The Ogre" and in "Touche" (reprinted in the collected poems as "Sympathetic Portrait of a Child"), the self is put forth dramatically and without excuse or elaboration as perversely attracted to very young girls, feelings ordinarily well masked. But the poetic force of the self will here and always be found in what is particular to it and not in what is conventional to poetry, and such emphasis is extended to sympathy with the lecherous if impotent drifters who study posters at the burlesque theater in "The Old Men."

The self, in short, accepts its own givenness and emerges by an unpredictable adherence to images of presentation. What is presented will have little or no force unless it is peculiar to itself and evocative of what it is to be a particular among the commonality. If perversity, peculiarity, or mere whim rules in a particular case, then agency has even gained by their specialness. Particularity liberates both poet and reader to further attention and to recognition, the pragmatic goal.

Many of the same or at least parallel acts of presentation still hold as Williams, preserving the presentational mode, shifts from self to a clearer emphasis on things or other people apart from the self. These poems, like the longer poems I have already discussed, share in the "outsiderliness" of the poems of self, since the self so seldom makes a world in which the poet acts or otherwise participates except as poet. Perhaps this is further expression of Williams's lifelong attachment to painting and to its emphasis on the presence of the artist as witness. If his presented self is individualized to itself, his physical world is largely and equally individualized and hence unrelated. It is a world of things, of scene, that exists as the poet's surroundings but that seldom extends to any other relationship.

The objects thus experienced may be single or plural, static or in motion, but the agency of presentation rules as completely here as in the poems of self, moving similarly to a poetic of perception that is often both narrowed and heightened by the objects' isolation. "Metric Figure" for example rests its poetic case in the interposition of "veils of clarity" and "veils of color" (*Others*, Feb. 1916, 139) to juxtapose a contrast of light and dark seen abstractly in the ocean with a more clearly formed vision of a sandy beach sliding down under the sea's surface to form a light-colored bottom. The world to itself here is of wholly aesthetic interest as it exists wholly in the "appearances" toward which Williams's commitment to Gaudier had directed him. The gain proposed by the poem is refocused vision, with no more than a latent suggestion that such vision is of use in making an otherwise ordinary presence more distinct. Such writing presumes no need to convert an outside world to any reasoned or derived harmony. The poem becomes agency working toward a proportioning of the nonhuman by aesthetic means alone.

A similar technique prevails in "Keller Gegan Dom" ("tavern versus cathedral," I take it, perhaps echoing those scenes as contrasted in Goethe's *Faust*), which opens by explicitly ordering the reader to "witness"—in this case, again, a series of interposed visions centering first on a young man hurrying to "confession" but shifting immediately to appearances of what he has to confess in the form of suggested assignations and thence to a newly framed conclusion suggesting a low bordello from which "trickles / the chuckles of / beginning laughter" (*CEP*, 147). The world here is something wholly outside, so much so that the action remains obscurely confined to whatever glimpses a sort of poetic voyeurism is made to reveal. Like the poems of self, both these exhibits reflect a manipulation of point of view as the poet selects certain "planes" of appearance to bring into juxtaposition, leaving such topics as "confession" or wrongdoing before us as no more than appearances. There is drama implicit in the poem, but it is only slightly enacted. If feeling or meaning is to flow from it, they must flow from means sparsely selected and obscurely arranged. Perhaps Williams's sense of the world in presentation of transcience or isolation of particulars, of scene's objectivity, leads thus to what might be called a response of fascination, or particularly of vision.

Beyond such reliance on presentation alone, however, Williams sometimes moves on to conversion of image, a structure that parallels what Linda Wagner has called "transitional metaphor." Like irony, we may say, metaphor in Williams is a figure more often of the whole circumstance of the poem than of specific utterance within it; it often functions as a framework by which the poem facing one condition of scene or self proceeds to convert that object to a new state and in doing so to find its own substance as poem. Such poems stand apart from the presentation poems with their simple or complex objectivity precisely as the planes of appearance juxtaposed in them are opened to subjective response, as indeed the very process of metaphor implies. If the presentation poems are largely descriptive in effect, however selective or fragmentary in their implication, so these conversion poems, as I may style them, move toward conclusion even though that conclusion is seldom more than a remaking of the specific condition with which they began. Thus they embody an action, one often though not necessarily enacted and completed by the poem, but one in any case upon which the poem's force depends.

A highly compressed case occurs in "El Hombre," a verse which Wallace Stevens was to use as a base for his own poetic variations.

> It's a strange courage
> you give me, ancient star:
>
> shine alone in the sunrise
> toward which you lend no part!
>   (CEP, 140)

We are still close to the presentational mode in this little work, and if the star addressed is taken to be no more than itself then the poem remains presentational. If the star and its condition, however, are taken to be emblems of the poet's condition (which the title implies and the giving "courage" to "me" enforces), then the sun is altered in meaning by the poem to become something like the history of poetic innovation, and by such alteration the poet is seen as adjacent to the "sunrise" in the arts going on all around him but to which he feels only a marginal relation. Read as metaphor, the poem becomes a testimonial, supported perhaps by the verse immediately following it in the magazine, "New Prelude," in which the poet declares he knows "only the bare rocks of today," but in which he alters the rocks as he writes, placing them imaginatively in a sea along with plants, fish, and a fresh air above, and embracing them, both his prison and his fulfillment now, as "sisters" (*Others*, Dec. 1916, 24–25). In both cases the figure is metaphor rather than simile. The likeness or second state of the object is inferred from the progression and context furnished by the poems themselves as guide. In both cases, again, the second state of the objects is distinguished from their original by the freight of subjective implication it carries.

There are six or eight poems in the *Others* groups that open themselves to such conversion of image, none perhaps more ambitious than the familiar "Spring Strains." The poem, again, is available to reading in largely presentational terms, functioning as a catalogue of sharply selected and perceived detail of a spring landscape—buds, twigs, birds, tree limbs, sky, sun. But as it proceeds an abstracting force is developed that converts scene to action. All its ingredients are drawn prodigiously toward opening and blooming by the power of the sun, identified as "creeping energy, concentrated counterforce" pulling the whole mass upward and outward—spring as invisible force rather than spring as visible scene. Spring is indeed "interpreted" here but only to the extent allowed by the sun which is itself part of the scene as it is converted to a second state to become a kind of battery driving forward the whole action that the scene itself and in turn has become.

If the presentation poems had found their outcome in rescuing for the visible what otherwise might be lost to the nondescript, these poems of conversion work more plainly toward extension of the visible by its own means to a condition compounding simple presence. Williams's poetic here is still rooted in the aesthetic but in an aestheticism extending itself pragmatically beyond what immediately meets the eye. In the concluding lines of "Spring Strains" the static whole is completed and fulfilled by conversion to action alone, by itself. Visible substance disappears or dissolves into the invisibility of movement in the abstract.

> On a tissue-thin monotone of blue-grey buds
> two blue-grey birds, chasing a third,
> at full cry! Now they are
> flung outward and up—disappearing suddenly!
>
> (*CEP*, 159)

The conversion poems are as fully grounded in efforts to poeticize the local as are the presentational, and their particular technique can be taken as another instance of the "new" at work. They accept local scene as itself but pursue it toward the metaphor inherent in it, bent, in particular, upon translation of that content, reconstructing scene without abandoning it.

Often enough, however, scene or self in Williams resists conversion and offers itself to simple discovery only as an unresolved cluster. In such cases Williams's poetic subject claims a place for itself resembling the one it commonly occupied in his fiction—the short stories or the Stecher trilogy. It becomes simultaneously a fact generating action and, in poetic action, a fact action also moves to create. Like the fiction, the poem of unresolved images (which, following Gaudier, might be called intersecting "planes") tends to allow the ambiguity it generates to be its outcome and, by Burke's pragmatic rule therefore, to foreground poetic agency alone. The pragmatics of the presentation poems lead most obviously to particularized disclosure, and the poems of unresolved images often share that effect. The conversion poems found resolution in a process toward change. In irresolution of image also such impulse may be present, but equally it is deflected by other presence within the work. The result is movement toward focus but one denied its full course.

The whole force of the local makes its presence felt in this last group as poetic obduracy and as an element Williams accepts for that reason. Scene, thus, for him cannot easily serve as resolution of conflict and is always at least a potential source of conflict—a presence known to be unalterable in itself but nevertheless accepted as that with which poetry must deal. This acceptance is the most basic premise underlying and shaping *Paterson* for example; by its terms that long work finds an almost necessary dynamics in the enactment, the dramatizing, of a conflict with scene. It may indeed be taken as affecting much of the poetry, sometimes finding a resolution in focused presentation or in conversion but often allowed to stand forth in its own right. Behind such conflict or within it lies the whole complex of the local, affecting Williams's writing—his commitment to the Passaic region although feeling that it was something of a contender; his resolution in favor of avant-garde writing and awareness although framing his life in the conventional pattern of occupation, family, and community. Again, and in short, he takes his position as unclassed member of the local present to him.

Across the body of his work examples of unresolved image range from the effective and the moving to the simply incoherent, and even the small sample of his early writing in *Others* suggests something of that range, including two of his commonly anthologized pieces. In "Pastoral" (one of three of his poems so titled) Williams is content simply to gather up four disparate cases and then finish them off with an open confession of inability to relate them. In the first of these cases, sparrows are seen hopping about the street, "quarreling / with sharp voices / over those things / that interest them." In the second an unspecified "we who are wiser" are described as keeping our thoughts to ourselves with no one knowing "whether we think good / or evil." In the third an old man "gathering dog-lime" walks the gutter with "more majestic" steps than, fourth, an Episcopal cleric approaching his Sunday pulpit. The poet concludes, "These things astonish me beyond words" (*CEP*, 124). Contrast exists, of course, in the combined vitality and dignity inherent in the sparrows and the old man set against the primness of the "we" of our secrets and the constraint of the Episcopal minister. Doubtless the poem is vitalistic in sentiment. Perhaps it is even a little sentimental in its unquestioning attribution of vitality to its low-life references. It seeks a certain kind of stock response. In fact, however, its content is hardly resolved at all. Its reader is left with the spectacle it presents, the judgment it inclines toward, and the poet's own astonishment, all as unfinished business. Its most obvious point is too easily assumed (If there is a better option, why is the worse given favor?), but what is most alive in it, perhaps, is the contrast it enforces, the unresolved coexistence of the contrary options it embraces. If the agencies of this work are too quickly given away to hortatory purpose, even so they remain an emblem of what the poet will encounter repeatedly as the unresolved experience his world generates—its unexamined division of itself against itself.

"Good Night" advances unresolved imagery a degree as it is more content to contain itself in suspension. Two planes of appearance are present within it, and the two are allowed to coexist without resolution and with each embodying the fullness of its own appeal. Unlike "Pastoral" such resolution as it affords is developed out of its appearances themselves. No reference to assumed values is required. The speaker is shown in his kitchen at night, with all there in order and even a bright decoration at hand formed by a bunch of parsley in a glass of water. Briefly then the tidy scene is interrupted by a fragmented recollection of "three vague, meaningless girls," immensely feminine in their presence, their garments rustling and "high-school French / spoken in a loud voice!" This interrupting image is given only nine lines out of thirty-four. Its details are unexplained, and the speaker of the poem turns from it back to the kitchen, drinking a glass of water, yawning "deliciously," and confessing himself ready for bed (*CEP*, 145–46).

Much of course depends on the presence and the sentiment of the "I" in the two poems, his "astonishment" in "Pastoral" contrasted with his general contentment in "Good Night." In the first he is stopped by contradiction, in the second by his personal pleasure in two unrelated things, pleasure indeed in their difference. The mildly wayward poet here both enjoys his waywardness and is reassured by the solidity and comfort of home. In a sense, each of the poems does find conclusion of sorts in its final statement. Neither, however, posits any possibility of resolution among the agencies which most fully develop each work—the emphasized images. Divergence in them is seen and left as divergence; perhaps this offers as good a clue as any to whatever sense of completion Williams brought away from each poem. Each exists as appearances which in themselves lead to no binding resolution. In the second, however, the poet is truer to his poetic agencies as he is content to frame them as a minor drama of awareness, as presentation, rather than as half-formed allegory of extrinsic purpose.

Others magazine published its final number in July 1919. Williams acted as editor and, in doing so, took upon himself a declaration that the journal's increasingly irregular course of publication was now at an end, a declaration set in blistering prose as a "Supplement" to the issue. The main tenor of his diatribe was the failure of *Others* and of domestic modernism in general to rise much above a quest for what he called "loveliness" in its efforts at a new poetry (for which he selected H. D.'s "Heliodora" as particular example), its failure to remake the aesthetic mode it had inherited in the direction of reality, of an aesthetic of truth. Williams was plainly conscious of his own intensity of effort in this regard, and the heavy limitation he felt hung upon the best of his efforts, but he was zealous in his dedication to his own direction. He confessed himself a "suburbanite, cowardly and alone"; he confessed himself a provincial cut off from Paris or London; he confessed a perhaps-undue longing for "the wealth of the world" that authentic poetry represented to him. At the same time, in the midst of what he took to be his limitations, he savagely defended his own authenticity.

> I sit a blinded fool, with withered hands stretched onto the nothingness around me. Perhaps this is a sickness. Perhaps what I call my singing is a stench born out of these sores. I deny that that makes any difference. AT LEAST I AM THAT. Or if the answer is that no one will listen to my singing or even call it singing I say that they cannot help listening and that— it doesn't matter one way or the other. Perhaps it is all a vain regret, an insane determination to walk forward and backward at the same moment, a clinging to a youth I never enjoyed except in mad athletic excesses and stillborn ecstasies of loneliness. AT LEAST IT IS THAT. At least I exist in that. (*Others*, Jul. 1919, 28)

It is the strength of such emotion and such doctrine that in fact seems most often to underlie his poems of unresolved image and to account for his acceptance of their openness—sometimes even chaos—of feeling and utterance. Williams was sure that poetry was being remade by his generation, or was in need of being so remade. His avant-gardism was unequivocal in this regard, and he was driven, thus, in varying moods to be sure, to the possibility of a remaking power. Both "Pastoral" and "Good Night" had been decorous enough in their procedure. His own final poem to appear in *Others*, "Romance Moderne," was to reach more drastically into the resources of mixed observation and emotion out of which irresolution of experience took its growth.

Its theme was the thwarting of erotic passion, a thwarting by mixed feeling itself. Its form, again, was a juxtaposing of planes of appearance that interposed large attention to a ragged and threatening landscape against counterimpulses of the passion itself. Its setting was an automobile in which the lovers, or would-be lovers, drive through the ominous landscape. Its action—a dramatic monologue occasional but not frequent in Williams—is the kaleidoscope of observation, feeling, and memory circling in the heart of the speaker, the lover. When coupled with his *Others* manifesto of situation and purpose, the work more than any other carries the reader close to the thrusting and unpredictable range of emotion out of which the poet was attempting to forge his work. As he himself was a mixed man writing out of mixed circumstances, so he would root his poetry in mixture. He was more interested in using poetic agency to maximize the mixture that was the poem's content—itself the drama for which form must find visibility—than in resolving it toward formal harmony or "loveliness."

Structure emerges as a series of quick changes. The landscape is exterior world imaging an escape into passion; the car's interior is both bower and prison for the lovers; the speaker feels bound by inhibitions inherited from childhood; he has a mad impulse to "punch the steersman," "twirl the wheel" and so send all of them to a grisly death in the ditch filled with a torrent of water; he fancies himself outside the car seizing a small handful of "the dirt of these parts" (*CEP*, 182), coupled with a burst of feeling that his love is divided, in one aspect a sun rising but in another a "grey morning moon." Such scattered images in effect are the poem. He recalls his wife's voice concerned about his dressing well, declaring she had married him "because I like your nose" (*CEP*, 183) (a favorite joke indeed of Flossie's), and the whole moves toward a grim *Liebestod* jostling wife against mistress in the lover's feelings.

> —I wish that you were lying there dead
> and I sitting here beside you.—
> It's the grey moon—over and over.
> It's the clay of these parts.
>   (*CEP*, 184)

The poem interposes its various and contending feelings, never able to escape them or even by its power to find perspective on them. It is an immersion in irresolution, a dilemma that can be neither resolved nor escaped. Despite its clear openness to charges of imitative form, Williams must have set store by this work and others in its mode since he included them in successive collections of his poems, and the immediacy of such writing remains a most characteristic aspect of it. At the same time, he gave little sign of resting in this or any other mode to which particular writing might bring him. Somewhat like the postcubist Picasso he once criticized in this regard, he would be an artist given largely to making the individual cases of his art as immediate presence dictated. Yet, he gave repeated expression to patterns of principle, perhaps most concisely in the final number of his own magazine, *Contact*. The declaration there (unsigned but giving every internal token of being Williams's work and accepted as such in Emily Wallace's bibliography) reduced the whole problem of poetic agency to a principle of direction and definition within freedom. The *Contact* manifesto contained three principles. First, "The object of writing is to celebrate the triumph of sense," and sense was declared to be "the ability to set a thing up against the moment and have it escape banality," the created thing in its own right. The second principle was "In writing, as in art generally, sense is in the form"; as "form," language becomes "possessed of a new flexible sense which makes it available to the artist for use in a structural unity such as he imposes." Finally, "form grows rapidly obsolete and must be replaced," and such replacement "seeks further for a liberation of pure form." I have been concerned here with three characteristic thrusts toward form in Williams—"presentation," "conversion," and "unresolved images." It seems clear, however, that he himself would hardly have been satisfied with such listing and would instead direct the argument not so much toward form defined as toward its root in "liberation," the wellspring from which agency emerged, the source, that is, which ensured form's continuing dynamic.

With presentation, conversion, and irresolution of image as its most salient features, Williams's poetry in effect was giving particular shape to the whole phenomenon of verbal act Burke had called transformation and which I have renamed "translation"—in Williams the translation of nonverbal space-time into verbal space-time. The special feature of this process was the immediacy it sought in virtually confining itself to the agencies he had made his own. Ruled out was the freedom or looseness of translation from thing which a more language-inclined technique afforded to a more conventional poetry. Shelley could think of a skylark, Pope of a snip of hair, or Arnold of an ebbing tide as no more than initial occasions, points of departure from themselves into elaborately associated utterance. Given his self-evolved agencies, Williams could think of scarcely anything without building his poem out of the terminal presence such a thing directly afforded. The image of dance he returned to so often evoked such offset of terminal presence against the thing itself. The guiding force of his method was implied in the second principle of his *Contact* manifesto when he spoke of setting a verbal thing "up against the moment" and having it "escape banalilty" in the primacy of what he called "sense." The criterion of a poem was the force of particularity and the re-recognition it created in comparison with the "moment" it rendered, its poetical presence as weighed against the presence it invoked.

Translation, of course, is not a reproduction of its original. It is a new entity, existing in a new medium, and holding attention as an existent in its own right. "The features of a landscape," Williams wrote, "take their position in the imagination and are related more to their own kind there than to the country and season which has held them hitherto" (*SE*, 18). Translation occurred from fact to the language of "imagination" finding its fulfillment only in that language. At the same time, translation presupposes an original and is finally validated by it. Translation exists only to the extent that its presence is reflective of a presence outside itself.

Spring and All of 1923, a volume mixing prose and poems, was in effect a wholesale treatise, liberally interspersed with examples, on poetry as translation from nonverbal to verbal presence. Its companion volume of that year, *The Great American Novel,* standing as no more than a duplication of the formlessness it treated, had documented Williams's need for such rules of procedure. The two placed side by side gave sharp distinction to what the attainment of form through agency meant to him. It could not be the business of poetry to reproduce the mixture that was nonverbal space-time, though the poet indeed bound himself to its presence. As translator he could not hope to succeed in what might be called a word-for-word reproduction of his original. He must find new words of course, but he must select them for their appositeness to his aim, his verbal sense of the things he dealt with. Having done so he must then proceed similarly to elect his own structure and texture of arrangement. As creator, he would be responsible for his choices, but he would be governed by his sense of the original as needing translation to make its presence apparent in language.

He began *Spring and All* with several pages of prose describing an imaginary holocaust reducing the world to a point where everything must be created over again, translated from nonbeing to being by the process of imagination, an effort thus to produce world but to do so by "using the forms common to experience" (*I*, 107). His argument, of course, was anomalous unless one supposed that his holocaust in fact left such form intact, and he went on—in a poem, "The Rose," for example—to reconstruct a rose not by seeking to duplicate or evoke any older presence of roses but by restating this rose in cubist terms he here associated with Juan Gris. The rose in past poetry had "carried the weight of love," but love, now, "is at an end of roses" (*CEP*, 249). The old order or imagery is exhausted; a rebirth, a "spring" is required. His goal, in short, was a newly stated rose, in this case one drawing on an imagination of cubism. Such a rephrased rose might again be able to sustain the weight of "love" if its emergence was seen not as rejecting the old for rejecting's sake but as recreating a rose to be newly amenable to so perennially renewable an emotion as love.

From the petal's edge a line starts
that being of steel
infinitely fine, infinitely
rigid penetrates
the Milky Way
without contact—lifting
from it—neither hanging
nor pushing—

The fragility of the flower
unbruised
penetrates space.
    (*CEP*, 250)

"Petal" has become "vector" as the flower's presence in space is restated in geometric terms amenable to love's extension and intangibility. Whether or not we want to see Williams in this effort as paralleling Gris's own cubist collage called "Roses" seems less to the point than his implied claim to have translated "rose" into new images while preserving "forms common to experience." As a conversion poem his "Rose" is particularly amenable to understanding as translation. About a third of the poems in *Spring and All*, however, attempt structures of unresolved image in a parallel reach for restatement, but perhaps only one of them very clearly attains success at such re-formation. In general, irresolution succeeded most clearly for Williams where it brought its content to a brink of resolution, where something unstatable but teasing was generated by its flux. Such poems, we may say, succeeded to the extent that like "Romance Moderne" or "Good Night" they implied a context having precarious identity but moving toward a possibility of internal shape. Among the *Spring and All* poems, "The Right of Way" finds episodic implication suggested by the title and developed in images strung upon the thread of an automobile drive providing views of an elderly man, a laughing woman, a small boy, and a girl "with one leg / over the rail of a balcony." The poet here is present in the poem as he had been in "Good Night," and, similarly, he is positioned in the scene—in this case "spinning on the / four wheels of my car / along the wet road" (*CEP*, 259). The ingredients of something are made visibly and clearly present. That "something" remains unstated, but its potential fascinates the poet and stays the reader in attention to itself.

Presentation of self more clearly dominates in "To Elsie" with its reaction to the effects of generations of poverty and social deprivation. That work is best read as a complex sense of poetic self in its world, in much the same way as "Spring and All" (beginning "On the road to the contagious hospital") is presentational of its own scenic content. It is, in either case, the presented self or scene by means of which focus is overtly achieved. Like "The Rose," each of these begins with banality seeking translation into remade image. "Spring and All" seizes upon mélange but directs it toward a single common property running through its whole content— "emergence"—and so, as is common in the presentation poems, focuses on a single ruling presence absent from the poems of unresolved image like "The Right of Way." "To Elsie" ranges equally over a miscellany—the human waste of the democracy—to approach its close in a straining of the imagination away from its subject toward its own country only to collapse into failure: "No one / to witness / and adjust, no one to drive the car" (*CEP*, 272). Poetry here exists by the imaging of personal inadequacy in all except the formal intent, which is focused upon the poetic voice and its sense of a helplessness present in scene and self alike.

Whatever the direction of its individual efforts, *Spring and All* as a whole was presented as a poet's manifesto in support of the kind of poetic presence reflected by its content. Such efforts at translation, surrounded by Williams's commentary on his aims, gave the book a literary existence similar to that of Anderson's *Winesburg* or Hemingway's *In Our Time* as a collection intended partly to display its own avant-gardism. In Williams's volume, however, the commentary bristled with strident declaration including much repetition of the central commitment to newly made form. As the famous red-wheelbarrow poem declared, much depended on the coexistence of the local and given with the formal patterning, here visual, the poem made present. *Spring and All* posed a holocaust, a universal collapse of an old world, as the reason for its effort, and in its course Williams relates his position to that of his friend Marsden Hartley in his book *Adventures in the Arts*. The painter too argued the universality of immediate experience and the amplitude of original patterning it presented. "I care more for [natural things] in themselves," Hartley stated, "than for any lengendary presences sitting under them." And he added, "I was constantly confronted with the magic of reality itself, wondering why one thing was built of exquisite curves and another of harmonious angles" (Hartley, 4). Such awareness led Hartley to Dadaism and its vehement rejection not only of "tradition" but of any concept of a privileged "art." "Nothing is greater than anything else, is what the Dada believes, and this is the first sign of hope the artist at least can discover in the meaningless impotence which has been invested in the term ART. . . . The artist has made a kind of subtle crime of his habitual expression, his emotional monotones, and his intellectual inhibitions" (Hartley, 247–48). *Spring and All*, similarly, was testimony of wholesale rejection and a consequent array of efforts at remade perception.

Shorter Poems, 1928–1941

Beginning as early as 1913 such poems give at least general indication of the thrust of Williams's work following his first appearance as poet accepting the avant-garde. The ensuing ten years can be looked on as forming his freest, least predictable, and most widely ranging period of poetic experimentation, with the best poems of *Spring and All*—the title poem, "The Pot of Flowers," "The Rose," "The Right of Way," "To Elsie," and "At the Ball Game"—as its apogee. His critical statements on Gaudier-Brzeska, that abolishing *Others*, and the concluding manifesto from *Contact* emerge as steps affirming his initiation into the avant-garde and efforts to move toward a definition of his own place within it. A certain initial phase of his work, thus, had been completed, and following such initiation his progress may be marked off by a number of other centers of effort, distinguishable at least generally by decades, and advancing experiment toward its inherent resolution.

For the short poems, there are three of these later phases. The late twenties and the thirties are often and usefully seen as dominated by his interest in "Objectivism," spurred by his close and continuing friendship with Louis Zukofsky, and marked especially by the prose-poetry combination of "The Descent of Winter" (appearing in Pound's magazine, the *Exile*) and by *Collected Poems, 1921–1931* and their swing toward evenness of control, in contrast with much of the formal freewheeling of the early twenties and before. It is this Depression decade, also, that brought Williams's social awareness, inaugurated in "The Descent of Winter," to a new degree especially apparent in *An Early Martyr* of 1935. The forties in turn, epitomized by the two volumes *The Wedge* and *The Clouds* (and otherwise much filled with work on *Paterson*), contained a widening of Objectivism and a substantial expansion of self toward a poetic meditation that had begun in *Adam and Eve and the City* of 1936. At the same time, Williams's preface to *The Wedge* and Zukofsky's participation in its forming attested the durability of his feelings still for poetry as the discovery and realization of form. Such commitment was to produce much evidence of itself during the decade. The advent of war increased further his awareness of history, politics, and personal judgment within their mesh. The fifties, finally, saw the fullest gathering of his poetry to date into two volumes of collected poems, along with reflection of aging and illness, and the intimate retrospect and assessment of his marriage—and indeed of much experience—that I have already examined. The thread common to all this continued to be poetic agency, however—Williams's unremitting attention to the how of his poetry as the means by which any of its other aspects must be generated.

"The Descent of Winter," again containing prose and poetry, may be put down as the third of Williams's longer works (or the fourth if we include *A Voyage to Pagany*) to find an impulse in the contemplation of the poetic self in its world that was to lead most directly to *Paterson* and the late poems. *Kora* had been an act of poetic play with such contemplating; *The Great American Novel* a retreat from it; *Voyage to Pagany* a consideration of alternatives and a rejection of them. "The Descent of Winter" finds its character in a new point of view, created in part by Louis Zukofsky's critical hand guiding Williams here for the first time in poetry and stemming also from a use of self-presentation as the single principle of the extended whole. The work continues the avant-garde impulse toward dramatizing the plight for the artist which avant-gardism itself had created and which Williams shared with numbers of his contemporaries, that of reconstructing poetry itself. Something of his originality in this regard, however, would here be displayed by his movement away from the tortured or bitter estrangement characterizing *A Portrait of the Artist*, for example, *Mauberley, The Waste Land*, or *In Our Time*. Williams remade their alienation into an acceptance of present world as vital fact, with the artist's task inseparable from that acceptance, though still in active search of its mode.

The effort reflected macrocosm and microcosm both. In 1927 the Williamses had sailed together to Europe to give their sons a year of education abroad (just as Williams and his brother had been given that opportunity in their youth). Williams stayed in Europe only briefly, returning to Rutherford by himself to spend the better part of a year without his family. "The Descent of Winter" began to take form during this separation, which seems ambivalently to reflect both the Williamses' questions about the future of their life together and, in Williams's own case, the emergence of a very great and heartfelt realization of his dependence on his wife and family. Certainly his prevailing sense of "outsiderlines" was reenforced by his loneliness at home. He also realized that he could not really adopt for himself or his art anything like an avant-garde flourishing of alienation. He needed Flossie, his medical work, his income, his feet on familiar ground: at the same time he pushed forward to express his inability to accept any or all of these rootings as sufficient occasion for his writing. The whole of "Descent" is contained within such self-presentation as these conditions enforced.

Its earliest poems, like a number that follow them, take the form of soliloquies addressed to himself: the sudden strangeness of his own clothing; the peculiarity on his return voyage of occupying a ship's cabin from which the second berth had been removed; a contemplation of his writing, literally at sea, as an entity formless and centerless as the ocean's waves. Such poems of self-presentation are complemented by brief presentations of scene or of items in it. Unlike much earlier writing, such presentations are self-sufficient and uncompounded renderings of selected, chiefly single or sharply isolated objects. The scenic poems perhaps predominate, but both they and the poems of self stress the isolation of the subjects they treat, culminating in the extended poem "A Morning Imagination of Russia" and a prose meditation upon it.

Taken out of their context, as they are in most later volumes, these poems seem largely uneventful. Indeed the poems and the prose hardly take shape at all without the context supplied by the whole as precursor to *Paterson* and sequel to *Kora*, a dramatizing of the poet as outside participant in his world, chiefly caught up in the question of how world may be translated into verbal form. The volume's detail is largely that of presentational image; overall it finds structure in irresolution of its images despite a possibility of social change it contemplates as transformational image. The prose passages combined treat several major aspects of subject beginning and ending with Williams's poetic situation: at the beginning of the prose he writes out of a mixed awareness struggling for focus and at the end he contemplates a vivid but not immediately helpful family inheritance figured in his mother. He divides himself thus between the poetic obduracy of the alien and that of the familial. Such subjects, then, are all counterposed against a narrative of the birth and early circumstances of one Dolores Marie Pischak of Fairfield, New Jersey, taken as epitome of the scene which he faces and its problem. Good poetry somehow must dissolve self and scene together into accomplished writing. Poetic genius is epitomized in Shakespeare especially as he could render a present world directly to his audience. Williams must recreate such a possibility in contemporary terms.

Central to prose and poetry together are some six pages on the subject of "Russia" as an image of the possible remaking of both scene and self. By 1927 and the writing of "Descent" he had been alerted especially by the execution of Sacco and Vanzetti and the organized protest against it to an awareness of Marxist Russia as an alternative to America's waste and self-destructive materializing of its own idealistic heritage, of its need for remaking. Neither here nor elsewhere was he to pledge any allegiance to a Soviet pattern of remaking, but following upon his deep sense of the kind of national self-destruction reflected in "To Elsie," Russia loomed as the image of a nation dedicated to renewal. But the renewal he sought for himself and his poetry would come from and by means of a grappling hold upon the existent, a remaking that held as strongly to things as to ideas.

The world of Dolores Marie Pischak reflected in "Descent" is not a proletarian world in the Marxist sense—lumpen-proletariat possibly. It is in its own terms a world of inherent possibility, some of it even realized, but it is a world contained to itself. The father is "young, energetic, enormous" (I, 242). His presence combines the anomalies that characterize the American democracy, anomalies Williams would seize upon for all his poetry and that might be seen as prerevolutionary, useful if redirected, but that equally claim attention and value for themselves. Neither here nor elsewhere will class conflict form any staple of his thought. Williams would, rather, habitually seek recognition for the poetic value inherent in a lower depths containing within itself the very virtues that the revolution might be seeking. Pischak, the father, poses the duality.

A man who might be a general or president of a corporation, or president of the states. Runs a bootleg saloon. Great!

This is the world. Here one breathes and the dignity of man holds on. "Here I shall live. Why not now, Why do I wait . . . ?

Oh, blessed love, among insults, brawls, yelling kicks, brutality—here the old dignity of life holds on—defying the law, defying monotony. (I, 242–43)

Throughout his work the poet muses upon his own isolation and that of the objects and persons he treats. His mind drifts to imagine himself part of a remade Soviet whole only to arrive at the vision of such a Williams as isolated and uncertain. He imagines measuring himself against the state by the "scales in the Zodiac," but retreats from such august dimension.

But closer, he was himself
the scales. The local soviet. They could
weigh. If it was not too late. He felt
uncertain many days. But all were uncertain
together and he must weigh for them out
of himself.
(*I*, 251)

As for America, he is equally unplaced and equally doubtful, "We
have cut out the cancer but / who knows? perhaps the patient will
die." He concludes, "We have little now but / we have that. We are
convalescent" (*I*, 252).

The world, in short, is as uncertain of reformation politically as
it is poetically, and indeed for Williams the two here run together.
Both reformations sought a fulfillment in translation, but both
posed the question "Translation to what"? The power of the poet
here is still dramatized as unequal to his self-elected task—except
perhaps in spurts or moments. The inventive power of politics is
hardly more certain. One fine moment of resolution in particular
fades off quickly into the detail with which translation—revolution—must grapple, and concreteness dissipates such a general aim
by its own unpredictability. Both politics and poetics look forward
to change; each faces the need that only invention can supply. Revolutionary politics no more than avant-garde poetry could be satisfied with preformed models. Agency was the condition of both.

The United States should be, in effect, a soviet state. It is a
soviet state decayed away in a misconception of richness. The
states, counties, cities, are anemic soviets. As rabbits are cot-
tontailed the office-workers in cotton running pants get in a
hot car, ride in a hot tunnel and confine themselves in a hot
office—to sell asphalt, the trade in tanned leather. The trade
in everything. Things they've never seen, will never own and
can never name. Not even an analogous name do they know.
As a carter, knowing the parts of a wagon will know, know,
touch, the parts of—a woman. Maybe typists have some special skill. The long legged down east boys make good stage
dancers and acrobats. But when most of them are drunk nothing comes off but—"Nevada" [a fellow passenger on Williams's transatlantic crossing] had a line of cowboy songs. (*I*,
254)

The task of "a soviet state" in renewal, presumably, would have to be the anomalous one of enforcing poetry, of making purpose out of means and bending means to such purpose. But it was only the Pischaks within this work who promised any such possibility. Any political purpose ignoring them would have to find its ideas outside of fact and hence outside of poetic illumination.

Williams had formed a friendship with Louis Zukofsky (then a graduate student in English at Columbia University) through the intermediacy of Pound. They had met, exchanged ideas, and formed a mutual esteem for each other's poetry and ideas about poetry. Zukofsky had been named by Pound to an editorial position on *Exile*, and one of the manuscripts he handled would be Williams's "Descent of Winter" in its original form. He found a great deal in the sprawling manuscript to reorder, much of it apparently tending toward what he saw as an excess which was intrusive and damaging to formal order, and he would continue to urge a heightened degree of control upon Williams. Williams in turn responded warmly to Zukofsky's blue-penciling here and, notably, in his *Collected Poems, 1921–1931*, published in 1934, and *The Wedge* of 1944. What apparently they most agreed upon was that a vital center lay more or less obscured in much of Williams's poetry, and that his writing often needed selection or reduction to acquire, by Pound's standard, a maximum "efficiency."

Williams's writing through the 1930s would indicate that Zukofsky's doctrine had taken root. At its core was an idea that Williams had already responded to in Pound and McAlmon and had seen reflected in Joyce and Stein, that poetry could be formed by enhancing speech through diction and rhythm. In addition, if less saliently, Zukofsky welcomed Williams's feeling that self and idea in poetry should be wholly inherent entities—poetry would be moral and enlightening to the extent that it cast light by its existence as speech. Like Williams, Zukofsky had been deeply persuaded by Pound's functional aestheticism.

Zukofsky's key terms were "image," "sound," and "interplay of concepts," and they were wholly the objects of poetry (Zukofsky, 29). The three mirrored Pound's extension of imagism into what he had called "phanopoeia," "melopoeia," and "logopoeia." The first and last of these were already living components of Williams's technique. As Zukofsky saw it, it was the binding power of speech as "sound" that lacked consistency and force in Williams's poetry. The whole of the triple measure did occur splendidly on occasion, as in "To Elsie," which Zukofsky felt was perfected poetry. In any case, it was the triple measure that was Zukofsky's rule and that he looked to for the begetting of all other poetic virtue. When it was realized, as Zukofsky sought to realize it in "The Descent of Winter" on behalf of self and scene, it effected writing that would enforce its interpretation of life by its own enlightening actuality—language to be dealt with as a translation of presence into its own presence. In a 1930 comment, it was this process that Zukofsky found in Williams at his best, with "poetic" awareness substituted for "social."

No outside program has influenced his social awareness. It is the product of the singular creature living in society and expressing in spite of the numb terror around him the awareness which after a while cannot help but be general. It is the living creature becoming conscious of his own needs through the destruction of the various isolated [*sic*] around him, and till his day comes continuing unwitnessed to work, no one but himself to drive the car through the suburbs, till they too become conscious of demands unsatisfied by the routine senseless repetition of events. (Zukofsky, 143)

The force of Zukofsky's emphasis is reflected in Williams's long and celebrated letter of 1932 to the fiction writer Kay Boyle. She had been experimenting with poetry and had complained to Williams of her inability to satisfy herself in regard to the formal completeness of her own work. His answer, filling seven pages of the *Selected Letters,* was an effort at deliberate and systematic survey of the problem as he then saw it. He had a year or two earlier published essays on Gertrude Stein and Marianne Moore in which he had emphasized his pleasure in their nonconnotative diction, in Moore's case her "wiping soiled words or cutting them clean out, removing the aureoles that have been pasted about them or taking them bodily from greasy contexts" (*SE*, 128). Such purification or deromanticizing of language was itself in agreement with Zukofsky's theory and practice and may be presumed still to hold in the broader approach this letter attempted. It was prefaced logically by Williams's rejection of "free verse." "Whitman," he said, "was a magnificent failure. He himself in his later stages showed all the terrifying defects of his own method. Whitman to me is one broom stroke and that is all" (*SL,* 135). In turn, Williams and all his contemporaries had to admit that they were writing in a masterless age. There was nowhere to look for any "tradition" since each tradition, Williams felt, must have originated from whatever native ground it found under its feet. Form, in short, had to be reinvented. The only place he could recommend in which to look was in the local speech or language. These two words, which recur frequently through the letter, in contrast with any critical writing of Williams predating 1928, attest Zukofsky's influence. He had, of course, earlier assumed the need of native language as central to his concept of the local. What he now made of it however, was the chief resource for verbal patterning, which was supplanting the imagistic and directly visual patterning he had found in Pound, Gaudier-Brzeska, and Juan Gris. But verbal structure he now declared to Boyle must always have been "inherent in the language." In his own case it required study of the line or "groups of lines" (*SL,* 130). Everything depended upon the individual's ability to feel his way into the common speech not for its own sake but for the formal patterning it might be made to yield.

Perhaps in no other single document does Williams make so clear his own sense of still working in agency, working toward an accomplished poetry rather than within one. The avant-garde, including himself, suffered from its own self-elected identity and the demands such an election created. The present age, he declared, "is a period without mastery. That is all," and he clearly meant to include his own efforts. "It is a period in which the form has not yet been found" (*SL,* 133). Perhaps reflecting Pound's doctrine set forth in his extended 1928 essay "How to Read," Williams thus gives primacy of place to that category of writers Pound had called the "inventors," placing them ahead of the "masters" and far ahead of other negligible groups. Pound had long before expressed his own admiration of "donative writers," those who added a unique quality to whatever they received from others, and Williams here extended such thought specifically to his own historic period. Though as poet, Williams felt, Pound himself had done no more than adapt classic lines to a modern necessity, and as such was neither really inventor nor master, he was probably still the best guidepost among his contemporaries. Others fell behind. Stevens, as prosodist, "has something more than his play with sequences of sound"

(*SL*, 132), but it was hard to say what. Eliot at most could offer no more than "the line as it is modified by a limited kind of half-alive speech" (*SL*, 134). Frost's "bucolic simplicity" seemed to Williams "a halt" (*SL*, 132). The letter declared its inability to do more than gesture toward poetic form, but its impetus was Zukofsky's emphasis on the whole structure of "sound" as the unifier of concept and image. There is no reason to feel that Williams made a master of Zukofsky, but he found him perhaps a particularly promising guide to invention. At any rate, his force was now being felt in Williams's work as together they sought to move "The Descent of Winter," given its multiple range of subject, toward a voice the work's presence defined.

As the thirties drew on, Williams's poetry tended to flow between the exacting and often abstracting drive of Zukofsky's objectivism—confining itself as structure to what its patterned speech rhythms allowed—and a breaking away from such strict constraint toward a speech felt as little more than oral presence, a poetry conversational or even confessional in its force. Williams's original drift toward presentation, conversion, or deliberate irresolution of image remained strong, but now a feeling for language controlled for its own sake was added. The difference this made was exemplified in a poem of which Williams printed two versions, one more condensed than the other as though he were not finally sure which kind of speech was better. The shorter version appeared to hold close to Zukofsky's recommendation of verbal "efficiency." The second, somewhat looser structure included, tellingly, a more generous element of sensory content than strict verbal pattern required. The occasion was Williams's perennial favorite, "The Locust Tree in Flower." The fuller version of the two poems ran as follows.

Among
the leaves
bright

green
of wrist-thick
tree

and old
stiff broken
branch

ferncool
swaying
loosely strung—

come May
again
white blossom

clusters
hide
to spill

their sweets
almost
unnoticed

down
and quickly
fall
(*CEP*, 93)

The subject was Beautiful Thing in its combined obscurity and evanescence. Image structure was clearly that of object presentation with overtones of a conversion of imagery to a second state suggesting the transience of rebirth and bloom. Verbal structure was that of common statement loosened in syntax and broken into lines to foreground image but, across the whole, also to assert a deliberate persistence of line pattern and interplay. The more condensed version of the poem, largely freed of dependence upon external reference and connotation, omitted the fourth, sixth, seventh, and eighth strophes almost completely and substantial parts of the others as well to sacrifice both specificity and overtone. The result was to "objectify" with a vengeance. The resulting work contained little more than patterned reference to colors and shapes attached to two nouns—"branch" and "May"—and the verb "come." Subject and image structure were sacrificed. The strictest aim of objectivism was to make an object that would compel internal reading, that would be as self-sufficient as possible.

Among
of
green

stiff
old
bright

broken
branch
come

white
sweet
May

again
(*CEP*, 93)

Reference was of little interest except as it contributed to structure. Though under Zukofsky's influence Williams's work inclined strongly toward object presentation as its image structure, the method in its purity would seek objectivity for the poem itself as a structural act.

In his *Autobiography* Williams summed up Objectivism as "an antidote, in a sense, to the bare image haphazardly presented in loose verse" and added that he felt "it was Gertrude Stein, for her formal insistence on words in their literal, structural quality of being words, who had strongly influenced us" (*A*, 265). But it was Zukofsky's editorial hand, by Williams's own testimony, that weighed in the *Collected Poems, 1921–1931*. The result was far more a "selected poems" than a collection. It included scant suggestion of the range of the author's exploration. Except for a brief appendix, it ignored Williams's publication before 1923 and offered less than half the poems of *Spring and All* and "The Descent of Winter." The newly collected poems were almost wholly glued to themselves as objects or to the objects they described. The selection excluded virtually any suggestion of the poetic person who had been emerging in Williams's early writing. What emerged here often seemed arbitrary, inhibited, and random. It was an unfortunate first "collection" for the poet, though he apparently gave full assent to it, and it drew almost universal dissent from its literary reviewers. According to Paul Mariani, Horace Gregory alone was able to see the book as a beginning rather than a résumé. Despite the prevailing rebuffs, however, Williams would never turn explicitly against Objectivism. Indeed, in 1944, he would again offer an amorphous selection, what became *The Wedge*, to Zukofsky for editorial pruning, and in this case he would clearly benefit by the judgment he received. Programmatic Objectivism itself perhaps had lost force by that time, though a generally beneficial impulse toward verbal control was retained. *Collected Poems, 1921–1931*, whatever its limitations as a survey of Williams's work, at least had the value of signaling a distinct direction in his poetry—an awareness of the poetically shaping power of speech.

Later publication of the thirties continued to vary between what can be seen as a stricter and a looser Objectivism. *An Early Martyr* of 1935 was also of Williams's books the one most noticeably given to poems of explicit social consciousness and to an extension of length in some texts. *Adam and Eve and the City* the next year moved sharply toward lengthening of form, which brought with it a conversationally retrospective emphasis. *The Complete Collected Poems* of 1938 and *The Broken Span* of 1941 added short poems of a recognizable kind to a continued interest in more extended works. It was often this lengthening of the poem that suggested Williams's continuing to play with technique within the general limits of a speech emphasis. In contrast to "The Wanderer" or "Romance Moderne," however, these later efforts, of which his elegy on D. H. Lawrence is a notable example, were characterized by attention to a calculated play of diction, line, and line grouping. Zukofsky had little or no direct part in the formulation of these books, however, and the general effect may be seen as reflecting Williams's increasing uncertainty of Objectivist orthodoxy. By 1941 or so, in any case, the two most prevailing influences on his technique had clearly been assimilated—the structuring of images within the poem according to general patterns of the presentation, conversion, or irresolution of image, and the statement of the poem in a verbal form that sought an exploitation of the denotative and rhythmic groupings of words derived from common speech.

Selected Poems

If his *Selected Poems* of 1949 may be relied upon, Williams came to see his poetry as reaching maturity after about 1930. Only a quarter of the book's content was drawn from the extensive earlier writing; half dated from the thirties, and a final quarter was drawn from the forties themselves. A second and posthumous edition of 1968 would increase the book by about a quarter with the addition of poetry of the fifties. The original selection was doubtless too exclusive—in regard to the earlier poems especially—but the book as a whole, and partly for that reason, needs attention in any discussion of Williams's technique. It shows him thinking of his poetry as something more than a pursuit of new effort—as an accumulation that needed to be given a shape. The *Collected Poems, 1921–1931* had in fact also been such a selection, revealing the poet's response to Zukofsky and objectivism. This second selection and arrangement of his own work by an author in his sixty-sixth year was far more liberal and inclusive than the earlier effort. Its perspective is therefore difficult to sum up readily; nevertheless its paradigm is that of presence within which agency reaches toward a delimitation and interrelating of the world its own nature has created. Such a poetic realm was definable chiefly as presentation and arrangement of direct poetic image and the shaping of a common tongue to imagistic purpose.

As a result it was most literally a secular realm, of its time and place, and shunning any transcendental gesture—philosophical, scientific, or religious. It was made up by a poetry as nearly as possible of presence alone, the presence of form measured as discovery or invention in each instance rather than as recall or allusion, and of meaning shaped by such formally constituted limits of reference. The result was to make of Williams as little of a "philosophical poet" as may be imagined, but *Selected Poems*, with its gesture toward what must be called significant form, moved nevertheless to establish a general paradigm of presence within which its various contents assumed a highly discernible pattern of reference. The presence of a certain texture of society, for example—a limiting of world to the ordinary—was important to almost every poem in the book. A feeling for religion was present chiefly as its own opposite, as a secularism that filled the scene but allowed religion as a fact of the scene it discerned. Like all of Williams's writing the *Selected Poems* was made up of life seized piece by piece at the moment, to which was added here and there a specific evocation of death. What may be called "nature" was also a part of this general paradigm as plant, bird, stream, weather, landscape, cityscape—all or part on occasion presented in their coexistence. The whole was completed by a range of persons, tenants of Williams's scene, manifestations of its indifferent but vital character. Little of this pattern existed as doctrine in the poems. It was compositely generated and limited by the agencies of image and its prosody. Nonetheless, the paradigm was clear: the democracy of spirit that was Williams's poetic world existing in a level, visible, plainly lit and unrelieved presence.

It was perhaps his sense of society that as much as anything else gave character to the whole. Like the Chaucer he admired and invoked on occasion, he assumed what was around him for poetic purpose, though unlike Chaucer he was often bitter. The note had been struck fairly often in his earlier writing, dating from his own Sturm und Drang of the twenties and the Depression years following, much of it excluded here. The desolation of "To Elsie," however, or, in the 1968 edition, the larger vision of "At the Ball Game" was included from *Spring and All* to state his sense of the democracy as the only social presence there was, though he was far from romanticizing it. Society was often enough a source of fear and distaste. It was on occasion a source of amusement and vitality. The crowd at the ball game, thus, is "moved uniformly / by a spirit of uselessness / which delights them." As for once they have been delivered "to no end save beauty / the eternal," so they have become "in detail" beautiful. But their mindless presence is no less felt. "The Jew" with his knowledge of pogroms senses it (*SP*, 31). It is as much "the Inquisition, the / Revolution" as it is "beauty itself that lives / day by day in them / idly—." For the moment, "the crowd is laughing / in detail." Now and always, however, it is "permanently, seriously / without thought" (*SP*, 32). This mindlessness makes up the social milieu extending through *Paterson*, the prose fiction, and indeed the whole breadth of Williams's poems.

Among writers responding to the American democracy, Williams's poetic perception of it strikes a unique note. He images it as crowd with as much uneasiness about crowd's nature as, say, Henry James, but with far more sense of present reality. Against Whitmanian transcendence he excludes any intimation of a spiritual presence or future. Against any Dreiserian vision he mostly excludes intimation of determinate victimage. He is often a heartless perceptor of the democracy. Presentation seizes upon what is there. When his democracy attains freedom and beauty they are often accidents. When it sinks into ugliness or cruelty that too is circumstantial. No doubt the crowd needs more space, means, cultural enablement than it has, but this poet knows himself to be in one aspect a member of the crowd and so knows how uncertain in fact the fruits of such improvement are. The crowd and all its members are present and inescapable. Democracy is fact not vision. In its uglier aspect, indeed, democracy is something of a cancer growing by multiplication of its own malformed cells. The poem "It Is a Living Coral" begins with a gracious enough natural comparison, though one that is as applicable to cancer as to an atoll, but it moves immediately to treat its subject—the historical art gallery in the nation's capitol—as "a trouble / archaically fettered." This coral is not growing gracefully. It is weighed down by a dome of iron "eight million pounds in weight" (SP, 56), which shelters "a sculptured group / Mars" crowning Washington with laurel. The general "jumble" of the exhibit is "superb / and accurate in its / expression / of the thing / they would destroy" (SP, 57) as it traduces any fructive or progressive notion of democratic history. At its end the poem celebrates Perry at the Battle of Lake Erie changing flagships to snatch victory from defeat, but with "the / dead / among the wreckage / sickly green" (SP, 59).

Williams's rendering of democratic society is as void of specific hope as it is of hopelessness. The dreadful and the vital are co-present. He absorbs the spectacle and translates it very much according to present appearance and present mood. There is little if any sense of future in him; the coral will grow as it will. The democracy as a whole contains better as it contains worse, but it is generically unable to discern between them and still be true to its nature. What it most offers is its growth, uncertain of character as that is. If there is positive hope it lies in change, but change entails the very process that is the society. In one of his striking conversion poems, Williams snubs religion only to seize upon a presence central in it, converting large C Catholicism to small c and offering that which results—including religion itself—as a living coral containing himself. It is hard to read "The Catholic Bells," thus, as a celebrative poem unless one adds that it celebrates little beyond the undifferentiation that lowercase "catholic" implies. The poet "listens hard" to the bells ringing and hence to the secular presence he feels they in fact celebrate. It is fall, and so "out" go the leaves and flowers, "in" comes the frost. "In" comes a new baby, and "out" goes the parrot he has replaced in his parents' attention (SP, 61).

The poem is almost a litany structured on the two prepositions. "In" come the announcement of a novena at the church and a somber young man hurrying to mass. "Out" goes the fall's harvest of grapes now nearly destroyed by the weather. "In," finally, comes the image of a friend, somewhat lost in deafness as her hearing has gone "out," but as attentive as possible to the life around her, which itself burgeons miscellaneously in her children and friends. "Oh bells / ring for the ringing!" the poet concludes:

> the beginning and the end
> of the ringing! Ring ring
> ring ring ring ring ring!
> Catholic bells—!
>   (*SP*, 62)

Society rather than any kind of religious or secular transcendence is the container here, and what it contains is everything, but figured as no more than what is available to present awareness.

Religion itself seldom occurs in Williams's poems as more than another fact of the life around him, one certainly that he stands apart from in his outsider's position. It does little to shape or characterize the general presence but is no less a part of the whole for that. As in the early "Pastoral," this may make it seem merely pompous. In two late poems—"For Eleanor and Bill Monahan" and "The Mental Hospital Garden"—it is allowed a more living presence, speaking however imperfectly to the old and ailing poet's response to the dimension it opens. Williams, finally, will not accept it, but, as in "The Catholic Bells," he is from time to time aware of it as present force. The bells do ring, the faithful hurry to their duties, and both together are part of the motion and change which are characteristic of the living coral, that American present which is the poet's world. On only two occasions in *Selected Poems* does Williams seek closer hold on it. Neither of these pretends to final grasp but together, one acting through presentation and one in a highly wrought structure of irresolution, the two open a vista into the poet's sense of the unassimilable but undismissable fact.

The central image of "The Semblables" is a red-brick monastery set down in a ragged suburb near a munitions plant and, itself walled off and tree shaded, joined to a full parking lot. Its presence is as anomalous in its setting as the faith it bespeaks is foreign to all that setting makes plain. Setting includes a dump, a polluted stream, open fields, and a cemetery. The monastery stands starkly in their midst, its cross turned green from the weather, a "miracle that has burst sexless / from between the carrot rows" (*SP,* 106). Certainly the lack of sex its discipline commands and the sexless divine birth it celebrates are central to Williams's sense of anomaly. The parentless children it cares for sing in their alien Latin tongue inside it like "the worm" (*SP,* 105) which has made a home by its very alienness in the social apple that nourished it. A "lonesome" cop stands guard on the outside over "that agony / within where the wrapt machines / are praying." (*SP,* 106). The word "wrapt" may be just a mistake or one of Williams's rare puns. The praying machines are absorbed in devotion surely; they are plainly wrapped away from real presence while contemplating, perhaps, an imaginary real presence.

The poem hangs from its title. The "semblables," the cloistered children, are no more than like a real thing, and for Williams they are engaged in a fictive exercise. The prayers are not real prayers since there is no god present to hear them. The children's isolation puts them in a false position which is stressed by the walled and guarded monastery itself. They are as blind inside their container as the worm inside his apple. However, they are there. Williams in some sense attacks religion here, but more plainly, as the poem's technique makes plain, he simply presents it as witnessed. As in the whole scope of presence within the *Selected Poems*—the capitol dome, the broad cityscape of "January Morning," the assorted and often unaccountable old and young men and women of other poems—religion is no more than present. The poem attaches idea to it only loosely and, obviously, from a distance.

What this poet needs to attain any hold upon religious reality is a shift of technique of the kind present in "Burning the Christmas Greens." In that complex and beautifully proportioned poem, unresolved images allow him to focus upon the strangeness of religion, to enter it as his light will allow. Religion is present in the work simply as the season; it is observed as ritual even though no belief is present, and thus it can be examined as action, wholly unlike the praying machines of the monastery. The action is threefold: the house is decorated for Christmas and hence transformed; the difference at first is enjoyed; then it all grows tiresome and the greens are burned, but the new movement of the now-dry boughs causes a surprised recognition of continued transformation. Even in his own agnostic household, Christmas is the occasion of rebirth. Religion here, as in "The Catholic Bells," goes along with the life of the coral in which all are involved and, by the changes it signals, makes that life visible and present. There is no final attainment, only process and its attesting of the reality Williams finds in the presence informing so much of his work. Here, in contrast to "The Semblables," religion is real to the poet because bent to share in a life which otherwise it seems to turn away from.

Much of the irresolution of the poem is sustained by a play of color imagery: the snow-white woods out of which green boughs have been cut; the transformation of the green to fiery red and finally to cindery black. It is the red fire which most holds force, perhaps, as its flames in their sanguine color echo the greenness of life which the boughs had at first brought into the house. Green has become red and the antipodal colors equally bespeak the occasion of Christmas as one of birth, of newness. Like the Brueghel of "The Adoration of the Kings," Williams has accepted the occasion "and painted / it in the brilliant / colors of the chronicler" (PB, 6). In doing so he has made his poetic translation of fact and so suggested that if religion can be opened to translation, it can find a place in his general paradigm. The final ashiness of the burning is not a terminus. Rather it is the fading out, with presence still felt, of the miracle of change which has been witnessed.

> Black
> mountains, black and red—as
>
> yet uncolored—and ash white,
> an infant landscape of shimmering
> ash and flame and we, in
> that instant, lost,
>
> breathless to be witnesses,
> as if we stood
> ourselves refreshed among
> the shining fauna of that fire.
> (SP, 111)

In its revised and anthologized form Williams's poem "Death" suggests something of the cost of his secularity. If society is at least growth, in whatever fashion, and religion real only when in fact it evokes renewal, death can be nothing in Williams's view except a cessation of these vital processes, a nothing that enforces completely the terminal character of his awareness. To be secular, clearly, is to be wholly defined by time and so to lose definition with the loss of awareness of time's presence. It is to enforce presence and to contrast it wholly with absence, which is the nothing that death paradoxically most prevents. Williams's bald and unforgiving poem originally contained references identifying as its subject the death of his forceful but inhibited father. Its revised form deletes these references to make the poem a travesty of eulogy on the death of a man afraid of love and guarding himself all his life from it. Death in this case is itself a translation, a restatement of the moribundity of feeling that life for this man had been. The tone is savage but also comic: "He's nothing at all / he's dead / shrunken up to skin." Rigor mortis is no more than a restatement of the rigor that had been his duty-bound life.

> Put his head on
> one chair and his
> feet on another and
> he'll lie there
> like an acrobat—
>   (*SP,* 44)

The poem's subject, dead or alive, bespeaks the place of death in Williams's world. It is terminus, but a terminus to be shunned as fiercely and as long as possible. It is nonreality that has nothing to contribute to reality except negation. If the subject here has died before his time—has done no more in death than confirm his life— that is because he has broken down the barrier to mix death with life.

There is little difference in tone, however, when Williams turns to a subject that elsewhere he celebrates as an epitome of life's strength and fullness—his English grandmother who had personified the American experience, bearing her son, losing her husband, immigrating to the West Indies, rearing her son (to be sure into the very dutifulness that Williams so raged against), and moving on to the United States to help rear her son's family. Her end was no less a blank terminus, however, except for the important suggestion that she accepted it properly—as properly present in time—out of a feeling of sufficiency of or satiation with life. Even so, there is no grace or dignity in her dying beyond the acceptance it marks.

Wrinkled and nearly blind
she lay and snored
rousing with anger in her tones
to cry for food,

Gimme something to eat—
They're starving me—
I'm all right I won't go
to the hospital. No, no, no
(SP, 94–95)

Her grandson tells her she has to be moved to the hospital, and she noisily protests the discomfort entailed. She scolds and chides "the young people" who despite their pretensions "don't know anything" (SP, 95). As the ambulance moves along, she looks out of its windows and asks what are "all those / fuzzy looking things out there?" The fuzzy-looking things are trees, she is told. She makes her choice. "Well, I'm tired / of them," she declares, "and rolled her head away" (SP, 96). That is all.

Perhaps nowhere is presentation more clearly an agency of form and reference combined than in those poems on death. Death here, by the nature of the poems and by its own nature as negative presence, can be no more than presented. In the one case we can learn that memory of the dead is cherished, though not from the poem. In the other, memory is occasion for scorn. But the two share the same response—that which a present blankness calls forth. By 1948 and in the title poem for a volume of that year, "The Clouds," Williams was ready to extend and reorder some earlier writing into what would clearly become his fullest utterance on the subject of death. In doing so, he would create a poem of self-presentation, of rumination upon negative presence. The image of the clouds filling part 1 of the extended work is wholly apposite as he seizes upon natural fact that in itself has little identity other than its presence. However central they may be to their ecology and however available to scientific understanding, clouds yield nothing to imagination except by a kind of Rorschach reaction. They can perhaps be read into; they can hardly be read from.

In this case they appeal to the poet's spirit of play as he figures them as "gigantic beasts" charging across the skies on whose back an imagination of the picturesque might fancy the dead to ride. Such imagination, of course, is not Williams's. At this moment and so in their presence, the clouds move only toward the "no-knowledge of their nameless destiny" (*SP*, 101). Section 2 invokes the *ubi sunt* theme to consider whatever life may be said to continue after death and finds it to be in nothing except the presence— bespeaking mind—that the illustrious dead may leave physically behind them. Spiritualism, in which Williams's mother considered herself an adept, is dismissed as one more religious illusion deceiving mind by claiming that, disconnected from tangible bequest, it can lead "beyond the clouds" (*SP*, 103). Religion reenters in section 3 as Williams recalls a priest seen in Italy at his offices and grinning at the American tourist "from his cloud" (*SP*, 103), content to ride as he may. So doing, he settles for projected vision. The brief fourth section turns discursively to the problem. Each life carries its value. Each life takes that value with it into death. So much may be clear. "But if they live? / What then? (*SP*, 104). But the clouds mock the question as in their ragged noncommunication they continue to tease and to make wholly fruitless any possible answer.

Williams's poems on death, in that they resist the severest temptation his own secular poetic raises, stand as the most strict enforcers of the ban against transcendence in his poetry. The worlds of mind and body alike exist only as presence. Neither can escape that limit. Like democracy or religion, death is perceivable only as present fact. To live or die in the world is to be present in time and place until presence ends. Such strictness will of course entail questions as to what poetic vision as a translation of presence can hope to accomplish that is not already accomplished by presence itself. Translation certainly will not abolish the value of the original presence. Its best hope will be, as in Williams's writing, to seek presence so that it is both truly phrased and, as the death poems suggest, most scrupulously attended to for its own sake. If presence is untranscendable, then the aim of poetry must be the acutest possible awareness within it.

Three further important parts of Williams's paradigm of presence are individuals, nature, and love. Love will not be much considered, however, until the poems of the fifties and their discernment of the need of constancy to make the secular world of this volume habitable. Of these three it is the persistence of the individual that is most central, as individuality itself will be in effect the crux of what Williams discerns in nature and love both. The individual, indeed, is a radical image of secular presence. Society, religion, and death alike are made up only of its instances. Williams's nominalism must decline any extrapolation from the individual, who delimits space and time by and to his own presence. His coexistence with others and with the world consists largely of arbitrary conjunctions. Like Leibniz's world, Williams's is filled with monads, atomized entities of countless number; and as is the case with any secular philosophy, encountering the "world" conjures up no more than encounter with the host that such entities comprise. Williams has moments of discerning hints of preestablished harmony among their number; otherwise randomness rules. But randomness may be made more acutely present as each such monad is brought more acutely into focus.

In "Death" Williams had railed against what he saw as his father's denial of harmonies that might have prevailed. Father and son had never seriously quarreled, and indeed they maintained a somewhat uncomprehending fondness for each other. They had lived for years in close conjunction, but each perhaps always sensed a separateness from the other. Long after the senior Williams's death, his son in a pair of poems dedicated to his mother and father—both of whom presented their inscrutability to him as he to them—attempted what presentation would allow of the individuality of each. Of this pair of poems it was "Adam," the poem on his father, that Williams included in Selected Poems. Its judgment remains cool and unattached. What interests the writing is the riddle which the presence of individuality could not help but pose. Object- and self-presentation combined were the poetic agencies. Not a great deal could be said about the individual as subject independent of the poet's own effort to translate the being he had known into language and its available judgment.

Adam, thus, was monad knowing nothing of windows. Growing up in the tropics, he turned his back on their luxuriance to practice his piano, practice his flute, and ignore the region's alien romance, bent above all on preserving his integrity from the careless allure of the region's exotic girls. In fact, Adam was to marry an exotic—a heavy burden, he was to tell his son as he lay dying. But the poem seeks only Adam's essence, his exclusion of the "paradise" where he had dwelt as he took on himself the burden of husbandry and parenthood.

He never had but the one home
Staring Him in the eye
coldly
and with patience—
without a murmur, silently
a desperate, unvarying silence
to the unhurried last.
                                    (SP, 75)

His duty was to live in a fallen world attempting as best he could to observe the rule it laid on him. Williams senior was a philosophic and religious man, the founder of a Unitarian group in Rutherford. He lived to support and guide his family. He spent his life with a woman whose combination of romantic impulse and complex motive must have been often incalculable to him. In both of the poems on his father, Williams preached something of a sermon against him. In both cases, however, as in his writing on his mother and his grandmother, he is most aware of individuality as isolation. His own family was a seemingly random assemblage of individuals walled off from each other to a measurable extent, each bending its energy to preserve the individualilty that was its own, tempered however by a strongly felt "harmony" of family tie that all succeeded in maintaining. The harmony held in its measure, as it would across so many strains hold Williams and his own wife together. It did little, if these poems are to be believed, to relate the individuals more nearly than family ties and their kind of knowledge made possible.

The point holds good in Williams's poem on his grandmother, "Dedication for a Plot of Ground." Presentation mainly rules once more: the bulk of the work is a chronology of her life, with the poetic self entering at the end of enforce judgment. What had been felt in Williams's father as coldness is treated here as a requisite busyness and devotion to duty. It is the other side of a similiar individuality. But the poem does not call for love or fondness—

rather for respect, a feeling that enters into Williams's feeling for his father more grudgingly.

> She grubbed this earth with her own hands
> domineered over this grass plot,
> blackguarded her oldest son
> into buying it, lived here fifteen years,
> attained a final loneliness and—
>
> If you can bring nothing to this place
> but your carcass, keep out.
>   (SP, 7)

Such individualism commands respect. It is the kernel out of which "world" is constituted. As the late poems would discover more plainly, there was indeed such "preexistent harmony" as family, but the power that harmony generated would then reveal itself only paradoxically to be what love was. There is little of love in any form in Williams's 1949 selection. What drew him to his father and his grandmother's memory, however, was not a direct but a residual emotion, one that only the late writing would find ways at last to bring more into the open.

There is greater fondness in others of Williams's poems on individuals, but the paradox holds as this fondness is so little productive of a binding. His elegy on Lawrence recalls the emotional excitement that the Englishman's writing had stirred in him, but recognition is measured out only in distanced strophes. Ford Madox Ford is remembered more warmly, but in the very memory is reduced to the self-indulgent personage he had been for Williams and others, most memorable for his violation of whatever harmony might have bound him to his friends.

> Thank God you
> were not delicate, you let the world in
> and lied! damn it you lied grossly
> sometimes. But it was all, I
> see now, a carelessness, the part of a man
> that is homeless here on earth.
>   (SP, 108)

An old school friend named Aigeltinger is remembered for his brilliance, but also for how it was destroyed in the drunken wreck he made of his adult years. Again, an incalculable entity. Mark Antony is singled out from the historic dead as an image of what the lover should be, but his ardor is as much textbook example as occasion of warmth. An old woman munching plums, among many other more casually seen individuals in the selection, is seized upon for the poet's pleasure but for little else. And, human beings aside, a sea elephant in the zoo is contemplated with an unresolved mixture of repugnance, pity, wonder, and finally dismissal for his irreducible and, in this setting, wholly anomalous individuality.

The individual for Williams is always immediately real but inescapably apart. He is the stuff out of which poetry would be made, occasion for the assertion of presence in its most unalterable form. Individuals existed only marginally as subjects of personal fondness or interchange. Instead, they were the human components of the democracy and its own incalculable character, the random monads that conspired to make religion or philosophy an irrelevance. Doubtless Williams's science can be aware of them as possible subjects for medical treatment, but science, physical or social, intrudes on the poems no more than society or religion to proffer a harmony for their reconciliation. Such harmony in the *Selected Poems* was both rare and ambiguous. The book's philosophy is coterminal with its virtual confinement to present image and hence to present time and place.

The term "nature," thus, is partly a misnomer for what Williams found to be present in the natural world—the final element in my paradigm of presence—since that world is so wholly unavailable to any version of nature as preestablished harmony. If Williams's "Adam" is the picture of a fallen man, what Adam most falls from in fact is an existence in a nature foreign to him. There are a number of poems on the seasons in *Selected Poems*, spring and fall particularly, and they are notable for their witness of season not as natural token but as matter for translation away from nature and toward whatever immediately human likeness it may be made to assume. "The Botticellian Trees," with "Burning the Christmas Greens" a notable venture into image conversion, alters the coming spring into a metamorphosis simultaneously from bare letters to words to music and from skeletal tree limbs to women's bodies moving undulantly under their clothing. Spring is Venus born, as the title suggests, rather than landscape restored. In other cases ugliness rather than beauty prevails as ugliness is not only the "nature" of much of Williams's Passaic region but what humans have made of their address to it. Nature has been no automatic guide. Wordsworth and the romantic tradition could seek to heal such a breach, but in Williams nature is mostly present as breach, as alienation, to be contemplated as in "The Clouds" for its inherent blankness. "To Waken an Old Lady" sees old age in an image of winter. The old woman's arousal from sleep is mirrored as birds, hungry in the bleak fields, find nature suddenly yielding them food, the seeds of a dry weed patch. It is the image of feeding, however, rather than any presence of nature that most accomplishes the change.

In "The Trees" nature is seized upon wholly as something apart from humankind and scornful of it, precisely for its separation from the natural whole. A little like Williams judging his father, the trees, pelted by storm, revel in a native condition and scoff at the human's indoor cautiousness.

> The trees—being trees
> thrash and scream
> guffaw and curse—
> wholly abandoned
> damning the race of men—
>
> Christ, the bastards
> haven't even sense enough
> to stay out in the rain—
> (*SP*, 59)

(The 1968 *Selected Poems* seems to make a grievous misprint here compared with all other printings of the poem, replacing "in" with "of" in the last line.) The trees see humans as "sapped of strength" and "wailing at the gate." The trees are wholly of nature and feel themselves the gainers thereby; the human condition is otherwise. The trees speak for themselves during much of the poem, and perhaps it is their voice that continues to be heard in the concluding strophes declaring "satyrs," "maenads," and "eagle headed gods" (*SP*, 60) to be fictions. The reality was men, "bursting the woods— / Trees their companions" (*SP*, 61). In any case, that reality has vanished. As the trees speak, their voices are strident with laughter at the human, but despite the vigor of their claim they remain outside of the human so far as this poem is concerned. They can mock man's fallen state, but they have no coherence or participation to offer in its place.

There appear to be only two exceptions in the volume to the general rule of nature, collectively, as blankness, and they are both much qualified. Flowers, birds, trees, seasons, to be sure, offer themselves frequently to Williams as sources of pleasure or suggestion depending on their ability to project human feeling, but "nature" as a supportive force is nearly absent. In "Lear" the poet, almost like one of his trees, rejoices momentarily in storm as an emblem of the whole and chides "pitiful Lear" for trying to "outshout" the tempest. What storm presents, however, is the other than human. Storm is a lesson in limits and thereby a reliever of anxiety, but it still is less than sustainer or abettor of human life.

> Today the storm, inescapable, has
> taken the scene and we return
> our hearts to it, however made, made
> wives by it and though we secure
> ourselves for a dry skin from the drench
> of its passionate approaches we
> yield and are made quite by its fury
> (SP, 126)

The human lot is to be "made wife" by storm, to acknowledge its greater strength, as sailing ships used to carry female figureheads, emblems of their yielding to what could be dealt with in no other way. Nature is to Williams the force that puts man in his uncertain place.

Williams's most extended grappling with his unyielding nature occurs in "A Unison," a poem that it is easy to misread as a kind of Wordsworthian celebration of nature's wholeness if one misses the point that what is being celebrated here is "a unison and a dance, joined / at this death's festival" (SP, 129). It is a poem of landscape offering mountains, matted greenery, and a grove of maples that seems "idyllic" except that all, imaged in a child's tombstone, is a "unison" of nothing more than mortality. What is a "music" and "undying" is still the fact of presence cherished by

Williams, but its cost is now plainly seen as death. Renewal demands cessation. Nature is a dance of life only to the extent that it is also a dance of death. It is a circular process containing man and his existence which does no more than confirm that existence as resource and limit both. Resource is invention, renewal. Limit is decay and terminus. The poem reaches for the whole in a succession of images leading to no other end.

> There it is and
> we'd better acknowledge it and
> write it down, not otherwise.
> Not twist the words to mean
> what we should have said but to mean
> —what cannot be escaped: the
> mountain riding the afternoon as
> it does, the grass matted green,
> green underfoot and the air—
> rotten wood.
> (*SP*, 129)

Humankind in Williams has no other scene, and recurrence here, beheld only for its presence, can do no more than yield itself to translation into the agencies of presence that are its most proper act of celebration.

VI PURPOSE

THE PRESENCE OF INTENT

In a book originally published in 1941, *The Philosophy of Literary Form,* Kenneth Burke brought together the long essay of that title and numerous other shorter essays to form what became perhaps his most compendious discussion of literature. He used the terms "chart," "dream," and "prayer" to indicate the three general aspects of literature that criticism might best be concerned with. The words themselves seemed chosen for picturesqueness, but each indicated a fairly clear-cut line of approach to the literary text. "Chart" suggested what Burke called the text's "realistic sizing up of situations" (Burke 1941, 7). Its operation was governed by an author's sense of the common reality he dealt with and, so to speak, his respect for it as reality. By "dream" Burke wanted to designate "the unconscious or subconscious features in a poem"—patterns of desire, fear, and all the inadvertent emotionality which at varying levels and in various ways gave the work affective import. "Prayer" then became a word for the text's "communicative function" (Burke 1941, 6), the means which an author found to embody the deep emotion of "dream" and the more public reference of "chart," whether for an audience or for himself as what William James had called an "I" seeking to clarify meaning and relationship to a "me" in an act of internal or subjective rhetoric.

In the four years intervening between *The Philosophy of Literary Form* and *A Grammar of Motives* Burke, as we have seen, broadened both his subject matter and its classification to produce the pentad upon which this study of Williams is based and to consider human "action" broadly rather than the narrower spectrum of literature alone. It is this broader canvas that has seemed generally appropriate for Williams, but the more specific concerns of "chart," "dream," and "prayer" are relevant to the question of literary purpose. All three terms carry strong purposive connotations as, respectively, they reflect elements of the "mimetic," the "expressive," and the "formal"—M. H. Abrams's influential terms for three ends that literature may be thought to fulfill. Like other poetry, Williams's eludes any reductive search for purpose. Equally, however, it may be made to yield a sense at least of intentionality if it is brought by Burke's terminology into a compass of aims that poetry in general has been seen to serve. Burke does not quarrel with Kant's denial of overt purpose to any form of aesthetic being, but his terms reflect the covert motives, neglected by Kant, from which literature may be said to spring. "Dream" relates to the subjectivity of what I have discussed under the heading of poetic agent. "Chart" then carries us to the subjective self in its scene, its "local," as it reflects the world present to it or considers the prospect of world relevant to itself. "Prayer" in this context often amounts to an effort to mediate the two in agency, imagery, and form appropriate to an expression of their coexistence; thus what has so far been seen chiefly as poetic means reveals a more subjective aspect.

The relationship of the three elements varies in Williams's poetry, but the thrust of dream—of emotional impulse—in relation to the more fixed proportions of chart is basic. Thus I begin with the unpredictable corners of the emotional life from which the poetry seeks expression against often resistant inhibition. This drive is given specific form in much of Williams's writing but finally exceeds any formal statement. It always lay beyond the termination of statement or figure and so remained perpetually compelling. I have spoken of the interplay of internal and external attention in *Paterson,* and such interplay may now be seen to mirror the clash within him of dream with chart, as may the frequent mind-versus-facts offset of the shorter poems.

As his *Autobiography* indicated, he himself saw his adult life as dividing from the start between chart and dream, situation and impulse, between conformance to the demands of the world he elected as his own and a freedom of poetry to which he would assign no transcendental powers. *A Voyage to Pagany* recorded his fear of letting go of his domestic world lest he fall into self-destructive excess and so records the same division in the opposite direction. Dream was the vital, sometimes ungovernable, sometimes even destructive impulse. He was despite his powerfully impulsive self the son of his father—an elector of marriage, family, a profession, and a pursuer of poetry only to the extent that such an established life permitted. His poetic rejections of his father, thus, may be seen in part as wails for the dream his father in him had somewhat done to death. He was in part a godlike "Kora," but in another part a Kora denied renewal most by a self-confinement to the commonly ordained. Poetry itself then became "prayer," a phrasing of freedom, a surrogate for the whole renewal of self he dreamed, but in part also the voice of elected circumstance, and of its resource as well as its limits.

Self-Expression: "The Pink Church" and "Russia"

The persistent purpose that prayer served for Williams, thus, was the means it afforded, if never quite finally, of serving the other states by lifting them into a sphere reflective of both, where dream and chart could be made to coexist reflexively. Prayer was thus the translation of dream and chart from unuttered presence to language. If in Williams's awareness there was an area designatable as outer life in which conformity to chart ruled, and a second area designatable as internal freedom in which the dream of renewal projected its claim, then his poetic effort was to fashion a verbal realm—prayer—that would find form and expression to unite the two in a single gesture, a single act mindful of both but beholden to neither. Earlier discussion of "scene," "agent," and "agency" has already reflected something of this multiple intentionality. My present concern will be to seize upon moments in Williams of a now-advancing, now-retreating, now momentarily poised drama of self-renewal and self-constraint, moments of dream displayed as a persistent subjective pattern.

A most moving poem of self-presentation called "A Marriage Ritual" must be quoted in full here, as it manages uniquely to freeze into the fixity of a moment the whole complex of purpose I am concerned with, the balancing of dream against chart and their common translation into poetic utterance, into prayer. Because it made its book appearance in *Collected Poems, 1921–1931* where Williams's writing was most ruled by Zukofsky's insistence on controlled form, it presents all its motives at a maximum peak of interplay.

         Above
the darkness of river upon
winter's icy sky
dreams the silhouette of the city:

This is my own! a flower,
a fruit, an animal by itself—

It does not recognize me
and never will. Still, it is my own
and my heart goes out to it
dumbly—

   but eloquently in
my own breast for you whom I love
—and cannot express what
my love is, how it varies, though
I waste it—

      It is
a river flowing through refuse
the dried sticks of weeds
and falling shell-ice lilac
from above as if with thoughts
of you—

This is my face and its moods
my moods, a riffled whiteness
shaken by the flow
that's constant in its swiftness
as a pool—

     A Polack in
the stinging wind, her arms
wrapped to her breast
comes shambling near. To look
at what? downstream. It is
an old-world flavor: the poor
the unthrifty, passionately biased
by what errors of conviction—

       Now a boy
is rolling a stout metal drum

up from below the river bank.
The woman and the boy, two
thievish figures, struggle with
the object . . . . in this light!

And still
there is one leafless tree
just at the water's edge and—

my face
constant to you
(*CEP,* 447–48)

Dream here—as often in Williams phrased as a dream of "love" in
danger of waste—is chastened, but it is also massively present.
Dominating the work's first half in the movement of love, the
dream is an uncertain preliminary vision of the city, which is also a
vision of love, "a river flowing through refuse / the dried sticks of
weeds / and falling shell-ice lilac / from above as if with thoughts /
of you—" The stream is colored by its neighbor and foil, the city.
Dream is fluid if polluted (like so many of the streams in Williams's
poetry), and this mixture is called "my face and its moods." It is a
supple presence, flowing and altering but nevertheless "constant"
in its movement. Like the Passaic falls of *Paterson* it is kinesis and
stasis in one. The stream is clearly in one aspect the city's opposite,
flowing in contrast to the old woman's and the boy's struggling and
fumbling. The river could be seen as pushing to be free of the city,
but that is not finally wanted. The poem's movement is from dream
to chart, from subjective impulse to objective closure, and the two
halves in their articulate prayer for mediation are at odds but inseparable. At the same time, as always, the poet in his own person
stands apart from what engrosses him—stream and situation alike.
Cherishing his separateness as the perceiving genius of the narrowing movement of the poem, its focusing upon a final natural object—a tree, leafless and just at the water's edge—he is himself constant in his own division between the work's two halves.

The poet here can neither abandon nor finally embrace the presence of chart—the city—nor can he abandon or embrace the
stream's free flowing force by itself. He would flow and change
with the latter—his "love"—but doing so he finds himself fixed in
the recurrence of its movement and the burden of its pollution. City

and stream alike share in imperfection. He would remain fixed upon the city, but he can do so only as he is sustained by stream's impulse to freedom and reflection of limit both. His final image yields the leafless tree, in a sense at the edge of stream and city alike—his own uncertain and less-than-fulfilled self, which has nevertheless devised for this moment the utterance that prayer for union has made possible. Love is the poem's impulse, but marriage and ritual are the forms its title confers upon it—marriage as the forming of love according to chart's demand and so both confirming and limiting what love's fluidity may be.

The work represents a balance that Williams—until his late poems—only occasionally attained when speaking of his feelings. The two sides of his uneasy unity both carry a powerful emotional charge, and his poetry was often an imperfect container of such force. The strain can be felt in many of the shorter poems I have already considered, and often the poem must settle for unresolved image instead of the closure that perhaps Zukofsky helped enforce in "A Marriage Ritual." Williams's poems of unresolved image frequently bespeak strain's presence, whether by their episodic construction or—in his early work especially—by the breakdown of dreamlike clusters of image, suggestive of influence from both Dada and surrealism, into unrelatable fragments. The emotional anguish of "Romance Moderne" will serve as a token of dream's force in this poet, his drive toward open, careless, even destructive feeling that was both attractive and alarming to him. Other poems in which self-presentation rules bespeak still the powerful waywardness of dream: the narcissistic dance of "Danse Russe," the pedophilia of "The Ogre" or "Sympathetic Portrait of a Child," the blank helplessness of self capping "To Elsie," the awareness of religion despite rejection of it, the furtive fascination with sinning of "Keller Gegen Dom." These and other texts speak for the presence in his work of emotional impetus that must be seen as a basic and pervasive poetic motive—a Faustian but troubled dream of self-gratification that would never die in him but that could live only when linked to contrary check and balance. It most often responded to prayer's demand when it was reduced to "thing," fact alone. Such poetic closure was figured in the leafless tree of "A Marriage Ritual" as a positioning of himself outside of the embroilment that emotion in itself offered.

There is one poem from Williams's earlier writing (where the force of dream in him is clearest) that contrasts with "A Marriage Ritual" and also lays bare the power of emotion so carefully framed there. The only poem that Williams would designate as "Portrait of the Author," its burden seems clearly to be the fear and trembling that a present vision of dream engenders in him. As chart the poem is clear enough in its concern with the coming of spring, renewal in nature standing here, as so often, in a hostile or at least less than clearly assimilable relation to the poet. Chart as the spring season is objective presence that might lead to either objective or subjective translation as the poet would decide, but here it leads only to impasse. The reason is that it is not chart but the tempestuous dream it arouses that wakes in him such complex feeling. Spring as situation is no more than another occasion of the calendar. Dream, clearly, is an anarchic force warping such chart into its own lack of shape and defying the power of prayer to give it shape other than its own tempestuousness. The poem maintains control by mounting itself as self-presentation and so gains locale at least; the poet speaks in a single and personal voice surveying his own dilemma, but poetic self here must note and record its own failure because spring so clearly is two disparate things at once—its natural presence plus a subjective presence for which neither chart nor any form of prayer will serve as adequate image.

The first stanza plunges into the dilemma.

The birches are mad with green points
the wood's edge is burning with their green,
burning, seething—No, no, no.
The birches are opening their leaves one
by one. Their delicate leaves unfold cold
and separate, one by one. Slender tassels
hang swaying from the delicate branch tips—
Oh, I cannot say it. There is no word.

What emerges is literally unspeakable feeling. "The world is gone, torn into shreds / with this blessing," and prayer struggles under the burden of such collapse. The second stanza reaches out for a "redfaced, living man / ignorant stupid." "Alone in this terror" with such a comrade and persona, the poet "clutches" him for company, begging him to leave the "polished plows" of wordaday spring and to speak ("say anything. I will understand you—) (CEP,

228) in the ungovernable force that spring embodies. What is most apparent is a huge broadening of the gap that had found a moment of resolution in "A Marriage Ritual." Poetic purpose is the same in both cases, to find expression for frontiers of feeling, for spring here is the reassertion of a life the poet yearns for but also finds confusing and terrifying—a chaos threatening personal and poetic integrity. As a poem, the work most tellingly overstates and overreacts to external cause. Clearly such response can come only from inside the poet as he defends against a vital promise he knows he cannot realize in himself, cannot even name. A similar doubleness of feeling was present in the earlier "Spring Strains," but there it overrode not only the familiarity, even the triteness, that chart affords but also found image dissolving in controlled gesture as speech passed coherently by way of image into the ineffable. Here there can be nothing more than reaction, confession of breakdown in the presence of internal conflict. A rage of impulse takes over to enact its own kind of image as overdetermined image rules.

> My rooms will receive me. But my rooms
> are no longer sweet spaces where comfort
> is ready to wait on me with its crumbs.
> A darkness has brushed them. The mass
> of yellow tulips in the bowl is shrunken.
> Every familiar object is changed and dwarfed.
> (CEP, 229)

This is not to say that purpose in Williams is a search merely for the expression of dream and its chaos. Purpose, rather, is reflected as the multiple address of poem after poem to the internal play that dream, chart, and prayer engender in him. He would be an innovative poet, no doubt, because in part the avant-garde he embraced centered itself in nothing so much as innovation, remaking the poem itself. But that requirement once faced and accepted necessarily threw him, and here violently, back into the tangle of personal motives that were particular to him—a lust for self-renewal, a fear of its anarchic prospect, and inescapably therefore his besetting concern with poetic agency as form, poetic prayer as both harmonizer and container. Williams in some massive sense was, surely, a poet of "things," but that commitment must be seen in the light of what such things—here, spring—could be to him. They were in effect often dream images with meaning and feeling heavily condensed in them and so irreducible to control by chart to exterior proportions. In this poet's psyche they were often answerable to psychic demand and the lust for what their presence evoked. He had not followed the path that the free subjectivity of *Kora* had opened to him. Instead he strove to shape these dream things—to reduce them where possible to objects alone; often to make of them presences around which a self-regarding self might circle. On occasion he found within them the capability of transforming themselves from alien to congenial presence. "The Botticellian Trees," for example, at one extreme, could handle spring gracefully by reducing it to composed figure of speech. "Portrait of the Author"— and it is a portrait of the author struggling—could move no further at the contrary extreme than relapse into the contest for resolution which was persistent poetic impulse.

The real obstacle to Williams's dream of renewal, in short, was the subjective war inside him between anarchic impulse and the internalized self-charted life he had laid out for himself in familial and social obligation and all they implied. Both "A Marriage Ritual" and "Portrait of the Author" are poems of a writer for whom exterior world can be radically out of focus with internal impulse. Exterior world is simultaneously agitator of impulse and enforcer of conventional rule. As chart, what it offers is alien to subjectivity except as prayer may find momentary framing for it. Given such stress, Williams often fell back into the turgidity of unresolved image evoked by dream. More occasionally he reached out to attempt reshaping chart, or to consider such reshaping—more nearly in accord with the heart's desire for freedom of impulse— but this effort at its best would result in little more than compromise.

A self much agitated by impulse was held in check by a self equally bound to control. He was, in a manner of speaking, dutiful son, husband, father, and doctor both in spite of and because of himself. He had justified his profession to himself because it brought in the kind of income he wanted, but it surely bespoke a deeper need for social place as well. He was faithful to its demands, tending his patients with energy and devotion, but in *A Voyage to Pagany* he made plain his contempt for its pretensions to status and special privilege. His practice was unfashionable, and though it provided him with a reasonable income he took no steps to climb the ladder that professional medicine offered—never, for example, becoming a member of the American Medical Association. At the same time there is little evidence to suggest that he saw the prevailing poverty among his patients as a socially remediable evil. His attitude toward them, his writing suggests, is that of an often brusque, often concerned, sometimes compassionate, sometimes even self-humbled superior. In most of his stories his patients appear before him, and perhaps he before them, as acts of God. Presentation and randomness rule in this respect both the reappearance of his patients with all their unpredictability of complaint and character, and his own reaction to them.

If on his professional side he presented mixed evidence of chart's social compulsion—and that chiefly when some particular untowardness forced his attention to it—his feelings as a husband were controlled by a heartfelt devotion to the "marriage" that is echoed so frequently in his later writing. Marriage was a fact which like his profession he bracketed in terms meaningful to himself but in that form made his own. As father he could and did write a treatise on a reform of education he thought might benefit his sons. In practice, however, the Williams boys were given a year of study abroad, like Williams himself, and were sent through traditional private colleges to make a conventional way for themselves in the world, the elder to become his father's medical associate and to inherit his practice.

It is hard to find social heterodoxy looming very large in Williams outside of his writing—apart from amatory affairs and some weekend participation in literary bohemia. In the writing it takes a more visible place and so stirs reaction from time to time. Chart, like dream, was a double-edged force. At home was his practical conformity to the society in which he lived, his membership in the imperfect democracy I have looked at in *Selected Poems*, evoking little warm allegiance and a noticeable amount of skepticism. He was dutiful to its demands and, simultaneously, unenthusiastic about either its presence or its promise. The democracy was no more than a sum of its parts. Particular patients, particular persons, particular events often stirred him as they touched his dream life, but they had a way of running their brief course in his writing and then disappearing.

In his writing, one noticeable exterior counterfoil to this mixture of reactions was the revolutionary symbol "Russia." The fact of massive renewal embodied in the Russian Revolution thus paralleled the dream of holocaust he described in *Spring and All*. He centered "The Descent of Winter" on his extended poem "A Morning Imagination of Russia" along with prose comment on it. At some time following the execution of Sacco and Vanzetti in 1927 he composed "Impromptu: The Suckers," which he did not publish until 1941, in which he bitterly attacked "the New England aristocracy / bent on working off / a grudge against you, Americans, you / are the suckers" (*CEP,* 316), but could conclude only "that this / is the kind of stuff that they can't get away / with. It is there and it's loaded" (*CEP,* 317). His 1935 volume *An Early Martyr* took its title from a poem protesting what he saw as official persecution of a friend he took to be a true radical, and included other titles like "Proletarian Portrait" and "The Yachts," both of which dealt with circumstances at least intimating a ground for revolution in America.

Despite such gestures, however, chart repeated a failure of renewal in common with dream. Neither in these poems nor in later ones could Williams find the heart to believe that the reordering of social chart which revolution sought could fulfill his quest. If he was a skeptical democrat, he was also a skeptical revolutionary. Both democracy and revolution failed to speak to the impulse of self-regeneration which in fact seemed lost as soon as any system was established, to be replaced by conformity. In regard to social change Williams repeated the division apparent in his other impulses—a deep desire for remaking coupled with distrust of it and doubts about visionary as opposed to actual fruits. The point is nowhere clearer than in two poems both making their first appearance in 1946, the year of beginning hostility between Russia and the United States following the end of World War II—"The Pink Church" and "Russia."

The former was perhaps Williams's chief official hymn to renewal, and was in fact set to music by Louis Zukofsky's wife, Celia Thaew. The color pink was itself a mitigation of Communist red, and though it finally led Williams to one of his few espousals of Communism by name (and so helped block his appointment as consultant in poetry at the Library of Congress), it at the same time

dissolved Russian renewal into a bewildering variety of other impulses to renewal. The "red" was heavily mitigated. Neither here
nor elsewhere was Williams anything of a Marxist except as Marxism was, in a particular aspect, a fact of regeneration in history.
Once an accomplished fact, however, it lost luster. Unlike the "Portrait of the Author," this renewal holds no terror for the poet, but
it is officially a general rather than a personal possibility, a cultural
rather than a personal opening.

The poem opens, indeed, with an invoking of religious renewal—"Pink as a dawn in Galilee"—routing the pagan tragedy
of murder embodied here by Aeschylus. What follows is a continuing mixture of impulses. These are interesting not only in their variety but in the degree to which that variety itself builds toward a
canceling out of any one of them as actual occasions for rebirth.
The Christian dawn gives way to "all ye aberrants, drunks, prosti-
tutes" (CLP, 159), the kind of low-life figures Williams's short
poems had often treated kindly as they so clearly embodied impulses to which he felt a response, or at least rejections of regular-
ity. They lead on to another kind of aberrance—"Poe, Whitman,
and Baudelaire"—in which the clash of larger aims is complemented suddenly by a wholly personal waywardness justifying
waywardness itself as a source of joy.

> Oh ladies whose beds
>   your
> husbands defile! man, man
>   is the bringer
>   of pure delights
>   to you!
> Who else?
> (CLP, 160)

The catalogue returns to the historical to invoke Dewey, James, and
Whitehead among philosophers, all perhaps seen as joining in
Whitehead's effort to expose the fallacy of "simple location"—an
argument Williams had admired in *Science and the Modern World*.
But the pinkness of the dawn is quickly given further location by
the invocation of "the nipples of / a woman who never / bore a /
child" (CLP, 161), the image of a virgin who suggests something of

whorish possibility, and is extended to Michael Servetus's heterodoxy and finally to the chorus of "Samson Agonistes" celebrating
Samson's mortal thrust toward freedom in unrhymed verse, Milton
at the last "singing among / the rest / like a Communist" (*CLP*,
162).

Williams's revolution is in fact incapable of public charting. It is
instead one more evocation of the subjectivity, the dream only of
renewal underlying his whole poetic impulse. But subjectivity of
itself could never become objective. *Spring and All* and "The Descent of Winter" had advanced no further in their arguments than
to the brink of regeneration. Paterson the city had been unyielding
to the dance of language Williams spun around it. Love itself was
aberrant by itself, as Williams came to confess, and was realizable
only in its regulated form as marriage; his own final study of renewal turned thus to what could be gleaned from the overlookings
of love's more hectic harvest. "The Pink Church" is not a poem
of revolution and not even, finally, a poem of renewal as much as
it is a poem of promise, of dream. That was the real center of Williams's emotional attachment. His image for it, anticipating a reconciling appearance in the late poems, was that of light. "The Pink
Church" celebrates the moment of dawning. It seeks to escape the
dark but hardly dares consider the sun finally risen. Instead, it her-
alds the translucence of jade, a light shining "through the stone, /
until / the stone-light glows, / pink jade / —that is the light and
is / a stone" (*CLP*, 159). This curious image catches Williams's
poetic moment with great exactness, a moment at which "light"
and "stone" are inseparable from each other. It is an image in
which both dream and chart are present, translating each into the
other's terms and so into prayer, an image bespeaking the desired
state.

Such unpredictable interplay of dream and chart is extended into
"Russia," with the difference that where dream is seen as both resource and limit in "The Pink Church," it is chart that receives such
attention in "Russia," a survey as it were of the revolution accomplished. What such accomplishment must continue to face at length
in the poem is what Williams here explicitly calls dream. He offers
only a little sense of what that dream is in general but in one brief
passage relates it to the specific subject at hand. Here as elsewhere,
Russia is his foil because, like the American democracy, it is estab-

lished and so unmalleable fact, and it is from contrast with fact that his dream springs. He regards the Russia of Stalin and asks, "must we begin to call / you idiot of the world"? As chart, Russia is as indifferent to subjectivity as Williams elsewhere had declared any given place to be. As for Russia, "When / you were a dream" and liberated from chart, "the world lived in you / inviolate" (*CLP*, 94). It is the vision of "The Pink Church" sobered now to fact but finding that fact is of as little help in renewal as disembodied dream itself had been. In the one case dream is extended to embrace every sort of image possible to it and to find completion in none. In the other it faces the single accomplished image and is equally unable to seize upon what it there discovers.

It is dream in this poem, indeed, to which Williams would waken Russia, dream given substance by the aspiration built into a humble Negro church he offers in his opening image, a thing for the revolution "to hold in the palm of the hand" (*CLP*, 93) and consider. Such a dream can only be alien to Marxism, clearly, and it is for this fact that the poet faults revolution, as bound to its self-created limits as any social order. The complaint is brought a little nearer home as Williams turns to consider the suicide of the poet Mayakovsky, who killed himself, Williams supposes, so as "not to embarrass you," Russia (*CLP*, 95). In either case—poet's suicide and Negro church—dream confronts chart and is driven out perforce. "The Pink Church" had celebrated the light that was the stone. The Russia of "Russia" has settled too much for stone alone. Williams ends with a second religious reference recalling a print of da Vinci's *Last Supper* he had noticed in a patient's house. He turns from the religious message of the work, however, to insist upon the background it includes, designed to accommodate and show forth the dream which the mural figures. Chart—here, specific place—is background, but it fulfills itself when it harmonizes with dream, when it becomes reality from which dream can spring and with which it can coexist. The poet makes his appeal on these grounds, beseeching the society of the revolution to readmit such openness to its structure. Williams here and elsewhere continues to hope, himself dreaming, that the Russian Revolution will bear such fruit. But the Moscow trials, the persecution of Mayakovsky, and a Russia itself now dependent on vast structures of alien factuality made the resource uncertain.

Form and Function: *The Embodiment of Knowledge*

Late in 1928 Williams began setting down notes for a treatise on education, seeking what amounted to social and cultural application of his practice and thought at that time. He was to continue work on this document intermittently into 1930, dedicate it to his sons, and then finally set it aside not to be published during his lifetime. But despite his abandonment of it and despite its fragmentary and disorganized character (which at one point led Kenneth Burke to reject it for publication), what he finally called *The Embodiment of Knowledge* takes its place in his critical writing as his most ambitious effort to project a broad overview of his calling. Its prevailing concern is as old as Plato, but it alters Plato to make poetry a superior mode of actuality because of its concreteness and immediacy. Opposed to poetry, "philosophy and science" suffer the countercharge of losing themselves in generality.

The argument was common to Williams's generation and in keeping with what he had preached and practiced elsewhere, but here he was to give more emphasis to poetry as prayer than anywhere else, and to prayer as embodiment of the local. *The Embodiment of Knowledge* confirms his placement of poetry in a condition of suspended commitment and connection. The work rejected philosophy and its like not only as abstract but as an effort at binding, at conclusive knowledge. To gain poetic knowledge was above all to be present at the act of poetry itself, at the translation of nonverbal experience. Philosophy and science dealt only with the results of this process. Williams changed the title of his work from the "humanization" to the "embodiment" of knowledge and gained specificity thereby. Poetry would be "embodiment" just as the experience it dealt with was embodied—in words. His was an argument for the primacy of prayer in poetry over dream and chart both, for language in a particular mode. The language of poetry took its shape from the immediacy of the occasion only. In that sense poetry was a prayer inseparable from the self and the scene calling it forth.

What most divided philosophy from poetry was that poetry does not drive toward "meaning"; instead, it yields an immediate "knowledge" as against "a moral, a burden, a lesson, a textbook, a thought, an idea, a narration" (*EK*, 119); poetry asserts its own existence. It is, Williams argues, like a chemical experiment in that, whatever consequences it may stir, it serves no end but its own accomplishment. Thus he justified the immediacy in which his poetry was rooted, though clearly he was endorsing no historically colored doctrine of "art for art's sake." His purpose rather was to separate poetry as absolutely as possible from the consequences that philosophy, or experiment elevated into "science," might propose. Present fact, poetic actuality, was the same as utterance; it was contact with presence translated into the "prayer" he sought; it could not exist in any form other than that of the verbal event it evoked. This was in effect to detach poetry from consequence and antecedent outside its situation, to make it sheer eventfulness, to see it as a prayer that had no bearing other than its immediate act of embodiment of subjective dream and objective chart, a translation of their givenness into its more malleable presence.

Thus, Williams was declaring poetry to be individualized utterance, random in relation to all other than its own sphere of being. In that state it necessarily suffered a philosophical truncation, but it gained what was most central to it, its presence as verbalized experience. I have argued that Williams found no comprehensive promise in either projected dream or reflected chart. He would espouse marriage as the nearest attempt at an ideal of human relation but made marriage wholly dependent on individual devotion to it. He made himself a citizen of his time and place but disclaimed any attachment to location other than that of presence. He would in his poems be caught by countless individual entities but would find little occasion for relation or commitment in any of them. Some acceptance of philosophy might have harmonized any or all of these dislocated moments, but, he would finally hold, it would do so only at the cost of erasing the individual act by which knowledge was in fact created. Philosophy was irrelevant to knowledge apart from whatever merely practical and therefore alterable generalization it might yield to the imaginative wayfarer.

Despite such disclaimers, however, there was still, of course, a view of life inherent in his program, one unpredictably composed of will, emotion, accident, changeability. In this treatise Williams cited his admiration for the view of the world Henry Adams had sketched toward the end of his *Education*. Multiplicity was the word for Williams also, but it carried one corollary that was foreign to Adams; Williams found multiplicity to be the necessary condition, against the unitary thrust of philosophy and science, making subjective assertion possible. If Williams's was a world in which nothing was more than its particular occasion, it was a world thereby in which every entity was unbound and so replaceable by another. He quite apparently exempted Dewey, Whitehead, and Einstein from his censure against philosophy and science, and this surely because he saw in them prospects of a human universe in which each entity was at the center of its own field of force, constrained thereby to singularity. He was in effect a philosopher of the openness he found endemic to his sense of poetry and was willing to accept lack of order and lack of relation in favor of the radical presence they made possible.

He avoided even this much philosophic commitment, however, by steering his discussion directly onto the subject of language itself. As he turned the argument to particular educational proposals, he in effect urged the value of replacing the study of philosophy and science with that of language. What he was after was a shift of awareness from the patterning that philosophy proposed in favor of linguistic prayer, language considered not as means to an end but as the act embodying knowledge. Philosophy, generally considered, subordinated language to "the idea which it is put forward to represent," and it was this subordination, with its parallels in science as in "history, religion, and the legislative uses" that he opposed.

As Williams would declare, thus, it is the "act" of writing with which he was concerned. Its reference or bearing is of small account. In some important sense he does his living in his writing and attaches commensurate value to it. Certainly it is poetic self's creativity and renewal that are found there. The world is part of the process but no more. "The tree as a tree does not exist literally, figuratively or any way you please for the appraising eye of the artist." The writer and the painter, he declares, share this condition together.

> What does exist, and in heightened intensity for the artist is the impression created by the shape and color of an object before him in his sensual being—his whole body (not his eyes) his body, his mind, his memory, his place; himself—that is what he sees—and in America—escape it he cannot—it is an American tree.

Render that in pigment and he asserts his own existence and that of men about him—he becomes prophet and seer—in so far as he is wholly worthy to be so. (*EK*, 24–25)

Like any prophet or seer the poet is what he is by virtue of his utterance, and like many of theirs his utterance will reflect heterodoxy. *The Embodiment of Knowledge* is a canvas of the ground required by such prophecy: first, a clearing away of what is seen as the empty orthodoxy figured as "Philosophy and Science," and then a staking out of the prophet's claim to his individual utterance. A more traditional poetic prophecy, like Whitman's perhaps, must find its ambience in such charting as a democratic ideal or common physical being might supply. Williams was more radically vatic. The prophetic voice or prayer would ground itself in its own being and the knowledge such being generated. Any student of art, Williams argued, had difficulty in conventional learning. His discipline—painting—confronted him with achievements already accomplished, and he was bound to their study. At the same time he must never be guilty of copying. What he learns from them is never more than "a barrier he must surmount if ever he is to do anything that can be called serious work" (*EK*, 10). Artistic form and poetic prayer were at one in this impasse. Their primary business lay in converting what had been discovered into what would be discovered, and it was thus that they were the embodiers of knowledge.

If the poet was in some sense a prophet, it was to the degree that his poetic means allowed hitherto unaccomplished revelation. "A writer," he argued "is a person whose best is released in the accomplishment of writing." I have argued that Williams's poetry was to him a surrogate self, an entity set apart from the embarrassments of natural self by what prayer rather than dream or chart made possible, and here he would be explicit on the subject. His writing, thus, was movement of self and situation toward reembodiment. The poet "does not necessarily think these things—he does not, that is think them out and then write them down; he writes and the best of him, in spite even of his thoughts, will appear on the page even to his surprise" (*EK*, 7). Language is itself the locus of renewal.

Williams's treatise was concerned with the place of poetry in the realm of what he called knowledge, and so it required poetry to be an advance upon what was already known. The poet's task must first of all be to exclude the already accomplished from his writing.

His prayer, ideally, would be one not heard before. If philosophy was an antagonist, so was existing poetry. The immediate aim was not so much to transcend as simply to break its bounds. "If we read alone," he argued, "we are somehow convinced that we are not quite alive, that we are less than they—who lived before us." Poetic prayer existed against such limit. Like a kind of chemical experiment it must, if it would add to knowledge, examine heterodoxy or even apparent anomaly. Such an aim—a translation of subjectivity into the objective presence of language realized—was of course a complement to Williams's dream of self-fulfillment. "WE are at the center of the writing, each man for himself," he declared (*EK*, 107), and that center needed a body to show it forth.

The picture throughout, thus, is that of a poet struggling toward the uniqueness of his own art. *The Embodiment of Knowledge* is a treatise more on what Williams sought than on what he necessarily accomplished. It is a treatise on purpose, but the purpose it spoke for bore powerfully on the actual composition of his poems, propelling them toward a frontier of utterance. If he could align himself with prophecy, that was because he sought testimony of an act personally accomplished and hence possessing personal validity. Clearly he sensed a validity for his poetic, but it was one that only he could ascertain. "For how can [the poet] be certain that his conviction . . . is so, unless he test it explicitly by statement?" (*EK*, 104). Poetry comes into being only by proving the intentionality driving it on. "Write that it may become clear—if possible, to escape ignorance and confusion" (*EK*, 105–6). If Williams would legislate away anxiety of influence, he is still harassed by an anxiety of formal accountability. Dream is powerful but amorphous. Personal chart is uncertain, public chart is restrictive. Language alone is the resource as it becomes the only mirror in which this poet can confront himself.

Poetic prayer thus furthers the intentionality of dream in Williams, simultaneously preserving him from engagement in the world and allowing him encounter with it. If *The Embodiment of Knowledge* is to be believed, the poet is a man on a raft of language seeking to stay afloat on a larger element that itself would engulf him. The early experimentation, the late poems of accommodation and harvesting, *Paterson* itself—all in their several ways combine to manifest his sense of a poetic prayer calculated to allow and preserve personal identity in a world largely barren of other resource. It is Shakespeare Williams chooses as an emblematic figure of poetic prayer. Shakespeare had already appeared as an icon in *Spring and All* and "The Descent of Winter." He now emerges as a whole embodiment of a poetry realizing itself in its agencies.

Williams would allow Shakespeare no other resource, contrasting him with Bacon, the other spokesman of the age. Here Williams made it plain that he recognized practical effects for philosophy as he made of Bacon "the head of a movement destined to come down through the centuries as one of the most fruitful in the history of the world" (*EK,* 69). Shakespeare's greatness, indeed, lay in part in his own participation in "a dawning scientific age" (*EK,* 112). As philosopher, Bacon was given credit as renewer and radical, but, granted thus their kinship, the difference between the two figures was the important matter. Shakespeare, Williams declared, possessed knowledge "without the dream," a dream here not only of subjective character but also of connecting and systematizing what he knew. Shakespeare was a great poet in part because of his ignorance of this possibility or his lack of interest in it. His matter, as poet, was the "pure knowledge" with which Williams was concerned. At the heart of his accomplishment lay his activity as dramatist and thus his participation in poetry's "active form" (*EK,* 69). In their whole concentration on a present reality inhering wholly in the language Shakespeare found for them, the plays were at once a witness to the dawning empiricism of the times and to poetry's ability to share naturally in it. They lived by presenting what was the case.

In summing up Shakespeare, Williams stresses his "solidity" and "opacity" (the latter term had been used by Pound to name what he thought was best in Williams's work, poetry as a window to nothing but itself and what its presence engenders). Shakespeare, thus, is a poet who, while he is most deeply open to the life of his day, is simultaneously most free of it. Life maintains no claim on him; he, rather, lays claim on it as far as he wishes. As person in his plays he is invisible; as interpreter he is present only in the plays' shape and texture. For Williams, thus, he is a poet fulfilled nowhere but in his writing and there finding what he most values. The image is a multivalent one as it implies an element of estrangement for the writer from his world and native self alike. Poetry may be prophecy, but if so it will be a prophecy in Shakespeare's mode, finding its application and source alike in its divorcement from the claim of any knowledge not generated by its images. Williams's treatise enforces severe limits, but to him they were productive limits. Poetry should not pretend to purpose other than its own, but hewing to such purpose it could then claim for itself what Williams here would describe as his own aim, to "embody America and myself in it" (*EK*, 47). The force of the claim lay in its verb. Shakespeare's local time and place are knowable by virtue of his poetry alone; Williams would aspire to perform the same feat for his own radically different time and place.

Mimesis: "The Desert Music"

Dream, subjective impulse, commonly moved Williams toward the freeing or renewing of himself, and his poetic shifts and turns on such a subject as the spring season, the presence of renewal, form an altering and multifaced testimony of such intentionality. Against such dream stood the restriction formed by his willed charting of his life's course in the world into patterns of limited flexibility. Outside this persistent internal contest lay also a more public aspect of chart, the social world he occasionally grappled with but left finally in a state of unsettled definition. It was, thus, poetic prayer, agency, form, that assumed primacy in his feelings about his art. He embraced art for art's sake, but only as a pragmatist. Renewal, a sense of self realizing itself, he would have. If renewal in life could be allowed only within limits, his aim must be shifted to poetry, the imagination, as primary realm. Since living offered only restricted possibility for impulse, poetry became its means, symbol, and substance. He himself would sum up the matter in *Spring and All.*

> But though I have felt "free" only in the presence of works of the imagination, knowing the quickening of the sense which came of it, and though this experience has held me firm at such times, yet being of a slow but accurate understanding, I have not always been able to complete the intellectual steps which should make me firm in this position.
>
> So most of my life has been lived in hell—a hell of repression lit by flashes of inspiration, when a poem such as this or that would appear.

The gap between chartable world and such framing of prayer was then plainly implied.

What would have happened in a world similarly lit by the imagination? (*I*, 116)

No one can say, since the world clearly is not so lit.

The prospect of chart in Williams, his summing up of his poetic situation, was imaged in his 1951 poem "The Desert Music." He had turned to its composition in a state of partial recovery from his first stroke. It was inspired by his trip through the Far West, just before his attack, that had led him across the southwestern desert to El Paso for a reunion with Robert McAlmon, his literary comrade of the early twenties. Although his speech was slurred and his movement impeded, he read it himself before an annual meeting of Phi Beta Kappa at Harvard in response to their invitation. Comment on the work has been much centered on the drama, thus, of its composition and initial presentation. The image—which we owe to Paul Mariani—of the partly crippled poet devoting himself to a poem bespoken by the very academy he saw as his foe, and presented to them as conscious challenge to poetic propriety, is indeed arresting. But neither this emphasis nor Sherman Paul's argument, welcome for its projection of the work against a broader background, seems adequate to account for what "The Desert Music" appears to claim. It is, I want to suggest, an encompassing statement of Williams's sense of his poetry in a world untransfigurable in itself. Early and late in Williams, the world is indeed often chartable as "desert"—the emotionally uncertain landscape of "The Wanderer" and the fiction, the American wilderness of *In the American Grain* and *The Great American Novel,* the scene fit only for holocaust in *Spring and All,* the secular paradigm of place spelled out by the *Selected Poems,* the unmalleable fact accepted at the end of *Paterson* 4, the landscape available to redemption by the personal act of conservation coloring the late poems. Against such "desert" in one sense, but in another wholly of it, stands, then, the contrasting image of "music." Sherman Paul revives the image of Beautiful Thing from *Paterson* to apply here, finding music to be a new personification of it. A differently focused view might suggest that the music Williams celebrates in his work is nothing less than the very poem to which desert gives rise. He had discovered that music is inherent in desert itself rather than in opposition to it.

Desert is a complex image for Williams. First of all it invokes barrenness of resource, but the desert out of which so much of his writing had grown to this date had clearly possessed some impulse. If we seek, thus, for a better awareness of chart in his work than he often allowed, the doubleness of this image comes to hand. In his impulse to renewal he indeed seeks the Beautiful Thing as Sherman Paul suggests. The only beauty to be found, however, as all his own argument suggests, will be whatever language is able to accomplish faced with the uncertain blankness which is factuality itself. Beautiful Thing, here as in *Paterson,* will be not so much any item encompassed by chart as the poet's discovery of his ability to function despite chart's blankness; desert itself is largely emptiness or irrelevance to human need. If one is a desert dweller, there is no alternative but to make fulfillment out of what is at hand. The poem is, thus, occasion of such a fulfillment in the absence of all other. Despite Wallace Stevens's claim, Williams here is not a cherisher of romantic idea perversely chaining himself to fact. He is rather a poet of partly willed, partly found situation, seeking to translate it into such music as his necessarily improvised agencies will allow.

The desert music is a "music of survival," a music the desert calls for first of all. Williams has opened himself to the Western land he has been traveling, "seeing the wind lift and drive the sand" (*PB,* 110), and he turns to thinking of McAlmon and of the Paris the two had shared so fruitlessly as writers. Memory here is no redeemer. Instead the poet seizes upon the present action facing him, which he discerns as an "imitation" of nature not as mimesis but as a paralleling of nature's action as engenderer. These early pages of the poem are patterned in unresolved images, one juxtaposed with another, and so less than logically formed. They introduce the ground of what is called a "music" that Williams joins with an evocation of dance: walking with his friends across the international bridge between El Paso and the Mexican town of Ciudad Juárez, he is stopped in his tracks by a human form huddled in a corner fast asleep. "Dance" is created by the encounter between poetic mind and this personification of the blank desert defying coherent reaction. "What a place to sleep! / on the international boundary," but such reaction is no more adequate than its opposite: "Where else, / interjurisdictional, not to be disturbed" (*PB,* 108). Two figures, one conscious the other unconscious, stand in partnership, and the two together make a dance figure of active against passive, beginning to call forth the echo of a music to be generated by such pas de deux.

The first three pages of the poem are structured wholly by the irresolution encounter begets. The poet meets desert, meets his friend after many years, meets the crossing into the unknown the border creates, meets the strange sleeper. Such music is properly unresolved, no more than an evoking of the chief components of the situation in which he finds himself. How are such components to be made present? The answer lies in the predictable quarter of prayer, "the made poem" (*PB*, 110), the act of finding what invention is possible. The first movement of the desert music, so to speak, is constituted by encounter with the chart that so untowardly presents itself. The first response is to capture what is thus presented as a material of imagination still exceeding resolution but available to awareness.

The tempo changes on the fourth page even though the poem is still rooted in encounter as Williams and his friends proceed to a brief tour of the foreign town. They are struck by the honky-tonks, the bull ring, the miscellany of wares in the market, the presence of other tourists, and a crowd of begging boys. But one kind of desert has been replaced by another. The emptiness of the open land has given way to a human jostle no less barren than its surrounding landscape, though by its human nature standing apart from it. Ciudad Juárez is hardly less empty of imagination than the desert itself; and its own music, the whining sentiment of popular Mexican tunes, affirms its inability to find expression for itself. A different human response is needed. The tour of the town, in its conventionality, has been more orderly than the opening passage, but order has been unproductive of active imagination.

This central section of the poem has moved to locate itself more coherently than the opening as the poet and his friends now begin to respond to the Mexican town's presence and so give the work a frame of action. Flossie Williams, who accompanies her husband, marvels at the colors in the town and at a tall woman tourist dressed in a mink cape. One of the party cautions the Williamses not to respond to the beggars. Someone notices a woman carrying a baby in a shawl draped from her neck. Response has begun to awaken and form the scene but still with the most tentative efforts. The party, as if overcome by even this much attention, takes refuge in a show-bar and the beginning of a striptease act that will prompt a first sign of awakening, but response is still jejune: "You'd have to be / pretty drunk to get any kick out of that. / She's no Mexican. Some worn out trouper from / the States. Look at those breasts." But the poet at last places himself at the center of the scene and is moved, "but not at the dull show" (*PB*, 114).

The dancer offers little to an audience, but something more important emerges for the poet as surprisingly and in a moment the scene finds embodiment in the dancer. Her weary triteness enacts the whole desert scene of Ciudad Juárez and the tourists in it. Her straight-out music contrasts with the Mexicans' songs about "their souls and their loves," not very visible entities. Her person, her heavy performance, her manifest contempt for the scene in which she finds herself, her very willingness to bare herself, all bespeak a "certain candor" (*PB*, 115). The poet is awakened by her vivid presence and charged with foolishness for grinning with pleasure. His answer is ready: "The music! / I like her. / She fits" (*PB*, 114). An image of desert has embodied itself in her presence, and it is in this respect she is like *Paterson's* Beautiful Thing. She is an apt image of chart. Her very dispiritedness bespeaks the truth in which all momentarily coexist. In his *Autobiography* Williams would record the sense of failure he felt in McAlmon. The whole of the visit to El Paso has been deadened with fatigue and lack of connection until now. The strip dancer alone has been the embodiment of what the general experience has begotten. The poet has yet to complete his own utterance, but in the dancer he has found at least passing formulation for desert dance and desert music which have come together to show their nature truly. Nothing has been at all redeemed or even improved, but something has been enacted. The intentionality that prayer affords has made itself manifest. Desert is present in cognate image.

The theme of the two musics—the "nauseating prattle" (*PB*, 115) of the Mexican songs against the fitting desolation of the dancer's music—now moves forward to structure the remainder of the poem. The dancer is in effect a demonstration against the derived and rootless dream the Mexican music offers.

> She
> at least knows she's
> part of another tune,

knows her customers,
has the same
opinion of them as I
have. That gives her
one up   .   one up
following the lying
music   .
(*PB*, 115)

Her "nakedness," Williams declares, "lifts her unexpectedly / to partake of its tune" and so to respond to desert with what is local to it. Her scene is closed with one more evocation of gods or at least legendary beings existing in debased form in the bedraggled modern world that dates back to *Kora in Hell:* "An Andromeda of these rocks, / a virgin of her mind" (*PB*, 116). Thus she shows forth the virgin-whore paradox that Williams will place at the center of his writing in *Paterson* 5 seven years later.

The party of tourists now leaves the bar, and, the presence of the dancer thus abandoned, the poet is dropped back into doubt about what he has sensed. Can so much be made of "an old whore in / a cheap Mexican joint" (*PB*, 116)? The street opens again with its trite and jarring images to enforce the doubt, and the party proceeds to a restaurant for dinner. There, and perhaps embarrassingly at the moment, the talk turns to the fact that a poet is present, and Williams is asked why he writes poetry. His answer is "Because it's there to be written" (*PB*, 117). Circumstances have lifted the cliché to immediate truth, however, and against any implication of romantic inspiration he says that such writing comes "Of necessity." As if to ward off further unanswerable questions he goes further: "I am he whose brains / are scattered / aimlessly" (*PB*, 118). The statement is exaggerated, but not altogether so. This poet is one who first of all knows poetry only when it happens, however unconnected and of uncertain consequence. His is the gift of knowledge of the immediate and its presence, and when for a moment the desert is matched by a human presence imaging and so recreating its presence, though not copying it, he is awakened. All around him is the "expressionless ding dong" of the Mexican music, but the surrounding chart of the city and desert mocks its saccharine expression. What he has seen and heard in the bar is another kind of sound, as much in contrast to empty dream as a remembered "deep cello tone" struck by Pablo Casals. In its presence, the knowledge it affords, the poet is for this moment of contact "speechless" (*PB*, 119).

The evening is over, and the poet and his wife walk back across the bridge only to encounter for the second time the sleeping figure they had met earlier. What had been no more than tentative dance then, however, is now more figurable, and the image undergoes conversion. The dancer's embodiment of the very desert in which the sleeper rests opens the view of a "birth of awful promise" (*PB*, 120). The sleeper is curled up like a fetus. To what will he wake but the desert city and the desert itself which surrounds him? "Shapeless" is his posture, "or rather returned / to its original shape, armless, legless, / headless, packed like the pit of fruit into / that obscure corner" (*PB*, 119). He is a second embodiment. If the dancer is desert realized in action, the sleeper as a kind of pregnancy is embodiment of desert's continuing to be desert. He is held in the "protecting music" which surrounds him—desert asserting itself not only as presence here but presence to come.

Dancer and sleeper together, then, lie behind Williams's concluding act: "I *am* a poet. I am. I am a poet, I reaffirmed, ashamed" (*PB*, 120). Leaving the dancer's presence had cast a pall of doubt, but doubt has been dispelled by the second illumination, his making of knowledge out of the second and separate encounter. He is "ashamed," surely, to have doubted the evidence of his own mind at work, and now, as if to confirm the confirmation, he has written at some length a poem itself embodying the whole sense of chart and embodying the prayer of restatement as translation toward such embodiment. Starting in irresolution he has proceeded on to more ordered but perhaps thereby rather barren presence. Barrenness, however, has been interrupted by what poetry for Williams is, the embodiment of knowledge—here, of the desert—and intuitive discernment of embodiment as generator of truth. Elements of barrenness again intervene but are again dispelled by the second encounter and, again, by the knowledge it evokes, so that what had been inertness only is transformed. Scene has imaged itself. The whole experience has become verbal embodiment of what the dancer and the sleeper themselves embodied, the presence and practice of a power making what can be made of what is present. The dancer and the sleeper are equally germane to their place and to themselves, as now is the poet, thanks to his act of recognition. His poem has been and remains as uncertain of feature and open in construction as the desert around it. It has fled any refuge in sentiment or grandiloquence to reflect in its presence only what its occasion has actually produced. Its voice finds its resources as they appear and as it alone can. To read "The Desert Music" as any sort of thrust at transcending desert or escaping it is to betray Williams's whole sense of what his poetry was and to betray the sense of this poem in its particulars. The dancer, the sleeper, and finally the poet himself are no doubt of a piece with the desert around them. Each of them, however, shares in the poetic gift of doing what chart as situation, dream as impulse, and prayer as enactment allow, but under the circumstances only that these particulars make available in their common presence. The poem can embody the situation and action giving rise to itself. It will disallow any further transcendence.

VII ACT

POETICIZING PRESENCE, TWO PLAYS

To perceive Williams's writing as act is finally no more than to see the effort to translate physical and psychic presence into poetic agencies he deemed useful to his immediate creative existence within them. In its raw state the presence he seized upon was often banal. The act of making poetry from it would be the finding and phrasing of whatever was necessary to separate such event from the power of habitual context and so assert refreshed being for it. Beyond that point particularity must fend for itself; the secular state such particulars made up had no framable implication beyond their collective existence. The desert world absorbed him by its ungainsayable presence, and he would consider no other. But the same desert world repelled him by its inconsequentiality, brutality, and thinness of subjective stirring. If present fact was to be positive resource, then, there was no alternative to the poet's facing it. Himself a part of it, he used his home-forged technique as an instrument not to provide escape or impossible transfiguration but to insist upon fact as constitutive of a creative existence—his own—that could tolerate no other home.

It is to his dramas, two of them in particular, that I turn to summarize this process, since it is in them that he most fully portrayed such poetic self, one moved by but doubtful of subjective dream, fascinated and repelled by objective chart, and in perpetual quest of the poetic means by which he could make his rhetoric a prayer accomplishing his own and his world's rerepresentation. In their fullness the plays reach out in one direction toward his own vocabulary of poetic action—of the "descent," "contact," and "invention" to which I have given precedence in some early chapters. Out of the same fullness they find relation to what I have borrowed from Kenneth Burke—considerations of "scene," "agent," "agency," "purpose," and now "act." Williams's terms share with Burke's a commitment to poetry as participation in a present reality. The plays are focused upon the poet in his present world, and their business is that of trying to realize the whole implication of the dilemma out of which his writing would be made—dilemma between that world as inflexible given and as poetic possibility.

The same dilemma is referred to by Burke as a clash of resource and limit. Williams's own repeated sense of his scene, himself, and his poetic means and their purposes is that they were resources for certain kinds of poetic action but not for others. His writing alternately presents him as innovating spirit and no more than struggling tyro. Invention did indeed represent for him the fulfillment of poetic agency, but he could not allow such fulfillment to poetic agency apart from the other and often contesting components of poetic action. Much must indeed be made of his insistence on poetic renewal, but much must also be made of the degree to which such renewal was a limiting of poetry to presence and its resources.

In its earlier stages my argument has led to the view that Williams's poetic act was sometimes generated by almost random encounter as material cause, and often enough limited for formal cause to no more than what encounter might immediately generate. Many of the resulting compositions can be gathered under my heading of irresolution of image. In other cases encounter has been seen to resolve itself into more developed stages, notably those of focus on self or object, or into movement toward the conversion of present image to a new immediacy of aspect. The plays introduce formal considerations different from those of the poems, but like the poems they will root themselves in their heroes' encounter with present fact (and the hero will often be hard to distinguish from the author), and thence proceed to an ambiguity of conclusion in which irresolution, presentation of self or object, and aesthetic metamorphosis of dramatic situation all have some part to play. The poems reflect the process which the plays enact, that of the poet coping with the poetic possibility inherent in presence. They share with the poems Williams's acceptance of himself as a man in the middle, a figure of the secular democracy that is his world who is partly beholden to its demands and judgments but who also is desperately restless within it, seeking relief in translating presence without abandoning it.

The poetry conjures up a welter of the dilemmas out of which Williams's plays will seek to draw their more ordered dramatic action. Like the poetry, they will largely fail of any deliverance from scene. Their business will be to enact descent and to seek the kind of contact within descent which occasions possibility of invention. In each case the playwright will accept a given state of affairs and, without altering that state, seek dramatic revelation of it. His characters in turn repeat his effort as, acting a given state of affairs, they seek self-realization within that condition. Poet and character both, thus, are seeable as agents within scene. Both together reach for agencies that will define a sense of purpose for them. Both, finally, will complete their efforts at action only insofar as such agencies allow, and neither will do more than reiterate the standoff between act and scene with which they began. The mode of the two plays I consider touches on the classic. In *Poetics* 18 Aristotle declares that pathetic tragedy is one whose motive is "passion," an immersion in the intractability of the given, a suffering of it. Comedy, he suggests in section 5, also finds "some defect or ugliness" to be inescapable dramatic presence, but in comedy the defect is finally "not painful or destructive." Williams's "Many Loves" and "A Dream of Love" will respectively enact these two modes—what Burke called "frames of acceptance"—and so pose options of response. These modes of using literature as "equipment for living" are described as "the more or less organized system of meanings by which a thinking man gauges the historical situation and adopts a role with relation to it" (Burke 1937, 1:3–4). In this regard, Burke argues, "the comic frame should enable people to be observers of themselves while acting" (Burke 1937, 1:220), a disinflating and so reconciling role Williams creates for himself as Doc Thurber in "A Dream of Love." Modern civilization, on the other hand, has often made tragic fatality a corollary of personal ambition, admonishing one "to *resign* himself to a sense of his limitation" (Burke 1937, 1:49), and it is this fatality that haunts the protagonists of "Many Loves."

The earlier of the two plays, "Many Loves," shapes up as pathetic tragedy when the idealistic playwright who is its hero faces the dilemma of his devotion to a dream of poetic drama. It is composed of three one-act plays Williams had originally written for a little-theater group in Rutherford, all as its title indicates concerned with the theme of love but otherwise unrelated. Williams was to seize upon these and, by framing them in verse, convert them into acts of his completed work, episodes in which their imagined writer, a character in the framing play, struggles to form his sense of the inchoate drama they present. He in turn is caught up in the dominant theme of love, as he and his leading actress have planned a secret marriage. He is fascinated by her perceptive embodiment of his writing, her actress's skill, but they must keep their hopes secret from the play's backer, a wealthy homosexual who is enamored of the playwright and anxious for his favor but whose ideas about the play are in full opposition to the playwright's.

In the verse play that encloses the three short plays it is the backer, Peter, who embodies one side of the givenness the playwright, Hubert, faces. Peter represents the given that Williams himself faced, or presumed he faced, in all his writing—that of superficial or downright false standards. Peter to begin with is at best indifferent to and finally contemptuous of Hubert's dream of realizing a poetic theater, and between them the two characters frame out a dilemma. Hubert is possessed by a finally ineffable and unrealizable conviction that poetry, the possible, can bring reality into the theater in such fashion that an audience will see it newly revealed. The aim of course was Williams's own, and what he wrestles with in the contest between Hubert and Peter is the demand laid upon the poet in his drive to render presence in its own terms. But Hubert is possessed more by an idea than by any reality he can present. Peter, who represents nothing if not the fixedness of reality, has no patience with mere hope. He knows theater as it is and its audience, knows that entertainment's values rule, and is contemptuous of what he sees as Hubert's innocence of things as they are, which as he will point out entails a devastating contempt for convention's rewards as well as its limits.

Toward the play's end it will be the villain, Peter, who will accurately if bitterly assess the dream which throughout Hubert has pictured as evidence of his superiority. Hubert struggles with the recalcitrant matter that is the stuff of his three short plays, recalcitrant even though it has been deliberately chosen by himself as especially requiring translation to lift it into poetic being. In the event, Hubert backs away from this demand to present his short pieces in a bald and literal prose, although Williams gives the framing play a loose verse structure. Hubert speaks of his poet's calling as a high one. To that extent he is romantically conventional enough.

I say: when we see,
on the stage, what we expect to see—
I'm not speaking of circuses
but something to turn our minds a little
to the light—it should project
above the coarseness of the materials . . .
something else, in the words themselves,
tragic without vulgarity. Seen—
in the mind! The mind itself . . . today,
without firearms and other claptrap,
in its own tragic situation. We can't
do this at once but must restudy
the means.
    (*ML,* 92)

Poetic translation here exists only "in the mind"; it is no more than possible. It is unfortunately only the idea of poetry with which Hubert is concerned, and by his own premises Williams cannot admit the idea of poetry without accompanying fact. Thus far Hubert speaks of poetry's freedom. In one brief moment, however, he will proceed to integrate idea with fact and so truly attain not poetic freedom but an image of his own embodiment—a true image, bespeaking his actual situation rather than idea alone. In that moment he makes act repellent just as it is vividly present; he seems almost to echo Hart Crane's bitter image of love as a burnt match skating in a urinal. "If I wish to present love / dramatically today," he begins, and the dialogue continues:

PETER: Yes.
ALISE: Yes.
HUBERT: I might do it—with a coalscuttle
PETER: How?
HUBERT: By spitting in it.
          (*ML,* 92–93)

The "coarseness of the materials" is clearly present, and Alise reacts in a way to suggest that the conventional purity of her love lacks the "mind" to which they are meant to appeal. "Darling," she can only say, "You mustn't talk that way" (*ML,* 93). The claim that actual image makes against unreal ideal here is too outrageously disrespectful. All three of the plays which Hubert has written and in which Alise is the star actress have been engaged in performing variations on just such an image, but she seems mentally untouched by the mordant poetry they and Hubert's image evoke. Hubert himself has reason within the play for such violence about given fact and possible translation of it. He is drawn to Alise, fascinated by her, but he is afraid of what Peter can do to him and his play, and at the play's end he will move both to marry Alise and accede to Peter's demands. His image of love as spittle in a coal scuttle is in its very grotesqueness a true desert music, bespeaking the emotional devastation present to Hubert, a rape upon dream's claim to adequacy.

Williams's drama ends with Peter's ironic stirring of himself to arrange a wedding for Hubert and Alise on the stage where all play out their roles. However, he demands that the wedding be followed by a night in which he and Hubert are together allowing him, as he puts it, "Le Droit du Seigneur" (ML, 100). Alise and Hubert may be allowed their stage marriage despite the nonmeeting of minds they display, and Hubert may even be allowed his vision of poetic drama, but only by acceding to the force which at this point Peter, as Hubert's financial backer, exerts. Though Alise is indeed Peter's rival and even enemy, he offers her a true if jaundiced view of Hubert's character as poet. Hubert is one who in the actuality of his image sacrifices the dream of love; his poetry takes precedence over his love. The poet, Peter suggests, is a kind of monster and Alise should know that. His real mistress is his election as poet. This election is his real life, and any wife of his must accept that fact. The act of poetry, as Hubert had declared, is an embracing act of mind translating whatever it meets into itself, without regard for other considerations. Meetings, descents into the given, are essential as they serve the poet's compulsion to translate them away from themselves and into his realm of invention. Williams himself, thus, had so translated father, mother, grandmother, and a host of less intimately encountered beings across the range of his writing. He had in his way sacrificed the whole city of Paterson to a penchant for "dance." His next play would so translate his own complex relationship with his wife, and the new translation of that subject in his late poems would be no less an act favoring poetry's need to husband its resources. Peter sums up the case and suggests its cause.

> He has
> only one ambition—to get out!
> Out from within himself, where he
> is freezing. There is only one door.
> Writing! Stop him and he'll destroy you
> as he'd eat a potato. Marry him
> and become his jailor—you'll find
> him thoroughly contemptible,
> not even human. This is the way
> it is—and you shall have, tomorrow,
> no part whatever in his life.
>
> (ML, 102)

The poet must slay near and dear for nearer and dearer, balance the given and the possible against each other so as to swallow them both into the translation, the new being which the poem represents.

For Williams, then, poetry is a translation of presence into images particularizing the poet's sense of actuality. It is an art accomplished for art's sake with its final cause that of the poet's fulfillment of the agencies by which he lives as poet. Made an actor in his own drama, like Hubert, the poet indeed becomes something of a monster. What he seeks is the restated presence satisfying his instinct; as Williams had so often declared, such translation for him was present deliverance from the "despair," the "hell," the "freezing," the arbitrary that was raw presence. Poetry could not remake such presence; it could not even escape it; but it could translate presence out of its own space-time. Williams's drama in this case will be completed by its three short plays. All will deal with love rather in the spirit of Hubert's metaphor, revealing it as a trap for the idealist and an exercise in manipulation for the masters of presence. Such patterning divests love of its consolation in favor of its dramatic possibility—possibility for the poet rather than the lovers. The three plays rely on object presentation as their poetic agency, object in this case including the persons of the drama. All three make their way, indeed, very largely by reducing person to object in situation. The love which the characters in the three plays enact thus emerges as little more than the given and the possible in confrontation with each other, echoing the contest which the framing play is also acting out.

All the short plays of "Many Loves" are concerned with the defeat or the compromising of love as an ideal—as pure possibility—just as the framing play is concerned with the falseness of an idealized poetry. All of them center in a female character who is played throughout by Alise of the framing play. In the first of them she is a drunken and promiscuous sloven of a wife ironically named Serafina and loved by an idealistic young man, clearly, for what he thinks he sees in her rather than for any quality apparent in its own right. She is, perhaps, a hardened version of Williams's Beautiful Thing, like the gang girl of *Paterson* or the strip dancer of "The Desert Music"; epitome of the scene that has bred her, she sets imagination into action. Her young lover is scarcely capable of formulating this vision, however, and indeed his failure seems to be that he distorts it, imagining by his idealization of her that he can redeem her from scene, convert her to suit the image he has of her. Certainly he is portrayed as an idealistic and neophyte "writer," and his romantic aim will be abruptly denied by Williams's scene-act dilemma at the action's end.

The second short play introduces a much larger cast including and once again centering on a female figure, Ann, the young daughter of a proverty-stricken farm family. She is bent on escaping from the drabness her scene represents. One possibility is her inept young lover, Horace, but he mismanages the elopement they had planned leaving the girl to be drawn almost hypnotically to a brisk and successful businesswoman, Agnes Breen, a lesbian, acted by Alise, who appears at the play's end as potential purchaser of the family's run-down farm and indicates a strong interest in including the young girl in her acquisition. Such homosexual intrusion, like Peter's attachment to Hubert in the framing play, seems to underscore the restriction of possibility to what presence happens to offer. If there is to be a change, it will come not out of Ann's attachment to her young man. Success in that direction is quashed by too many counterfactors. Love again will depend on the power represented by the businesswoman's wealth and its power to detach Ann from her native scene. Personified by a blind and brutal father who is most interested in selling the farm to Agnes, scene's force can be altered only by counterforce. At the play's end it will clearly be such power emanating from Agnes Breen that will draw the hardly cognizant Ann into its fold. Ann scarcely dreams what Agnes wants of her, but within Agnes's aura she can sense a power which she thinks can assist her own drive toward change and remaking of herself. To the audience such a possibility must appear compromised at best since Ann in effect is to be included in Agnes's purchase of the farm. To Ann herself, besotted by the possibility of deliverance through ideal love alone, the situation remains clouded, indeed distorted by her own so clearly unbalanced ideality, as great as that of the young lover, Laddie, is in the first play.

The third of the three short plays again presents its vision of love as engendered out of circumstance close to home. The cast shrinks to two persons only, a frustrated suburban housewife and a poetically if also cynically inclined doctor whom she has called in to treat her only child. The play divides rather clearly into two halves. Throughout, both the housewife and the doctor develop a conversation during which they fortify themselves by recourse to a bottle of cheap wine. The play's earlier part is dominated by the housewife as she unfolds her unshakable sense of being an outsider in her world. A harum-scarum drawn by men and the idea of a "good time," she rejects herself as a mature and capable woman, thus completing the trio of aberrant females Alise has enacted. The doctor sees her for what she is, though he falls nevertheless into her flirtation pattern by revealing his own sense of wanting and needing deliverance from the ordinary but of being inhibited by conventional ways. As a boy, he says, he once went so far as to plan the rape of a little girl by whom he was smitten, fulfilling himself thus as male conqueror. When the time came, however, he could only fumble and fall away from his end. He and the girl made friends, and he has come to regard his intention as a sort of madness which has now passed. The housewife is enthralled by his seeming to be a kindred spirit and plays up to him, but in the end she is unceremoniously repulsed by the doctor when her ailing child appears and calls them both back to the "normality" which is their fate. Each short play portrays the folly of naive dreaming in ignorance of what the given will in fact allow. The three, along with Hubert's story, make a pathetic tragedy on the subject of imagination gone wrong by misreading the dilemma that in fact it faces.

The result in "Many Loves" is an antiromanticism produced by the obduracy of scene in the face of act, though the work is given its form, of course, by the very act which is thus resisted. Williams cites Shakespeare's "Let me not to the marriage of true minds admit impediment" as his epigraph, but with heavy irony. The mind may indeed seek fulfillment or creativity, but the only end to which it can find access is that generated by impediment itself. As the whole work is given unity by its framing play on the subject of poetry, it can be no other than a tragic vision of poetic dream grounded in irony of circumstance. The poet's pride will be humbled by a fate his own defining of poetry creates. The three short plays extend this pattern beyond the limits of poetic action alone as they concern themselves with a pride of love. But like Hubert's poetic dream, love suffers appropriate penalty for its romantic hubris. Such tragic coloration in Williams's poems is not often explicit, but it is widespread. We have only to think of the radical secularity of the world I have sketched out in *Selected Poems* where, although not formulated as a drama, the interplay of given and possible is enacted in a variety of expressive gesture. The effect in both the short poems and *Paterson* is that of driving the poet toward recognition of the ground at hand as the forming power of his poem. Poetic possibility beckons him on as a liberating force. In the end, however, he must settle for recognition within scene, chastened by its power, and give up hope of liberation from it. Such recognition had played a part in the work of his major contemporaries also. Unlike Pound, however, Williams would only skeptically propose alteration to scene. Unlike Stevens he would seek no life of the mind searching out its own terms. Unlike Eliot he would feel no radical sense of dispossession as a result of scene's presence.

However, if a degree of pathetic possibility is thus implied for poetic act or renewal in general, it stems from imagination's misreading of presence and is uninterested in forcing conclusion any further. The second of Williams's plays I consider, thus, "A Dream of Love," accepting the same obduracy of presence as "Many Loves," will turn it into comedy. Here descent makes for contact and invention and so for recognition as an enabling force for the protagonist rather than as one confirming descent's power alone. If "Many Loves" is a pathetic rendering of circumstance's power over aspiration, "A Dream of Love" will be a comedy of the restorative power of expectations reduced to proper measure. Poetic action was a twofold process including agent's impulse as well as scene's inertia, and impulse could turn its translating power away from chart to exert its remaking force on dream itself. Presence thus would be no less affirmed, but it would be affirmed as resource of action rather than as impediment to it. "A Dream of Love" will be no more a play of redemption than "Many Loves," but it will impel its chief characters, through the very portal of death toward deliverance from estrangement, as it finally allows them to face clearly the degree to which they and their world are not just limited by presence but in effect constituted by it. The pathetic and the comic elements in Williams are near allied. They combine often in the tragicomic wryness of recognition. They differ chiefly in that presence seems to confirm the projector as blind victim in the tragic, and, to enlighten him as to the reality that is his in the comic.

"A Dream of Love" is written close to the autobiographical bone of Williams's relation with his wife. It portrays a marriage much troubled by philandering and the complicated feelings of both husband and wife. The pair are deeply attached to each other and cannot really envision divorce. At the same time both are unhappy within marriage. Myra, the wife, knows of her husband's wandering and struggles to find some ground upon which she can establish acceptance of him and his ways. Doc Thurber, the husband, is a compulsive chaser and can no more control his impulse than Myra can find emotional acceptance of it. The play thus opens on a pattern of entrapment, or certainly of emotional blockage, seeking the means by which such a life can be made livable by the two sharing it. The play is Williams's most extended grappling with the problem that haunted his own marriage, and that also, it makes clear, deeply involved his being as poet. The presence upon which the piece opens appears to be beyond any possibility of change. Both characters are bound to it. At the same time, both grope for revisioning, for translation of its terms into a new vocabulary of feeling and understanding acceptable to both. The situation poses a demand for what Williams saw as a poetic power or rephrasing of what itself could not be altered.

In the opening scene Doc and Myra face each other at the end of a wearying day. Both are tired, both reach out to each other for support, but their efforts clash and they are led to a final effort at phrasing what each of them seeks in their marriage. Myra declares that it was Doc's calling as a poet that created a "first dazzlement" (*ML,* 122) which has bound her to him ever since, and the scene moves quickly to her asking Doc to read to her from his poetry, a gesture toward the writing which is of great emotional weight for them both. First, however, Doc backs up to recall his own feelings upon their marriage—not really love for Myra but a hope for love itself. The mismatching that has taken place is thus given clear formulation as the play's root—Myra's attachment to what is freest and most self-fulfilling in her husband along with his own primary devotion to his poetry but only secondary devotion to the wife who has made it possible for him.

The play poses the dilemma that Peter described in "Many Loves," that Harold Bloom in his discussion of Wallace Stevens has described as a dilemma of solipsism. The poet finds vital satisfaction only in his art, obedient to the romantic demand that he live only his poetry, that it be wife and all to him. Williams himself made it plain that he regarded his medical practice as no more than supportive of his writing. Here in "A Dream of Love" Doc Thurber suggests something of the same feeling about his wife. The two poems from which Doc reads to Myra are far from ruling her out of his life, but together they make no more than an equivocal place for her within it. Both poems are absorbed in love as an emotion of absence. One of them, a passage from Williams's "Perpetuum Mobile," directly asserts the emotional standoff in which the play's opening is rooted. Beyond that it suggests the inadequacy of the poetry, as yet at any rate, sufficiently to extend love beyond dream so as to face presence. The lines Doc reads are in fact sentimental in this situation as they remain some distance from its heart, his own infidelities. In their fashion they repeat the presence of romantic pathos which had so filled "Many Loves."

—a dream
we dreamed
        each
    separately
        we two
of love
    and of
desire—
that fused
in the night—

    A dream
a little false
toward which

```
        now
    we stand
        and stare
    transfixed. . . .
    And so
        we live
        looking—
        (ML, 122–23)
```

In this first scene Doc and Myra are no more than victims of the presence their marriage has created, solacing themselves a little mawkishly with self-dramatization. That sense of things is underscored by the second poem, "Love Song," in which a lover sees the whole world suffused by the yellow color generated by the sunset into which his beloved has traveled in a westward journey. Williams himself once referred to the verse as immature, as "cryptic" and "shy" (IW, 23). Its emotional pitch is high, but it is wholly a response to the beloved's absence. Both poems thus are about a union not complete in fact, indeed cherished because of the element of absence infusing it. Neither poem can offer much more to husband and wife than occasion for sighs and regrets.

An only equivocally more present love for Doc appears in the second scene in the presence of Dotty, his typist. She is married, has not yet given herself to him, and so at the moment is hardly more present than Myra, and much of scene 2 is worked out in a kind of buffoonery in which Doc pursues Dotty as best he can in her husband's presence, retreating only after he has managed to arrange an assignation with her for the next day. The attraction of Myra exists for him as a pursuit of the past, of the love for which Doc says he married her. The attraction of Dotty lies in the future and a mixed but momentarily powerful promise of union. From such a beginning the play will proceed as both its chief characters are inducted into the reality of what they seek. Doc will understand why he pursues such wavering flames as Dotty, and Myra will understand that he is a being for whom presence can hold no satisfaction unless it is subject to remaking, renewal.

The play's machinery is complicated, as perhaps it must be to serve the purpose of double recognition it seeks. Doc dies during the frenzy of love he enjoys with Dotty, but in Act 3 his wholly earthy spirit returns to make his involvement with her and what she means to him as clear to Myra as hindsight will allow. His approach to her is accompanied by quotation from a third poem, "Rain," which proffers the suggestion that Myra's love for him was an enveloping and nourishing power but more maternal in its force than connubial. Free love, like poetry, he declares, is a dealing with raw material. The beloved is appealing because of what the lover may make of her. Marriage is wholly another matter. As Williams's late poems in *A Journey to Love* will suggest, marriage needs constant refreshment as much as love does, but its refreshment serves the ends of fidelity and self-abnegation. Like poetry, love heightens self-presence, effects a deliverance from the hell of circumstantial encasement.

Self-presence is not easy to make clear. Doc phrases it as the need of a man to protect his integrity "as best he is able, by whatever invention he can cook up out of his brains or his belly as the case may be." He must produce "a woman out of his imagination to match the best. All right," he adds, "a poem" (*ML*, 200). Doc can neither change his own ways nor as yet bring Myra to see the need they serve in him. She drifts contentedly off to sleep and so misses all his explanation. Her own turn at finding reality will come in the next scene which she prepares for by rousing herself to repeat her demand for a dramatic and present enactment of what Doc has found in such as Dotty. He has given an idealized account, and Myra has found it unreal. If there is to be true poetry, it must be actual, not merely ideal, presence. She is a doubter for whom vision must be confirmed by tactile presence.

The play now moves to satisfy her demand in a next-to-last scene by conjuring up a flashback of Doc and Dotty together, he perfervidly rousing passion in her by stating all over again his sense of the centrality of creative effort to love and poetry alike. As his lover, Dotty will become his poem. Myra, who in the play's course has been emotionally felled by Doc's death, finds recovery in the revelation such dramatic enactment affords of his nature, and even of the rightness of his dying as he did. He is no more than a clumsy grappler with marriage. His effort at eloquence has been unable to move her, but at the play's end embodied demonstration of his half-fledged emotional nature and need enable her to recognize her own virtue as mistress of presence and to face her life as it is. The business of poetic action has been accomplished, to reconcile perception to the presence of what is, and so to assert the continuity of life in the face, even, of death. Doc must have his exercise of imagination in the flesh. By her own gifts, Myra will accept it enacted in all its insistent incompleteness and so accommodate to its reality. Both have been right in their quarrel, as each must cling to his or her need and imperfection both. The play has combined pathetic and comic elements which Williams balanced and rebalanced in working out several versions of it, but it ends on a note of mutual affirmation for both characters.

Williams's imagination exists in the pathetic mode (*Paterson* 1–4 is a notable example) when it calls upon unfulfillable aspiration as its ground for action. *Many Loves* is wholly an exercise in this mode as all three protagonists in the short plays find love to be a frustration and a defeat. They are victims of unreality, of a thrust toward transcendence through love, as is Hubert, their creator, in his own unrealizable vision of a poetic drama and a union of perfected authorial and thespian skills to be consummated in his marriage to Alise. Williams's shifts to the comic mode (as in *Kora*, "The Desert Music," "Asphodel," *Paterson* 5, and many of his short poems) when the ground for action becomes that which Aristotle poses for comedy, the incomplete, imperfect, but benignly present. "A Dream of Love" is comedy in this sense. Doc dreams of love in the play's first two acts to emerge there only as what Williams in the subtitle to the play's earliest draft called an "innocent blackguard." His early notes for the play indicate that his original plan called for Doc to be converted to monogamy, to become a "whole man and the man whole." This aim, however, seems not to have survived into any of the texts. The center of action in all of them instead shifts to Myra in the final acts, and all are concerned with her gradual return to composure and wholeness after Doc's death. In the printed text of 1948 her recovery is made explicit in an added scene through her act of accepting Doc for the wayward creature he is (*Direction*, 105–6), and in a 1954 typescript (Beinecke) this comic realism is further emphasized by a concluding speech in which Myra's acceptance of her husband is effected in her declaration that men in marriage are no more than children depending on a mother. Aristotle's comic reduction is clear, and it is present at least implicitly whenever Williams's writing contents itself with a revelation of presence in its own right, free of idealistic or romantic illusion and the pathos it begets.

Drama, then, must be the enactment of presence, for better or worse—the comedy of settling for what is there, or the tragedy of pathetic illusion. Outside of drama, the whole of Williams's poetic accomplishment finds reflective being in a territory uneasily mixed of such presence and possibility. In *Paterson* he declared that the province of the poem was the world, and so posed a complex problem for himself. Such a slogan reverses the prevailing romantic proposal that the province of the world is the poem, but Williams's whole effort was to demonstrate the combined futility and falseness of such doctrine. Poetry is no less indispensable to him than to his more romantically minded compeers, but it is indispensable for a reason wholly different from theirs. Poetry exists in him to make the world as it is faceable, to assert possibility of action within the unalterability of presence, and to proclaim the possibility of meaningfully restating the constant.

With what image, then, can I conclude so as to leave a focused sense of such combined impulse and qualification? The negative aspect of such poetry, its denial of romantic transcendence, is surely its clearest facet. In the terms of Coleridge's distinction between fancy and imagination, for Williams imagination is a fanciful lie, and fancy, restricted to play with "fixities and definites," is a realm from which neither poetry nor any other mental act can successfully escape. Far from being trivial, such fancy is for Williams the breath of life, the only breath indeed that life will allow to infuse it with congenial being.

Williams's best and most sustained utterance to this effect is his middle-length poem "Writer's Prologue to a Play in Verse," though there is no extant verse play with which to connect it. In effect it is prologue to his whole sense that poetic action must remain within presence and move toward that for which it may hope to find image. It is in one sense a blueprint of poetic limit as Williams saw it, but it is more powerfully than usual for him a statement of poetic achievement as he understood it. At its center stands the figure of the auditor or reader to whom it is addressed, who in Williams's world must learn to face poetry not as revelation but as an occasion of disclosure arrived at by the rejuggling of bits of the world which encloses poet, poem, and reader alike. Do not trust the poem, Williams urges; do not lean upon it for solace. Approach it with as much skepticism as you would any other secular act.

Accept the convention as you would
opera, provisionally; let me go ahead.
Wait to see if the revelation
happen. It may not.
Or it may come and go, small bits
at a time. But even the chips of it
are invaluable. Wait to learn
the hang of its persuasions as it makes
its transformations from the common
to the undisclosed and lays that open
where—you will see a frightened face!
                    (*CLP*, 14)

The first pleasure and profit of poetry is dislocation, defamiliar-
ization. The second and last is the reforms they achieve. Poetry is
not a bridge leading beyond these effects. They can be terminal only
insofar as the knowable world that encases the poem lays terminus
upon it. Williams's is as complete an abjuration of romantic fulfillment as modern poetry will yield, and it is perhaps such abjuration
that has made his writing of importance to later poets themselves
skeptical of what they see as romantic lie. Doc Thurber in "A
Dream of Love" at one point recalls a Sunday school teacher who
discussed Plato with his pupils, but recalls him as an ineffective
prophet whose religion was one of flight from presence. That way,
Williams asserts, is the death of poetry, of love, of virtue of any
kind, because it is a way requiring ideal rather than actable belief.
Romantic transcendence can find small basis for itself beyond that
of wish, of will toward itself. A postromantic poetry must indeed
seek belief, but it must direct its search in a way that includes belief's requisite, experience.

But believe! that poetry will be
in the terms you know, insist on that
and can and must break through everything,
all the outward forms, to re-dress
itself humbly in that which you
yourself will say is the truth, the

exceptional truth of ordinary people,
the extraordinary truth.
                    (*CLP,* 14)

Such truth is in one aspect comic:

                    And how
you shall laugh to see yourselves
all naked on the stage.
                    (*CLP,* 15)

Williams's poetry flees any and all fictions of invention, in favor of invention at its actual work in actual presence. It focuses on whatever it regards and finally on the poet and the reader as the only directions of appeal it can conceive and sustain. It is an appeal dependent through language on something that exceeds language, the reader's sense of his own presence within presence. That reality is mostly unalterable: much of it must always remain irrelevant or marginal at best; but some of it is always closely present and so local, demanding of constructive attention. Poetry makes such presence present as itself, though this time with pathetic overtones.

                    Believe it, to be
proved presently by your patience.
Run through the public appearance
of it, to come out—not stripped
but, if you'll pardon me, something
which in the mind you are and would
be yet have always been, unrecognized,
tragic and foolish, without a tongue.
That's it. Yourself the thing
you are, speechless—because there is
no language for it, shockingly revealed.
                    (*CLP,* 13)

The business of poetry lies between itself and its reader. Its aim is to awaken the presence of the reader's poetic self, to insist upon it, and to insist upon it as fancy not free of but in the world and struggling against banality. Poetry would form itself on the reader and his being-in-presence as themselves the stuff by which a human universe can be kept before the mind's eye, by which indeed the poet suggests he has kept his own universe human.

> Yourselves! Within yourselves. Tell
> Tell me if you do not see there, alive!
> a creature unlike the others, something
> extraordinary in its vulgarity,
> something strange, unnatural to
> the world, that suffers the world poorly,
> is tripped at home, disciplined at
> the office, greedily eats money—
> for a purpose: to escape the tyranny
> of lies.
> (*CLP*, 13)

The poetry of presence, contrary to Williams's assertion, would in fact strip both reader and poet, would presume their need for stripping to the condition most radically germane to their existence, that of being in present truth. Williams's poetry embodies the truth not of adhesion to the meaning of what is said but of apperception of all that in time and space is thus embodied. The poet, as distinguished from Emerson's seer, is an incarnate eyeball, only in the light of his moment finding focus within the presence enclosing him.

VIII CONCLUSION

DWELLING AMONG THE PIECES

Where then does Williams emerge? Of what and to whom can he be said to speak with poetic authority? Given his poetic limitation of himself, does any constructive vision appear? Though one recent answer has been that, properly edited, he may be taken as a poet for young readers, his immediacy and simplicity serving as a bridge into poetry's world, J. Hillis Miller and others have given him more adult status by including him among "poets of reality," aligning his work with that of his major contemporaries. Much opinion has accepted him as a poet of vitalistic assertion against the routine and the ordinary, but this line of appreciation is one I find subject to qualification. In another direction, he has often been extolled for his nativism and so rather ironically given a place alongside such figures as Whitman and Sandburg whom he so much distrusted. In fact, no one of these classifications seems adequate, all the more so in that each has to impose on his variety what seems to be a narrowing limit. Each offers a qualified "Yes, but only this" as the best claim for his poetic validity.

If no one of these responses is satisfying, however, taken together they may serve to point to a large accomplishment for him. His is an imagination of accommodation. The interinanimation among the terms of Burke's pentad is a notion which enables us to seize upon an active and assertive poetic being in Williams. The world his poems create is both diverse and monotonous, both broad and flat. His denial of transcendence is not only a cutting off of alternative to presence; it is a limit upon presence itself, confining it to the poet's own presence within it. At the same time, spread across the two volumes of collected poems, the collected *Imaginations,* *Paterson,* and *Pictures from Brueghel* is a variety of feeling and reaction to presence that, along with much overlapping, brings into existence a poetic personage. This poet finds eye, voice, and feeling that is unique to himself and, particularly, is at the business of leading a native existence, of being at home among the pieces of a world that is his, and that he perceives and shapes to form a range of experience horizontally available so to speak, and so available to poetic definition.

It is not hard to detect a progression of mood across his poems. A certain brashness, or ardor, or impatient raggedness of expression is common in his writing of the 1920s and earlier. The more frequent evenness and control in his poetry of the next two decades manifested Zukofsky's influence. The whole is then completed by the retrospective coloration of the 1950s. Out of the midst of the more finished expression, however, erupt *Paterson* and "The Desert Music," marking between them Williams's most central writing as they come to grips with what most obsessed him, a "striving / to re-establish the image" (*PB*, 70). The striving was for "re-establishment," which I have argued implies both preservation and alteration of what is considered. The strife is not against the world, which he accepts as his own, but rather in conjunction with it toward enhanced realization. It is in this sense that Williams makes a unique place for himself among his contemporaries. Largely turning his back on the anxieties of descent and incompleteness, major themes in Eliot, Pound, and Stevens, he replaces them in *Paterson* and "The Desert Music" with an anxiety of aspiration that finds a degree of ease in the coexistence of poet and subject, which early and late assumed shape for Williams as "the dance." Williams doubtless retained a large measure of romantic impulse toward transformation in his poetry. If we are to speak of accomplishment in this regard, however, it might best be figured as transformation coexisting with fact. The world is present not to be remade or shrunk from as neutered or hostile; it is present to be reimaged in terms it itself yields.

His final and posthumously published volume, *Pictures from Brueghel*, devoted its first third to a presentation of previously uncollected poems, numbers of them clearly stemming from his last years, which contrast with the rest of the volume in largely freeing themselves from the triadic line and in returning as a kind of last word to a revival of subjects and forms prominent in his earlier work. Among them is one poem, "The Dance," which may be chosen as epigraph to Williams's whole poetic effort and achievement. It is, properly, a poem of motion and conflict, of encounter and of patterning, though not of resolution between the forces set against each other. Its subject is the perdurable American one of winter and of snow falling among trees that we find in Bryant and Emerson, J. R. Lowell and Frost. The dance it figures is manifold: snowflakes patterned within themselves and in relation to each other, framed and divided by branches and twigs; the mind patterned within itself and in relation to the storm; the self patterned in relaton to its partners; the self patterned in relation to its own nature; and ruling all, "the flurry of the storm / that holds us, / plays with us and discards us." In the midst of all, the poet maintains poise in himself and in his expression, "dancing, dancing as may be credible" (*PB*, 33). The qualifier "credible" largely separates him from his predecessor poets on this theme, excluding Frost's sense of limit in scene. Credibility is a curious sounding aim for dance, but one that exactly distinguishes it from mere gyration, random motion uncertain of pattern. The poem is celebratory of at-homeness with bits and pieces; it does this by projecting and holding them against patterns that are less than definable but that offer ground for belief in their presence.

Williams greatly distrusted any pretense toward ordering the world he lived in beyond what presence of order it itself made available. Like the Brueghel he celebrates in this final volume he himself worked between two principles and by virtue of their counterpositioning. Brueghel's art had been greatly stirred by his exposure to the sophistication of Italian painting and by the widening of visual experience his visit to Italy had made possible. On the other hand, returned to Flanders, his eye would be filled again and again with the presence surrounding it there, notably of course the village life that was native scene. The result was interplay, an interaction of life and art, of the transitory and incomplete with the permanent and completed. The dance, Williams would say in his poem, was "sure." It was the stuff of Brueghel's and of all life, and Williams's admiration for Brueghel grew most certainly out of the painter's seeming to offer him a mirror of his own case.

This is all the more plain in Williams's lack of attention to the moralism that often motivated Brueghel's work. In this and other respects he responded to the painter as a kind of sixteenth-century Williams, an artist bent to his own ground, and there is much in Brueghel, of course, to support the view. In the series of ten poems he called "Pictures from Brueghel," Williams does include both "Landscape with the Fall of Icarus" and "The Parable of the Blind."

Both are narrative, even allegorical, but in both cases it is the arrangement of the content that holds attention. In the case of "Icarus," for example, Williams's poem contrasts with Auden's work on the same theme, which gives two-thirds of its lines to a general consideration of suffering. Williams devotes all his lines to the painting, observant of the spring season marked by the plowman in the foreground, the sea, the ship, the sun that has melted Icarus's wings, and, finally, "a splash quite unnoticed / this was / Icarus drowning" (*PB*, 4). The irony is no less in one poem than in the other, but for Auden it forms occasion for homily. In Williams, as in Brueghel, Icarus's death is one event among several others. Icarus's failure does not cancel out the plowman's tillage or the ship's sailing. Art is a dwelling among the world's pieces without pressing for general conclusion about them and without poetically seeking to dissolve their multitude into dominant symbol. It is a negative capability coinciding with Williams's early love of Keats.

The story of Icarus, doubtless, comes down to us as a moral tale, and neither Brueghel nor Williams avoids the fact. Neither, however, maximizes it as Auden does. Williams's scene is one in which death, even the pathos of youthful effort so ended, is unremarkable. It may indeed be noticed as sad irony, but such notice in itself is not the stuff of art, which, rather, reaches out to reimage the event. For both poets, of course, Brueghel achieves a magnificent originality by giving Icarus's fall a particular scene, one the myth says nothing of, and it is this newness and its presence that capture Williams especially. The failure of Icarus happens along with the success, so to speak, of the plowman, the ship, and even the sea. Wings dependent on wax fail: it is not a matter for lucubration. And the same assumption of the finality of presence, except for its being reimaged as itself, fills his poem on the blind men "leading / each other diagonally downward" to the bog awaiting them. Williams calls the painting "horrible but superb." But is it, indeed, pathos or comedy? And the question may even be raised about Icarus's fall. Falling, by itself, is limitable to neither reading exclusively. Again, Williams's eye is taken by the bits out of which Brueghel's picture is made—its subdued coloring, the blind men's staffs and other belongings, a peasant cottage and a church in the background. Neither the painting nor the poem, however, is concerned so much to resolve judgment as to see fully what is occurring. The blind faces are raised, Williams notes, "toward the light" (*PB*, 11), and extrapolation of the irony is withheld. The work of the artist in both cases is to frame disaster by the familiar with which it is surrounded. Perhaps a key to Williams's sense of Brueghel and himself is found in "Haymaking" where, he notes, "the living quality" of Brueghel most emerges, its "covert assertions / for art, art, art, / painting / that the Renaissance / tried to absorb." To Brueghel in the midst of it, however, his subject and his art join in "a wheat field / over which the / wind played" (PB, 8), its stems, no doubt, moved to dance by the air's force.

Poetry may indeed assert foreground as central to its being, and to do so it may relegate other consideration to the background. Williams, like Brueghel, asserts a middle ground of awareness, one upon which focus is nearly impossible in itself and which, consequently, most often comes into being by interplay between foreground and background. The poetic claim lies somewhere indeterminately between Icarus and the other figures in Brueghel's work and in Williams's poem. The blind men more plainly fill their work, but behind them is a peasant house and a church, and ahead of them still is country bog. Again, both painting and poem find their dynamic in the interplay between such items of assemblage. Neither Brueghel's nor Williams's world is allowed preordained perspective of the kind that Auden imposes on his work. Speaking of "the old masters" on the subject of suffering, he ordains judgment: "they were never wrong" (Auden, 3). But the very assertion creates doubt once it is lifted from the poem back into general presence. The world Williams rejoices over in Brueghel is one in which middle ground, interaction of bits, is called upon for aesthetic duty rather than any perspective commanding the order of their presence.

A further image of poetic at-homeness among dispersed pieces, which are taken as true representation of the world, occurs in two of the volume's poems dedicated to the adoration of the Magi, an image also found in Paterson 5, where it had a place in the spread of the virgin-whore paradox. Here two other aspects of the image are explored: Brueghel's presumed religious skepticism despite his having painted on a religious theme, and the inherent diversity of the scene as the Magi offer their gifts. Williams is unimpressed by the symbolism conventionally attached to the gifts and regardful as a consequence of their inappropriateness to the occasion. The piecing out in the first poem is classic Williams as it issues in the diversity between given fact and mind's address to it. Givenness for Brueghel here is twofold. In the first place is the authority of the Italian painting which he accepts as model but also as point of departure. In the second is what Williams takes to be his doubt of his subject's truth. The result is a work finding its being in an indefinable middle ground between the attitudes. On the one hand "mastery of the painting" occupies him, but against both the commitment inherent in such mastery and the conventionality of his subject stands "the alert mind dissatisfied with / what it is asked to / and cannot do." In part Brueghel accepted what was given "and painted / it in the brilliant / colors of the chronicler." But, so accepting, he also reimaged and posed against convention what Williams sees as counterforce, "the downcast eyes of the virgin" (*PB*, 6). Do they, within their scene, register acceptance? awe? a covert mockery? detachment from the whole? Neither mastery of theme nor mastery of technique is finally the end. That, rather, is the indefinability of the virgin's expression, and such invention is the real object "for profound worship" (*PB*, 6). Brueghel seizes upon his subject for independent play of mind among the pieces within it and from their offset generates renewed vision of commonplace matter.

The second adoration poem stands outside of the Brueghel series to become a work in its own right. But "The Gift" returns to the parent theme again to explore the range of its detail across an open span of implication. The birth this time is seen as that of "the god love," in Christian as in pagan iconography portrayed as an infant and here confronted with the familiar but nevertheless inept offerings of gold, frankincense, and myrrh, "rich gifts / so unsuitable for a child / though devoutly proffered" (*PB*, 61). As in "Icarus" or "The Parable of the Blind," it is the picture/poem's content—the spread of pieces—out of which aesthetic is generated, this time by dint of what Williams will call a "miracle" but which turns out to be nothing more than the addition of a third bit to complete the pattern, the mother's milk which sustains new birth. But the Magi's gifts are not balanced by or resolved into the mother's gift. What remains is mixture. Praise of love's birth must perhaps always be as arbitrary as any bouquet of flowers or golden ring. But in such case, "All men by their nature give praise. / It is all / they can do" (*PB*, 62). The gifts of the Magi clutter the scene. The virgin and child remain encased in their own perfection. The poetry of the

occasion lies in acceptance of the unlikeliness, the inappropriateness, but the inevitability of the Magi's gifts along with the ragged
stable which is the scene and even the workaday ass so extra-
neously at home in it.

The poem as mixture rather than resolution, as suspension between foreground and background, is pervasive throughout Williams's writing and most clearly offers ground for summarizing his
distinction and worth. In the series of longer works including *Kora
in Hell,* "The Descent of Winter," the five books of *Paterson,* and
"The Desert Music," for example, suspension is maintained between poetic self and poetic scene as major components, with the
two alternately serving as background and foreground. Self dominates in the first two titles. It finds less certain placement in *Paterson,* dominating in Books 1 and 3 while more largely giving way to
scene in Books 2 and 4. But both of these groupings maintain the
suspension between self and scene and allow movement also toward foregrounding of poetic agency, an element which will rise to
dominance in Book 5, where it will stand in suspension against
poetic self. "The Desert Music" returns to poetic self primarily, but
a self wholly given character by the desert it faces and seeks to deal
with. In these poems, as in all of Williams's writing, the reader sees
foreground against background and must feel out their relationship. Scene, self, and agency alternately move forward or back as
the poet holds all in awareness by implicit or explicit attention
within the compass of his writing.

Williams could declare on occasion that he disliked speaking of
"poetry" and preferred to speak and think of "poems"—individually accomplished utterance. Nevertheless, I will suggest that his
work emerges with clearest distinction as a body of poetry rather
than as a collection of individualized and completed poetic wholes.
At almost any of its moments it depends for its success on a recollection of the background that any immediate utterance evokes.
Even in *Paterson,* for example, the five books of the poem are dependent on each other for the poem's total effect. The work is cumulative rather than progressive. Like the totality of Williams, it
stands as a field of interest rather than a structure. What is true of
the long poems is even more forcibly true of the shorter works assembled in the two volumes of collected poems and the whole first
third of *Pictures from Brueghel.* In marked contrast to Wallace Stevens, say, Williams is a difficult poet to anthologize. An editor can

make a larger or smaller selection of titles from Stevens each of which stands by itself as poetic utterance. This is to say not that any part of Stevens sums up the whole, but that he strongly inclines toward the individual poem as his base of poetic action. He grounds the poem consistently in agency. Williams's base, to the contrary, is the totality of what Burke includes in his pentad. The pentad, suspending one of its parts against another, shifting its ratios, is the structure his poetry has to offer. In contrast to Stevens, his is an open and fluid personality shaped by his scene and his agencies of the moment. Thus he generates what Burke calls a dramatistic presence, dominating and in turn finding alternative and varying expression in a shifting overlap of parts.

If the long works ranging from *Kora* to "The Desert Music" form one segment of this whole, a second is made up of the shorter poems stretching up to *The Desert Music* and *Journey to Love*, volumes of 1954 and 1955. Here both scene and self are broken into many bits reflecting a variety of moods and scenes that range from the opaqueness of total descent into occasion, to the detachment of clearly framed utterance. Between these extremes stretches a whole range of writing finding clearer or more elusive contact with its occasions and emerging as clearer or more elusive examples of poetic invention involving self, scene, and agency. Thus Williams becomes the poet suggested by his own *Selected Poems*, a work itself as much marked by its omissions as by its inclusions but offering at least serviceable entry into the broad and variegated totality generated by his shorter poems. He is a writer here whose "text" lies across a range of composition. To read him in this segment of his writing is to move back and forth across the pieces. In this he resembles the Pound of the *Cantos*, the Lowell of *Life Studies* or *Notebook*, or the Berryman of *Dream Songs*.

The one remaining segment of his total is made up of the two late volumes, *The Desert Music* and *Journey to Love*. The title poem of the first apart, these are largely dominated by the triadic line and by a centering in a poetry of old age. Even this unity, however, creates a poetry of suspension within itself, as age finds its character against the more youthful and strenuous concerns of the earlier poems. It is that background from which age emerges in the late poems. These are eloquent on their immediate subjects because they have the whole of the earlier writing and its concerns in view. And the counterposed stresses of the fiction back them up specifically, just as the short stories make positive background for *Paterson*, or *The Build-Up* makes particular background for this late writing, or the short stories as a whole provide a summary background for the world that Williams's poetic self in general faced as counterforce in all of his writing.

Toward the end of "The Desert Music" Williams proclaimed, "I am a poet." But it seems clear that he depended greatly on his own terms for that estate. I might now define these as interplay between background and foreground to seek out a middle ground as imagination's realm. Background is what is assumed as given. Foreground is what may be made of it by refocus, translation. The two enact their dance with greater or lesser elegance and completion. The moral, if we are to find one in Williams, is that mankind exists nowhere but in a world so constituted. Williams seeks to be a poet of truth, and this is the truth he clings to. Any rhetoric ignoring it will be bound to falsehood. Although the tone prevailing in *Pictures from Brueghel* is one of reconciliation, Williams's poems across their breadth offer much variety in his sense of being at home. In "Writer's Prologue to a Play in Verse" he had found that home was where one was "tripped" as the office was where he was "disciplined" (*CLP*, 13), and his writing is dotted throughout with the reality of deprivation and discontent. To dwell among the world's pieces may be to find one's ease, and Williams's poems often do this. Being at home may equally if unpredictably be a finding of denial, exasperation, beauty, revelation itself. Home is where one lives. It is its unpredictability that Williams makes his own, seeks to image in his poems, and, by doing so, assert as manageable human state.

INDEX

INDEX

Designed by Richard Hendel

Composed by Graphic Composition, Inc., Athens, Georgia

Manufactured by Bookcrafters, Chelsea, Michigan

Text and display lines are set in Sabon

Library of Congress Cataloging-in-Publication Data

Duffey, Bernard I., 1917–

A poetry of presence.

(The Wisconsin project on American writers)

Includes index.

1. Williams, William Carlos, 1883–1963.—Criticism
and interpretation. I. Title. II. Series.

PS3545.I544Z5865   1986   811'.52   85-40760

ISBN 0-299-10470-2